LEARNING TO
Write
WRITING TO
Learn

Theory and Research
in Practice

Roselmina Indrisano · Jeanne R. Paratore
Boston University, Boston, Massachusetts, USA

EDITORS

INTERNATIONAL
Reading Association
800 BARKSDALE ROAD, PO BOX 8139
NEWARK, DE 19714-8139, USA
www.reading.org

Library of Congress Cataloging-in-Publication Data
Learning to write, writing to learn : theory and research in practice / Roselmina Indrisano, Jeanne R. Paratore, editors.
    p. cm.
Includes bibliographical references and index.
ISBN 0-87207-576-1
1. Language arts. 2. English language–Composition and exercises–Study and teaching. 3. Language arts–Correlation with content subjects. I. Indrisano, Roselmina. II. Paratore, Jeanne R.
LB1576.L374 2005
808'.042'071–dc22
                                                                        2005003019

Second Printing, February 2006

Contents

Section Two: Writing in the Middle and Secondary Years

In Tribute to James R. Squire

Roselmina Indrisano

Learning to Write, Writing to Learn: Theory and Research in Practice honors James R. Squire—visionary, scholar, teacher, writer, researcher, and friend. The contributors to this collection who were privileged to know Dr. Squire offer these tributes to his life and legacy.

WE BOTH MET Jim Squire when we began our careers in higher education at Boston University. Although we met him separately and in different years, we each had the same instantaneous attraction to him. We knew that we had met a giant in the field and a much-larger-than-life human being. His gregariousness drew us both into his world of warmth, humor, and savvy. We frequently commented to one another that Jim saw the future; he instinctively knew a promising finding from research that would become a staple of educational life. He'd say, "This research will hit classrooms in five years, and it will be so good for teachers and students." He never missed in his predictions, and he never missed an opportunity to take a chance on an idea that fascinated him or a person who captured his attention.

He took a chance with both of us, again separately, while he was the publisher at Ginn & Company. He signed each of us to our first publishing contract and then rooted for us and supported us from that moment on; he always seemed delighted with our careers and the careers of so many scholars who were starting out at that time. He always wanted to know what was new and what our thoughts were on the topics of the moment, from classroom management trends to whole language, to literature policy, to high-stakes assessment. No new idea or unique trend passed him by without his reflection and subsequent expressions of passion in his point of view.

We always enjoyed working with Jim, and we were fortunate to have had several wonderful opportunities to do so. Our time together working on both editions of the *Handbook of Research on Teaching the English Language Arts* (Flood, Jensen, Lapp, & Squire, 1991; Flood, Lapp, Squire, & Jensen, 2003) was filled with precious moments we'll always treasure. Each session spent together in the hotel suites and meeting rooms of America was a wonderful history lesson; we lived the history of the profession with him through his stories, insights, and commentary. We both came from institutions where the history of the International Reading Association (IRA), National Council of Teachers of English (NCTE), and National Reading Conference (NRC) were cherished, so our chats with him filled us with delight as he filled in the missing pieces with glorious detail. All the luminaries of the field who had gone before us came to life through his words; he was the grandmaster storyteller who had us mesmerized time and time again.

To say that Jim was a doer with political savvy who changed the course of history in language arts instruction for the better is as much an understatement as to say he was an extraordinary scholar and thinker. He was so much more; he was a visionary and a pioneer who blazed the trail for all of us. He was never fearful of saying exactly what he was thinking.

When Jim was asked to write a piece on teaching literature in the 1990s for *Literature Instruction: Practice and Policy* (Flood & Langer, 1994), he said he had been waiting a lifetime for the opportunity. In his paper, after he cataloged previous failed attempts to legislate literature policy from colonial America to Nazi Germany, to the politics of contemporary America, he went on to conclude,

> Better to have policy dealing with literacy, not literature. They are not the same. Affirm literature's importance, of course, but let decisions in what and how to teach remain with the classroom teacher. Aesthetic experiences with literature cannot be legislated; any attempt to impact the teaching of literature from an external limited base will create more problems than we need. (Squire, 1994, p. 174)

Yes, Jim was clairvoyant, steadfast in his beliefs, and wise.

Jim, for your wisdom, your friendship, your guidance, and your mentoring, we'll always miss you. You taught us well.

James Flood and Diane Lapp

I MET JIM in the 1970s at an NCTE convention. From that time we connected regularly. I came to Ginn to discuss the design of basal textbooks—I wasn't an author, but an interested observer. Jim was fascinated with the possibilities of enhancing the instructional power of teachers' manuals by exploring alternatives to the interrogate-respond-evaluate pattern. The inertia of the system stood in the way, of course, but he was patiently persistent.

Jim was smart, he was practical, and he was passionate. I remember attending a conference at Asilomar, near Monterey, California. The California school system had recently gone through another "restructuring," probably in the student testing system, that turned everything upside down. Jim offered the concluding comments following several presentations about implications of the new requirements. Most of the presentations had a slight edge but focused on how to deal with the matter in ways that would preserve quality education. Jim stepped to the podium, written notes in hand. He glanced at the notes, he looked out at the audience, and he fairly trembled—which for Jim's size was impressive. He began to talk in restrained tones, reviewing the new program and the presenters' recommendations. Within a matter of moments, his voice rose, the papers rattled in his hand, and his voice quivered in anger and frustration. His main point was the unfairness of the program for students and teachers, most especially those in greatest need of quality schooling.

I wonder at times how Jim would speak about current state and federal policies and practices. Jim was a kind man, and he did not speak ill of anyone. But beneath that exterior was an intensity of commitment that I came to respect and admire. We miss his presence in so many ways.

Robert C. Calfee

IN AN AGE of "fast capitalism," Jim Squire's work may have appeared anachronistic to some. He often sought to remind us of the precedents for our ways of thinking, as when he spoke about the 1966 Dartmouth Conference—which rejected the transmission model in favor of a growth model—or about efforts within progressive education or even earlier to define what matters in education. His voice at times must have seemed quaint to those concerned only with a narrow definition of "what works." He attended to the research of those such as Walter Loban, who conducted a classic study of language development from kindergarten through grade 12. This attention evoked long-term, committed scholarship in a time when many sought only efficient experimental designs and the rapid generation of publications. Similarly, Jim's concern for literature, for aesthetic experiences, and for an appreciation of the complexities and personal meanings of literacy were incongruent with uncritical emphases on new techniques for instruction or assessment.

It is ironic then that Jim's ideas and even more—his strong sense of values, his personal energy and commitment—have had far more influence than that of most of his contemporaries. This influence extends from the larger issues he continually kept in the forefront to the details of particular methods and theories. For me, his presence has been one that shaped my career and continues to influence it since his death.

I first got to know Jim in the early days of the Center for the Study of Reading (CSR) at the University of Illinois, Urbana-Champaign, while I was researcher at a partner organization, Bolt Beranek and Newman, Inc., in Cambridge, Massachusetts. As a young researcher, I was mystified by the dichotomies of IRA and NCTE, reading and writing, learning-to-read and reading-to-learn, and elementary and secondary as they played it out in organizational structures and research paradigms. I remember being asked to represent the CSR at an NCTE meeting, with questions about where the CSR or I stood on these dichotomies, questions I only dimly understood at the time. In that context, I found that Jim was a person who was not only comfortable and confident himself in the different worlds, but who could also help others see areas of common ground and help to build common enterprise toward the deeper values that were shared. This ability to bring people together toward a common purpose was one of Jim's special strengths, and he showed it in many other areas as well.

Early in the history of CSR, there was a focus on analyzing texts that children read. These analyses were at times insightful and representative of the best linguistic and psychological research. They were also a bit naive with respect to the sociohistorical context of schooling. And they were often too critical in the bad sense, that is, unfairly negative, without suggesting any constructive alternatives. The publishing industry might well have ignored that research, thus furthering one more unfortunate separation of theory and practice. Jim played a major role in setting up a different option, one in which publishers and researchers engaged in dialogue. Through a series of conferences, which led to collections of research articles and one-to-one discussions, there was a productive conversation facilitating learning on both sides. The results spilled over into teacher education, instructional designs, and research conferences. Looking back two decades, one might quibble with specific research findings or talk about how the landscape for educational publishing has radically changed, but I doubt that Jim would be bothered by that. What he would rightly emphasize is the enormous value of bringing together people with diverse views to explore those differences and to seek common ground.

Jim was very supportive of my own work at that time, inviting me to participate in various conferences, connecting me with others doing interesting work, and providing helpful critiques. But his impact on me went beyond friendly mentoring. He saw before I did that the work I had done critiquing the misuse of readability formulas or analyzing children's stories was running its natural course. About that time I began work with Andee Rubin and Allan Collins on Quill, a computer system to support children's reading and writing (see Bruce & Rubin, 1993). I still remember a meeting with Jim over 20 years ago in which he helped me to see that my heart and potential lay in studying the impact of new information and communication technologies on literacy, an interest that persists to this day. Despite (or should I say because of?) his strong historical sense, Jim was one of the first to see the potential of these new technologies. I know that Jim played a similar role for many others, neither attacking nor praising blandly but helping them to understand themselves.

One other experience encapsulates much of what Jim was about. Jim and his wife, Barbara, were the consummate dinner hosts. My wife, Susan, and I were fortunate to attend several delicious dinners at their home. These soirees exemplified the integrated approach to learning and life that Jim promoted. The food and setting were excellent, not to mention Barbara's beautiful quilts. There was personal warmth together with intellectual excitement. I remember meeting Charlotte Huck, Martha King, Jeanne Chall, Lee Indrisano, and many others there, getting to know them as caring people, not just as names on book spines. Jim helped me as a junior researcher come to understand the field in a richer and more nuanced way. Most important, the Squires showed through these dinners and in many other ways that one could combine high moral standards, a commitment to children, intellectual integrity, and openness to new ideas. In contrast to those who would reduce learning to simple lists of skills or blind quantifications, Jim's work and life remind us to acknowledge our finiteness and to keep the wonder alive.

Bertram C. Bruce

WHAT TO SAY about Jim Squire? What a legacy! His absence leaves a gaping hole in our field and an irreparable void in those who crossed his path.

I had the good fortune to know Jim professionally as well as personally. In each way, he was larger than life. As an English language arts professional, he was equally at home in and made valuable contributions to the research, teaching, policy, and materials that helped shape our field and give it integrity. Because he admired and knew the value of each of these areas to the improvement of education, he constantly and creatively provided opportunities for dialogue and joint imaginings. He looked ahead, always dreaming of more and better and catching us up in his journey. One day a call or letter from Jim would arrive, and before we knew it, we were meeting with people and writing in collections of his creation that give breadth, history, and vision to our field.

As if that wasn't enough, Jim was also the kindest, friendliest, warmest, and most constant people-lover I have ever met. Once he considered you as a friend, he never let up. Cards, gifts, and conversations were constant reminders of his presence in our lives. He easily shared his time and the details of his life as he fixed himself in ours. We felt like extended family.

Why do I use the plural nominative instead of the singular? For many years, I understood that my husband, Arthur Applebee, who had known Jim since his high school days, had a special personal, as well as professional, bond with Jim. And I imagined that Jim's kindness to me was by spousal affiliation. Only as the years went on, and through many conversations with others, did I realize that this was Jim—both provocateur and family to his immense coterie.

His contribution to the 20th-century English education, and the people in the field he touched, is astounding.

Judith A. Langer

JAMES SQUIRE WAS one of the pioneers in the area of research on readers' responses to literature. Prior to the 1950s, there had been little study of how readers actually respond to literature, the notable exception being I.A. Richards's 1929 study *Practical Criticism: A Study of Literary Judgment*, which examined university students' responses to poetry. And given the dominance of a New Critical approach that dismissed the idea of individual differences in readers' responses, particularly affective responses, as irrelevant to a text's meaning, there was little theory of response, other than that of Louise Rosenblatt's *Literature as Exploration* (1938).

In 1956, Squire completed his dissertation at the University of California, Berkeley, entitled "The Responses of Adolescents to Literature Involving Selected Experiences of Personal Development," which served as the basis for the 1964 NCTE publication *The Responses of Adolescents While Reading Four Short Stories*. In this study, Squire examined how 42 15-year-olds' responses varied according to differences between four short stories and six different points within each story. Based on a content analysis of the responses, he found that the adolescent readers responded in highly unique ways, responses not related to differences in gender, intelligence quotient (IQ), or reading ability. Readers who were highly involved in stories were more likely to judge the literary value of the story; readers made few connections to their own lives, and they experienced difficulty in interpreting stories. As they moved through a story, readers adopted a "happiness binding" stance in which they predicted positive story outcomes. This study was one of the seminal published studies that focused on how readers varied in their responses, leading to challenge, assisted by work in England by James Britton and D.W. Harding, of the prevailing focus on New Critical analysis.

Squire's content analysis methods and his findings had a strong influence on subsequent literary response research in the 1960s and 1970s by researchers such as Dwight Burton (1968), Charles Cooper (1969), Don Gallo (1968), James Hoetker (1971), Jerry Johns (1970), Dianne Monson (1966), Ben Nelms (1967), Alan Purves and Victoria Rippere (1968), Fehl Shirley (1969), and James Wilson (1966)—all of whom made major contributions to theories of teaching response-based literature.

During this same period, Squire and Roger Applebee were conducting one of the first national studies of English instruction, which was published as *High School English Instruction Today: The National Study of High School English Programs* (1968). In this study of 158 schools, they found that while about half of English instruction was devoted to literature instruction, there was no clear consensus on the purpose or approaches, and that 9th and 10th grades were devoted to thematic instruction; 11th grade, to American literature; and 12th grade, to British and world literature—a pattern that remains in many schools 50 years later. At the same time, Squire and Applebee (1969) were studying British English curriculum, which they found focused much more on writing, drama, and literary response than did the American schools they studied. These survey studies served as the basis for Arthur Applebee's (1990) national survey work on the teaching of literature in the 1980s and 1990s.

And given the strong interest in the innovative nature of the British approach to literature instruction, Squire (1968) edited the proceedings of the 1966 Dartmouth Conference, a major meeting of thinkers from Britain and America, *Response to Literature: Papers Relating to the Anglo-American Seminar on the Teaching of English at Dartmouth College, New Hampshire, 1966*. This publication provided American readers with insights into ways in which writing, drama, and classroom discussion could be used as tools to foster literary response.

These studies led Squire to recognize the need for a change in teaching literature at the level of the school curriculum and teacher education. As an editor at Ginn & Company, he was instrumental in launching the Responding Series, a textbook series for teachers by authors such as Alan Purves, Charles Cooper, and James Hoetker that focused on ways of fostering literary response in the classroom based on a well-articulated curriculum model of different types of literary response and ways to evaluate growth in response as described in *A Guide to Evaluation* (Cooper & Purves, 1973). He was also instrumental in fostering the publication of Alan Purves's *How Porcupines Make Love: Notes on a Response-Centered Curriculum* (1972), which became widely used in literature methods courses.

All of his contributions have had a profound influence on literature instruction in American schools. While many of the traditional approaches to literature instruction remain, literature classes are much more likely to feature students actively engaged in response activities, engagement based on both the research theories of response that Squire promoted in his work. In a preface coauthored with Ed Farrell to *Transactions With Literature: A Fifty-Year Perspective: For Louise M. Rosenblatt* (1990), Squire wrote,

> Concern with the responses to literature written expressly for children and young people has led, during the past fifty years, to an awakening of interest in such literature, to the establishment of critical standards by which it might be judged, and to its increased use in our classrooms. Concern with the transaction between book and reader has led to a reappraisal of how literature is most effectively taught and to the development of strategies to enhance the transaction. And concern with reader response has broadened research to include attention to the nature and process of the literary transaction and the ensuing literary experience. (p. vii)

James Squire was one of the early pioneers in instigating this concern with literary response, work that sparked many others to follow in his footsteps.

Richard Beach

WHEN A CAREER looms as large as did Jim Squire's, his touch points of influence are incalculable. So we chose one quality that made him seem larger than life to us, and that was Jim's ability to acknowledge, initiate, and grow the budding professional. Jim Squire never got too busy to ask what professional projects you were involved in. He never got so important that he couldn't stop to meet a new professional, and he never got too self-saturated to listen intently to folks who knew far less than he. He connected your ideas with others' and still let you think you'd come across something splendid. In a great big enthusiastic voice, he would say again and again to people who needed to hear it: "That's a great idea!" And then he'd tell them why. In the many metaphors for the role of teacher, Jim Squire was a gardener—growing and tending his profession.

Nancy Roser and Katherine Bomer

OUR CONTRIBUTION TO this volume in honor of James Squire's legacy to research and practice about language and literacy focuses on professional development. As such, it provides yet another lens on his remarkable contributions to our field and adds yet another dimension to the range of his vision and influence. Professional development was a passion for Jim. Throughout his career, he worked on promoting professional development: first as an English supervisor at the University of California, Berkeley; second during his years as executive director of the National Council of Teachers of English; and third as director of research for Ginn & Company. For some 15 years, during his years with Ginn (later to become Silver, Burdett, & Ginn), Jim organized what is arguably the very best professional development conference on reading and language arts our field has ever known. Each summer, Jim invited school leaders—superintendents, curriculum directors, district language arts supervisors—from around the country to spend the better part of a week at Asilomar Conference Center in Pacific Grove, California, at the southern end of Monterey Bay; summer "reading camp" they called it. And aptly so, because it was reading (and writing and language) research and practice dawn to dusk. You had to rise with the morning sun in time for breakfast and the first session of the day, and sessions went well into the long summer evenings in this picturesque locale. There was some downtime, but the participants were supposed to complete readings and other homework assignments during that time.

Jim would invite a sprinkling of Ginn authors—not because they were Ginn authors but because they were doing interesting research. Let's be clear: There was a marketing subtext in that Ginn & Company clearly wanted these school leaders to adopt Ginn products—not because those leaders were so well hosted or so vigorously marketed but because they would see the link between the research presented in these conferences and the research underpinning the Ginn series. And there was always one evening during which leaders could attend a voluntary session about the Ginn Reading Program. But most of the plenary session presenters were not associated with Ginn or any other publisher. They were invited because they were doing research that Jim thought this audience of school leaders needed to know about in order to create effective district-level programs for reading and language arts.

Jeanne Chall, who was a good friend and Jim's sometime teaching partner at Harvard, came every year to serve as Jim's cohost and universal respondent to all presentations. The format varied between lectures, open forums, and small working groups charged with the responsibility of digesting the information and transforming it into action plans for their districts and schools. Jim was in his element at these annual events—getting everyone organized so meetings could start on time, making sure speakers stopped on time, asking the penetrating question that others in the audience were too timid and polite to ask, providing a contextual fabric to weave all of the presentations together, ranting and slapping the podium with his open palm when he became impatient with a policy or a practice that he thought was getting in the way of good instruction. And the presenters argued with one another and sometimes complemented (and occasionally complimented) one another.

The defining features of these conferences were excellence and integrity, and Jim personified both. The schedule was as demanding as the content, but neither was as demanding as the expectations placed on the participants for what they would do with the knowledge they gained. Jim's Asilomar conferences were in great demand, both by the participants invited to attend and the scholars invited to share their work. Attending Jim's summer camp was a feather in anyone's cap.

Another face of Jim's professional development work happened inside the editorial offices at Ginn & Company. For all of the editors, junior and senior, Jim ran the equivalent of a doctoral seminar on research in language and literacy. He handed out reading assignments, with the expectation that folks would read them in preparation for a discussion and deconstruction of the key ideas. He invited scholars from all over the country to lead daylong seminars on their research or on its application to the development of materials for kids and teachers. Long before we had evidence for the characteristics of effective professional development, Jim had an intuitive sense of what the research would eventually reveal. He knew that educators needed to have a voice in shaping the agenda, that the professional development had to be site based (in this case the site being a publishing house), and that participants needed to stay on a topic long enough to develop some depth. Just as he was in so many other aspects of his career, Jim was a visionary in professional development, and he would anticipate the understandings we would develop much later on. Would that he were still with us to help us in the difficult task of applying what we know about effective professional development to the vexing problems of reading reform, especially as it plays out in our most challenging schools.

P. David Pearson and Barbara Taylor

BRILLIANT SCHOLAR, SKILLFUL teacher, passionate speaker—these are all phrases that describe Jim Squire, and yet they are insufficient in portraying the treasure he was. He was like a giant teddy bear, not only in appearance but also in effect. As a child relies on a familiar and love-worn stuffed animal for comfort, many among us found in Jim's oral and written words not only scholarly wisdom but also professional warmth and reassurance. His words not only taught us about research and theory; they also convinced us that if we worked together we could make a difference; and Jim did everything he could to create contexts in which we could and would collaborate. An invitation from Jim—whether to participate in a conference, a publication, a symposium, or a dinner—was virtually always a joining of familiar and unfamiliar voices, an opportunity to learn from those we knew and others he wanted us to get to know. He was truly special—a deeply thoughtful scholar teacher, a passionate and compelling speaker, a kind and generous person. When I think of Jim, I think of the often-cited words attributed to Sir Isaac Newton: "If I have seen further, it is by standing on the shoulders of Giants" (Letter to Robert Hooke, February 5, 1675/1676). In the field of literacy, Jim is one of our giants. Knowing him, and knowing his work, was quite simply a privilege.

Jeanne R. Paratore

Reading the tributes written by my friends and colleagues for the first time in their entirety, I was gratified to note that the theme of this book, theory and research into practice, and the authorship, theorists and researchers collaborating with practitioners, reflect two of the most vivid threads in the tapestry of the legacy of James R. Squire.

Like James Flood and Diane Lapp, I met Jim Squire when, at the end of one of the first presentations I made as an academic, while I was still critiquing my effort, he startled me by saying that he wished to speak with me about becoming an author of the Ginn Reading Program. The reason for my response was twofold: first, because I was already an admirer of this remarkable scholar, and then because I had begun my teaching career as a liberal arts college graduate who relied substantially on the teachers' manuals of the Ginn Reading series.

That invitation led to one of the experiences I most cherish—the opportunity to work with an author group comprising Theodore Clymer, Dale Johnson, P. David Pearson, and Richard Venezsky, all of us led by Jim Squire. His plan for the preparation of a reading series was characteristic of his approach to matters of teaching and learning. Each author contributed to a document titled "Research-Based Decisions in the Ginn Reading Program." Conclusions from theory and research in the critical areas of our work were summarized and referenced to the literature, and the document served as our guide. I continue to keep the last edition with which I was associated and use it as a model as I work with students and teachers.

Like Robert Calfee and David Pearson, I was a participant in the Asilomar conferences, where the effort to join research and theory to practice was again pursued. Researchers and theorists presented their classic and contemporary work to school administrators and curriculum leaders, followed by discussion of the implications for the practice of education. The highlight of the week was the concluding session, when Jim presented his brilliant summary and reflections and his clarion call to participants to use what they had learned during the conference in the service of children and adolescents.

Like Bertram Bruce and Judith Langer, I was a fortunate dinner guest at the Squire's salon, where the gourmet food was joined with conversation that was equally savory. For me, there was an additional gift: I was the person who drove Jeanne Chall to these events. After a lakeside house became home to the Squires during the benevolent seasons in New England, Barbara and Jim, Jeanne, and I met each month at a different restaurant, taking turns setting the date and arranging the venue. Needless to say, the scheduling was the challenge, the friendship the treasure. As I drove home, I invariably reflected on the spirited dialogue between two sages, Jim and Jeanne, and I was reminded of President John F. Kennedy's observation following the White House Dinner for America's Nobel Prize winners—"the most extraordinary collection of talent, of human knowledge, that has ever been gathered together at the White House, with the possible exception of when Thomas Jefferson dined alone" (April 29, 1962).

Like Richard Beach, I have been enlightened by Jim's research on response to literature, lessons that are reflected in the chapter of this book written with colleagues who participated in the poetry institutes at Boston University, a project that Jim approved with the enthusiasm that marked his devotion to the printed word.

Like Nancy Roser and Katherine Bomer, I observed Jim Squire's ability to acknowledge, cultivate, and grow the budding professional. Shortly after Jim's retirement, Jeanne Paratore and I were fortunate to have Jim join us at Boston University as a visiting researcher. In a series of seminars, he taught our students the history and contributions of the significant theory and research of the 20th century. He influenced their dissertations and, just as important, their work with students and teachers.

During that year, Jim and I coedited *Perspectives on Writing: Research, Theory, and Practice* (Indrisano & Squire, 2000). That volume is both inspiration for and companion to this book. Each of the contributors hopes that this book is a worthy tribute to James R. Squire, whose extraordinary, diverse, and enduring contributions were joined in a quest to assure that teachers and administrators use classic and contemporary research and theory in the service of future generations.

In behalf of the authors of this text, "I count myself in nothing else so happy / As remembering my good friend[s]" (William Shakespeare, *Richard II*, 2, 3).

REFERENCES

Applebee, A.N. (1990). *Literature instruction in American schools.* Albany: Center for the Learning and Teaching of Literature, State University of New York at Albany.

Bruce, B.C., & Rubin, A.D. (1993). *Electronic quills: A situated evaluation of using computers for writing in classrooms.* Hillsdale, NJ: Erlbaum.

Burton, D.L. (1968). *The development and testing of approaches to teaching of English in the junior high school* (Final Report Project #H-026). Tallahassee: Florida State University.

Cooper, C.R. (1969). *Preferred modes of literary response: The characteristics of high school juniors in relation to the consistency of their reactions to three dissimilar short stories.* Unpublished doctoral dissertation, University of California, Berkeley.

Cooper, C.R., & Purves, A.C. (1973). *A guide to evaluation.* Lexington, MA: Ginn.

Farrell, E.J., & Squire, J.R. (1990). *Transactions with literature: A fifty-year perspective: For Louise M. Rosenblatt.* Urbana, IL: National Council of Teachers of English.

Flood, J., Jensen, J.M., Lapp, D., & Squire, J.R. (Eds.). (1991). *Handbook of research on teaching the English language arts.* New York: Macmillan.

Flood, J., & Langer, J.A. (Eds.). (1994). *Literature instruction: Practice and policy.* New York: Scholastic.

Flood, J., Lapp, D., Squire, J.R., & Jensen, J.M. (Eds.). (2003). *Handbook of research on teaching the English language arts* (2nd ed.). Mahwah, NJ: Erlbaum.

Gallo, D.R. (1968). Free reading and book reports—An informal survey of grade eleven. *Journal of Reading, 11,* 532-538.

Hoetker, J. (1971). *Students as audiences: An experimental study of the relationships between classroom study of drama and attendance at the theater.* Urbana, IL: National Council of Teachers of English.

Indrisano, R., & Squire, J.R. (Eds.). (2000). *Perspectives on writing: Research, theory, and practice*. Newark, DE: International Reading Association.

Johns, J.L. (1970). *Expressed reading preferences of intermediate-grade students in urban settings*. Unpublished doctoral dissertation, Michigan State University.

Monson, D. (1966). *Children's responses to humorous situations in literature*. Unpublished doctoral dissertation, University of Minnesota.

Nelms, B. (1967). *Characteristics of poetry associated with preferences of a panel of tenth grade students*. Unpublished doctoral dissertation, University of Iowa.

Purves, A.C. (Ed.). (1972). *How porcupines make love: Notes on a response-centered curriculum*. Lexington, MA: Xerox College Publishing.

Purves, A.C., & Rippere, V. (1968). *Elements of writing about a literary work: A study of response to literature*. Urbana, IL: National Council of Teachers of English.

Richards, I.A. (1929). *Practical criticism: A study of literary judgment*. London: K. Paul, Trench, Tubner.

Rosenblatt, L.M. (1938). *Literature as exploration*. New York: D. Appleton-Century.

Shirley, F. (1969). Case studies of the influence of reading on adolescents. *Research in the Teaching of English, 1*, 30–41.

Squire, J.R. (1956). *The responses of adolescents to literature involving selected experiences of personal development*. Unpublished doctoral dissertation, University of California, Berkeley.

Squire, J.R. (1964). *The responses of adolescents while reading four short stories*. Urbana, IL: National Council of Teachers of English.

Squire, J.R. (Ed.). (1968). *Response to literature: Papers relating to the Anglo-American Seminar on the Teaching of English at Dartmouth College, New Hampshire, 1966*. Urbana, IL: National Council of Teachers of English.

Squire, J.R., & Applebee, R.K. (1968). *High school English instruction today: The national study of high school English programs*. New York: Appleton-Century-Crofts.

Squire, J.R., & Applebee, R.K. (1969). *Teaching English in the United Kingdom: A comparative study*. Urbana, IL: National Council of Teachers of English.

Squire, J.R. (1994). Literature and public policy. In J. Flood & J.A. Langer (Eds.), *Literature instruction: Practice and policy* (pp. 170–175). New York: Scholastic.

Wilson, J.R. (1966). *Responses of college freshmen to three novels*. Urbana, IL: National Council of Teachers of English.

Contributors

Bonnie B. Armbruster
Professor, Department of Curriculum
   & Instruction
University of Illinois at Urbana-Champaign
Champaign, Illinois, USA

Soledad Concha Banados
Research Assistant, Intergenerational
   Literacy Project
Boston University
Boston, Massachusetts, USA

Richard Beach
Professor of English Education
University of Minnesota
Minneapolis, Minnesota, USA

Katherine Bomer
Independent Literacy Consultant, K–8
Austin, Texas, USA

Bertram C. Bruce
Professor of Library and Information
   Science
University of Illinois at Urbana-Champaign
Champaign, Illinois, USA

Jennifer Hauck Bryson
Grade 3 Teacher
Chelsea Public Schools
Chelsea, Massachusetts, USA

Robert C. Calfee
Distinguished Professor, Graduate School
   of Education
University of California, Riverside
Riverside, California, USA

Renée M. Casbergue
Professor of Education
University of New Orleans
New Orleans, Louisiana, USA

Ana María Chacón
Program Coordinator and Research
   Assistant, Intergenerational Literacy
   Project
Boston University
Boston, Massachusetts, USA

Elizabeth A. Close
Director of Educational Outreach, Center
   on English Learning & Achievement
University of Albany, State University
   of New York
Albany, New York, USA

Sharon L. Comstock
Doctoral Student in Library and Information
   Science
University of Illinois at Urbana-Champaign
Champaign, Illinois, USA

Julie Coppola
Assistant Professor of Education
Boston University
Boston, Massachusetts, USA

Sunday Cummins
Literacy Consultant and Doctoral Student
University of Illinois at Urbana-Champaign
Champaign, Illinois, USA

Catherine J. Dawson
Literacy Specialist
Lowell Public Schools
Lowell, Massachusetts, USA

Rita ElWardi
Educator/Staff Developer
Hoover High School
San Diego, California, USA

Douglas Fisher
Director of Professional Development, City
    Heights Educational Collaborative
San Diego State University
San Diego, California, USA

James Flood
Distinguished Research Professor
    of Language and Literacy Education
San Diego State University
San Diego, California, USA

Nancy Frey
Assistant Professor of Teacher Education
San Diego State University
San Diego, California, USA

Tom Friedrich
Doctoral Student in Literacy Education
University of Minnesota
Minneapolis, Minnesota, USA

Joanne George
Grade 2 Teacher
Lowell Public Schools
Lowell, Massachusetts, USA

Molly Hull
Language Arts Teacher, Grade 7
Farnsworth Middle School
Guilderland, New York, USA

Roselmina Indrisano
Professor and Chair, Department
    of Literacy and Language,
    Counseling and Development
Boston University
Boston, Massachusetts, USA

Merri Jones
Grade 3 Teacher
Frank M. Sokolowski School
Chelsea, Massachusetts, USA

Barbara Krol-Sinclair
Director, Intergenerational Literacy Project
Chelsea Public Schools
Chelsea, Massachusetts, USA

Judith A. Langer
Distinguished Professor
University of Albany, State University
    of New York
Albany, New York, USA

Diane Lapp
Distinguished Research Professor
    of Language and Literacy Education
San Diego State University
San Diego, California, USA

Diane MacLean
Grade 3 Teacher
Lowell Public Schools
Lowell, Massachusetts, USA

Sarah J. McCarthey
Associate Professor
University of Illinois at Urbana-Champaign
Champaign, Illinois, USA

Susan McPhillips
Grade 1 Teacher
Lowell Public Schools
Lowell, Massachusetts, USA

Roxanne Greitz Miller
Postdoctoral Scholar, Graduate School
    of Education
University of California, Riverside
Riverside, California, USA

Jeanne R. Paratore
Associate Professor of Education and
    Program Coordinator for Reading
    Education, Department of Literacy and
    Language, Counseling and Development
Boston University
Boston, Massachusetts, USA

P. David Pearson
Dean and Professor
University of California, Berkeley
Berkeley, California, USA

Mary Beth Plauché
K–2 Teacher and Team Leader
Metairie Park Country Day School
Metairie, Louisiana, USA

Wendy L. Ranck-Buhr
Literacy Administrator
San Diego Unified School District
San Diego, California, USA

Nancy L. Roser
Professor of Language and Literacy Studies
University of Texas at Austin
Austin, Texas, USA

Anamarie Tam
Teacher Specialist
Glendale Public Schools
Glendale, California, USA

Barbara M. Taylor
Guy Bond Professor of Reading
University of Minnesota
Minneapolis, Minnesota, USA

David J. Williams
Language Arts Teacher
Hopkins High School
Minnetonka, Minnesota, USA

Introduction

Jeanne R. Paratore

At this point in time many, perhaps even most, policymakers believe that the best approach to school reform is high-stakes assessment. The underlying claim seems to be that teachers may know how to teach, but for some reason, they choose not to offer their students the quality of instruction that will lead to high levels of achievement. The reasoning is apparently that, when faced with the threat of accountability, both teachers and their students will work harder, and the by-product of this hard work will be higher levels of achievement. Many literacy experts dispute this line of thinking, particularly as it relates to the teaching of writing. George Hillocks (2002), for example, argues that, although high-stakes assessments may influence what is taught, they do not teach teachers how to teach. Rather, changing the ways teachers teach writing requires changing the ways teachers understand the process of writing. The landmark studies of Janet Emig (1971) and Donald Graves (1983) were catalysts for substantial changes in both the number and types of investigations related to writing. As a consequence, knowledge about the acquisition and development of writing abilities has grown substantially, and noteworthy changes have occurred in writing classrooms (National Assessment of Educational Progress, 2002). Nonetheless, overall levels of writing achievement, as measured by the most recent National Assessment of Educational Progress (2002), indicate that work remains to be done. This book represents one attempt to respond to the need to continue to support teachers in their understanding of writing development and in their implementation of excellent instruction in writing and, by so doing, improve students' writing achievement.

The result of collaborative effort of researchers and teachers, each chapter provides explicit descriptions of what is commonly termed "theory into practice"—ways that research comes alive in classrooms. Each authorship team reviews research and theory related to a particular area of writing development and applies the evidence to instructional practice. The descriptions of recommended practices are supplemented in various ways by each of the author teams, including transcripts of classroom discourse, samples of student work, and teachers' responses to particular instructional practices.

We have clustered the chapters within two sections: writing in the early and elementary years and writing in the middle and secondary years. We note, however, that although chapter authors have chosen particular classrooms in which to exemplify the application of research and theory in practice, the fundamental ideas in each chapter can be readily applied across a range of age and grade levels.

In the first chapter, Renée M. Casbergue and Mary Beth Plauché review the body of research literature related to children's early writing development and the instructional practices that support beginning writing. The authors address multiple aspects of emergent writing, including children's understanding of the

Learning to Write, Writing to Learn: Theory and Research in Practice edited by Roselmina Indrisano and Jeanne R. Paratore. Copyright © 2005 by the International Reading Association.

forms and functions of print, the manner in which print conveys meaning, and the connections between letters and sounds. Detailed descriptions of classroom environments and activities that support each of these aspects of writing development are drawn from Mary Beth's K–2 multiage classroom. Writing samples include children's representations of both narrative and informational texts and demonstrate the increasing complexity of children's writing attempts as they mature and move toward the more conventional writing typical of the primary grades. Some samples include pieces of writing drawn from a single child's work over time, while other samples illustrate the varied ways that children of different ages and developmental understandings of writing respond to the same instructional activity.

In the second chapter, Nancy L. Roser and Katherine Bomer continue the exploration of writing in the primary grades. They note the substantial and meaningful changes in the ways we understand early writing development, and in ways helpful to novice and veteran teachers and researchers alike, they "make the intricacies of terms and teaching seem both real and manageable" by walking us through the daily routines in Katherine's K–2 multiage classroom. They use children's oral and written language (and their own skillful commentary) to make the process of learning to write come alive in remarkable ways. Through examining Katherine's organization, planning, goals, opportunities, instruction, and the responses to writing in her classroom, they make primary instruction tangible, its struggles transparent, and its links to theory and research both useful and stretching.

In chapter 3, Julie Coppola, Catherine J. Dawson, Susan McPhillips, Joanne George, and Diane MacLean address the particular challenge faced by young children who are learning about two aspects of language: how to speak a second language and how to represent one's thoughts and ideas in that language in written form. The context for their work is a yearlong, schoolwide effort to improve writing instruction for children from linguistically and culturally diverse backgrounds in an urban elementary school. This chapter is notable not only for the detailed explanations that help the reader to understand and replicate the types of instructional actions they planned and implemented but also for the authors' acknowledgment of the long-term nature of meaningful change. In keeping with this understanding, they present a teacher-generated plan to continue their work to improve writing instruction.

In chapter 4, Roselmina Indrisano, Jennifer Hauck Bryson, and Merri Jones present a classroom writing project that grew out of a collaboration with Robert Pinsky, U.S. poet laureate, 1997–2000, and the national Favorite Poem Project. The authors give a detailed description of a university-based Poetry Institute and then describe the ways Jennifer and Merri, both elementary-grade classroom teachers, engaged children in reading, written response, and the creation of poetry; the extension to the families and other members of the community; the support and resources provided by the principal and the Title I director; and the outreach to teachers in their district and other professional communities. Samples of the writing of students and parents help demonstrate the power of this work.

In chapter 5, Bonnie B. Armbruster, Sarah J. McCarthey, and Sunday Cummins turn the focus from learning to write to learning to use writing as a tool to help students learn content. As in each of the other chapters, these authors begin with a brief review of research on writing and learning in elementary classrooms. They explain that, based on their understanding of existing research and theory, they were interested in knowing how the evidence has influenced instructional practice in local elementary classrooms, and they take us with them on several classroom visits so that we, too, can see what is happening. The examples they find and share include a variety of forms of writing, and the teachers we meet are at once enthusiastic about the possibilities and challenged by the barriers that they confront in their daily routines. Armbruster, McCarthey, and Cummins conclude—and we, the book editors, agree—that their classroom observations and conversations effectively tell us what is known but also underscore what is yet unknown about how to support children in their development as writers. As such, they provide some clear directions for future investigations.

In chapter 6, Jeanne R. Paratore, Barbara Krol-Sinclair, Ana María Chacón, and Soledad Concha Banados expand the early learning context to include parents and other family members in the home setting. The backdrop for this work is a family literacy program in an urban community in which immigrant parents are learning to use writing to mediate their own and their children's literacy and language learning. Using samples of parents' and children's writing and excerpts from interview transcripts, these authors help us to understand the situations or circumstances that cause adults and children to choose to write at home and the factors that influence their choices about language, genre, and form.

Chapter 7 marks the transition to an examination of the ways excellent teachers apply research and theory in middle and secondary school classrooms. Despite the shift in grade level, however, several of the earlier themes persist. Just as authors of earlier chapters have remarked on the complexity of the writing task for young writers, James Flood, Diane Lapp, and Wendy L. Ranck-Buhr acknowledge "the complexity of what writing encompasses in the middle schooler's life" and how this interacts with "the complexity of the middle schooler's swirling psyche." They begin with a description of a professional development program designed to support effective instruction in writing, and then, with two urban schools as context, they describe how teachers work together to bring effective practice from the professional development workshop to their middle school classrooms. Foundational to the work described by Flood, Lapp, and Ranck-Buhr is an underlying premise that middle school students are both exciting and excitable—and that they deserve teachers who can effectively join a love of teaching with the depth of understanding necessary to help them to develop both the motivation to read and the powerful literacy skills necessary to meet the demands of today's society.

In chapter 8, Douglas Fisher, Nancy Frey, and Rita ElWardi take us into urban secondary school English and content area classrooms where effective instruction of writing is the norm. They include a description of the ways effective secondary school English teachers teach and support students' writing as well as the types of writing instruction that can and should occur in content area classrooms. They choose a few of the practices to explore in depth, and they ground each of these in the experiences of their students. Their detailed student profiles, accompanied by samples of their students' writing, clarify and deepen our understanding of what writing development looks like in secondary school students.

In chapter 9, Richard Beach, Tom Friedrich, and David J. Williams help us to continue our exploration of the development of writing by turning the focus to the actions we take, as teachers, in responding to our students' work. They review theory and research on different ways of responding to writing that foster self-evaluation and revision leading to writing improvement. They begin with different theories of revision that range from simply changing text to rethinking or altering beliefs and ideas. They then turn to various methods of providing feedback during the writing processes in teacher and peer conferences and written or online comments. They explicate the various methods for supporting revision using examples of feedback to students' writing from David's work with students in his secondary English classrooms. Their chapter concludes with a summary of the practices that they suggest will lead teachers to provide more effective support for revision and, in turn, lead students to more effective writing.

In chapter 10, Elizabeth A. Close, Molly Hull, and Judith A. Langer turn our attention to the interdisciplinary nature of writing acquisition and development. They explain that they have chosen to use the chapter as a "reawakening...and also as a call for more relationship-focused instructional research." Indeed, as you read about their Partnership for Literacy—a project intended to engage teachers as active investigators into the effects of their teaching on students' learning—we believe that you will be drawn into their work in ways that will prompt deep thought, serious reflection, and likely changes in approaches to teaching and learning.

In chapter 11, Bertram C. Bruce and Sharon L. Comstock argue that new technologies have changed the ways we "communicate, create, and collaborate," and they remind us that new technologies have been the catalyst for

> new genres that are now becoming as commonplace as the computer. Hypertextuality is no longer a buzzword of academics or postmodern literati, but an accepted form of both fiction and nonfiction; online diaries have flourished in a networked environment that offers both anonymity and audience for creative construction of identity; and blogging has reached professional culture, with corporations and libraries alike posting to the world.

To help us to understand the influence new technologies have had (and continue to have) on the teaching and learning of writing, they take us into classrooms, libraries, and community settings in which technology is not only expanding the environments for writing but also changing how the craft is practiced. Through detailed description and intriguing and engaging writing samples, they help us to understand how we might use technologies to develop writers in and out of school, and in much the same way as Armbruster, McCarthey, and Cummins, they help us to understand how much more we need to learn about these new literacies.

In the final chapter in this section, Robert C. Calfee and Roxanne Greitz Miller conclude our exploration with a focus on assessment. They argue that in the current accountability climate, writing is either ignored or constrained by on-demand tasks or arbitrary rubrics. In response, they describe an approach to assessment that builds on classroom-based, authentic writing tasks that have the potential to reveal students' ability to effectively organize and present information. Throughout the chapter, they emphasize what they describe as the "classroom teacher's crucial role in the implementation of cognitively demanding, transformative instruction and assessment."

Finally, whatever the merit of various instructional practices, achieving change in classroom instruction is, in the end, primarily a function of the quality of professional development. Although the importance of professional development is addressed in several chapters, in the epilogue, P. David Pearson, Barbara M. Taylor, and Anamarie Tam take this as their primary focus. In exquisite detail, and with a window on one school in particular, they walk us through the procedures and elements that they have learned lead to meaningful and important changes in teaching practices. Although the work they describe is largely grounded in reading instruction, they argue, and the book editors agree, that the fundamental principles and lessons they learned are equally sound and valuable in the context of writing instruction.

As we began this introduction, we noted that some educational experts argue that high-stakes assessment is a misguided tool for meaningful instructional reform and that, instead, professional development may prove to be a more beneficial investment. We share that point of view, and we offer this text as one means to assist teachers in their efforts to help children become accomplished writers.

REFERENCES

Emig, J. (1971). *The composing processes of twelfth graders*. Urbana, IL: National Council of Teachers of English.

Graves, D. (1983). *Writing: Teachers and children at work*. Portsmouth, NH: Heinemann.

Hillocks, G. (2002). *The testing trap: How state writing assessments control learning*. New York: Teachers College Press.

National Assessment of Educational Progress. (2002). *Writing: The nation's report card*. Retrieved October 31, 2004, from http://nces. ed.gov/nationsreportcard/writing

.

SECTION ONE

Writing in the Early
and
Elementary Years

Chapter 1

Emergent Writing: Classroom Practices That Support Young Writers' Development

Renée M. Casbergue and Mary Beth Plauché

It was early in Micayla's first-grade school year when terrorists struck the World Trade Center in New York, September 11, 2001. Even though she lived in New Orleans, Louisiana, and her family shielded her as much as possible from the horrible details of the event, it was clear that she was deeply affected by what she had witnessed on television. As a means of helping Micayla and her classmates cope with their feelings about the tragedy, the children were invited by their teacher to share their thoughts by drawing and writing about the attack. Even so early in the school year, first graders like Micayla were able to produce powerful pieces that revealed the breadth of their knowledge about the events and the depth of their responses (Figure 1.1). The simple yet genuine emotion expressed in her writing, "I do not like what happened and I wish that it didn't happen," is in stark contrast to the incredible detail apparent in her drawing.

That Micayla was able to use writing so effectively for such a personal purpose may surprise those unfamiliar with the research on children's early writing development. Yet many characteristics of her writing—from her inclusion of more information in the picture and her oral description of it than in the text to the way she used phonemic spelling and reversed the orientation of some letters—are typical of emergent writing development. The pages that follow illustrate the developmental milestones that typify early writing and offer a glimpse into one multiage classroom that provides multiple opportunities for writing and writing instruction that support that development.

Early Writing Research

The development of writing is an evolutionary process that is situated within the broader development of children as social beings. Learning to write is essentially a social process that "entails learning to differentiate and manipulate the elements of the written system (e.g., letters and words) in order to engage with, and manipulate, the social world" (Dyson, 2001, p. 126). Many researchers have

Figure 1.1　First Grader Micayla's Drawing and Writing Sample

I do not lis with a P N

and I wish that it din

h a P I n

I do not like what happened and I wish that it didn't happen.

documented how naturally young children engage in writing when they are surrounded by print and when they interact with more knowledgeable language users (Baghban, 1984; Bissex, 1980; Schickedanz, 1990). Writing begins early in life as toddlers and preschoolers experiment with "mark making" (Schickedanz & Casbergue, 2004). During their earliest writing attempts, they become increasingly purposeful in their use of crayons, markers, and other writing implements as they gain better motor control and begin to recognize that their marks can be used to represent concepts and objects in their environment.

At the same time that young children learn to control their mark making, they also begin to learn how to compose meaning. Composition begins first with oral language, as children tell about events in their lives and share knowledge with others (Dyson, 2001; Roskos, Tabors, & Lenhart, 2004). There is also a significant connection between children's engagement with books and children's ability to compose. Children who have listened to many stories, have talked about them with family and teachers, and have begun to read on their own have an intuitive sense of story grammar and expository text structure; this deep understanding of how writing works filters into the writing they do themselves (Casbergue & Plauché, 2003; Duke & Kays, 1998; Kamberelis, 1998, 1999; Pappas, 1991; Snow & Ninio, 1986).

Emergent writers thus have a lot to learn about print as they become increasingly competent in its use. They need to learn its forms and its functions, how it conveys meaning, and the links between meaning and form (McGee & Richgels, 2000). Regarding form, they must learn that graphic patterns called "writing" differ from graphic images called "pictures." They need to learn that symbols used for writing are constructed from a mix of straight and curved lines and that varying the combinations of those lines yields different letters, each with its own name and sound. Regarding function, emergent writers need to learn that writing can be used for a number of different purposes and across many different contexts (Schickedanz, 2003). In terms of meaning, they must learn that what they want to say can be said in writing and that print, more so than pictures, is a precise and efficient way to convey meaning to others. Finally, emergent writers must learn that letters represent sounds that, when combined, represent words. Armed with that knowledge, they will have begun to make the link between meaning and form.

Chrissy's Writing Development

A close examination of one child's writing as she progressed through kindergarten illustrates the extent to which children's understanding of the aspects of writing emerges as they experiment with expressing themselves in print and receive instructive feedback from teachers and peers. Chrissy began the school year using a mix of letters, mock letters, and scribbles to write (see Figure 1.2a). At this point, she had become aware of print in her environment and knew how to write her name conventionally. She used the letters in her name frequently and flexibly to create lines of print that resembled conventional writing, although she demonstrated no awareness of the alphabetic principle, selecting letters based on her familiarity with them rather than their sounds. She also drew on less mature forms of writing, using invented symbols that looked like letters and lines of mock linear writing to complete her piece. Her reading of this composition, "I got another new dog. His name is Mambo. He always jumps on me and he licks my face," suggests that she "romanced" her writing; that is, she made up a story to go with the print, even though it appeared to have no inherent meaning (Gardner, 1980).

Eventually, however, Chrissy abandoned the mock letters and mock linear writing that characterized her earlier pieces and resorted to using only real alphabet letters, as can be seen in Figure 1.2b. This shift in form often occurs as children become more aware of the details of print in their environment, and especially as they come to recognize that a finite number of letters comprise all of the writing they see (Schickedanz & Casbergue, 2004). The writing in this sample was still nonphonemic, however, as Chrissy apparently chose letters at random to produce writing that she determined to be of sufficient length to represent a story. Her reading of the story upon its completion was, "Bart Simpson has a sister and he doesn't want his sister around him. And there is a mean guy that wants to kill him. My dog...then my dog, whenever he sees people, he jumps up and down." It is not clear that Chrissy wrote with intent—that is, she still may not have planned what she intended her writing to say before she began. More likely, the fact that her teacher ascribed intent by asking her to read her writing aloud once again prompted her to make up a narrative to go with her text after she finished writing. The two distinct subjects of her story, Bart Simpson and her dog, may have evolved because she didn't believe that she had "read" enough (relative to the amount of print) when she had completed the narrative about Bart.

From a social perspective, Chrissy's earliest kindergarten compositions demonstrated her determination to participate in an activity that was valued in her classroom—daily journal writing. Establishing herself as a writer, and thus a full

Figure 1.2   Chrissy's Early Writing Samples

A. Early Kindergarten Writing Sample

I got another new dog. His name is Mambo. He always jumps on me and he licks my face.

B. A Later Kindergarten Writing Sample

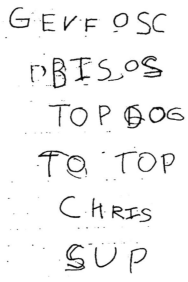

Bart Simpson has a sister and he doesn't want his sister around him. And there is a mean guy that wants to kill him. My dog...then my dog, whenever he sees people, he jumps up and down.

participant in the literate life of kindergarten, was probably a more important goal than conveying any particular meaning through the writing itself.

As would be predicted by research on early writing development, Chrissy did eventually break through to alphabetic writing. Figure 1.3a illustrates her early attempts at using the alphabetic principle to write as she created semiphonemic spellings to say, "My dog is Mambo," choosing letters to represent the most prominent sounds in words or syllables. Contrast this with the sample in Figure 1.3b, in which her spelling was more fully phonemic and thus included letters for most of the obvious sounds in the words she tried to write: "I like Christmas, and I like Santa Claus, and I like my presents." In both samples, consonant sounds were more easily represented than were vowels, and long vowels were better represented than short vowels, which are hardest to hear. Figures 1.3a and 1.3b also illustrate the difficulty children often have determining word boundaries, primarily because the divisions between words are often difficult to hear in the connected speech on which writing is based. Thus, even though Chrissy was now intentionally writing real words to convey a specific message, she did not include any spaces between those words.

Note also that her messages were longer when she wrote first and made up a narrative later. Once children begin to focus on inventing spellings for the words they are using, the task of writing becomes much more tedious. As a result, the quality of their messages often suffers. Children who previously had concocted elaborate stories appear to regress and write only simple statements with little elaboration. This seeming regression is not due to a loss of narrative ability but is instead indicative of the aspects of writing on which children focus during different developmental phases. Whenever children begin to give their attention to some unfamiliar aspect of writing, other aspects that had appeared to be under control may be set aside.

Figure 1.3   Chrissy's Attempts at Phonemic Writing

A. An Early Attempt

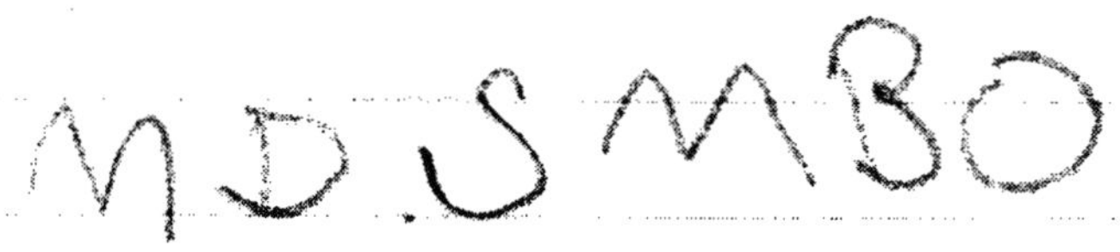

My dog is Mambo.

B. A Later Attempt

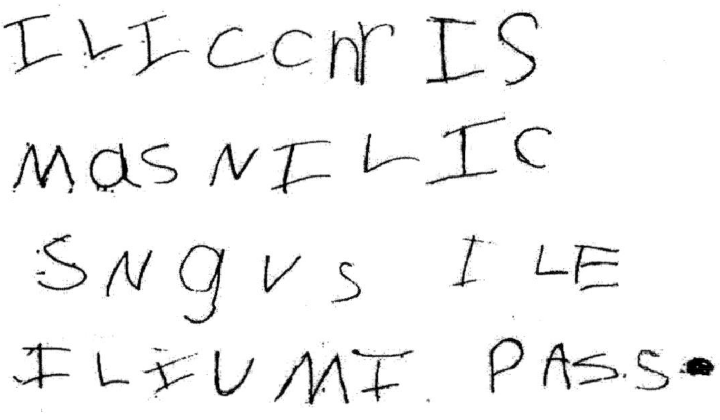

I like Christmas, and I like Santa Claus, and I like my presents.

Figure 1.4   A Sample of Chrissy's Improved Writing Skills

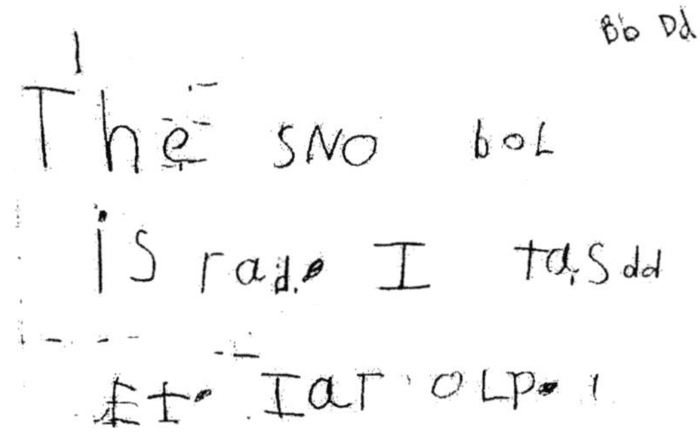

The snowball is red. I tasted it. I ate it all up.

Figure 1.4 further demonstrates this phenomenon as Chrissy again wrote a brief message: "The snowball is red. I tasted it. I ate it all up." Note the growth in other aspects of her writing, however, as she demonstrated mastery of spaces between words (indicating growing awareness of word boundaries), more comprehensive phonemic spelling, and basic punctuation, including capital letters at the beginnings of sentences and periods at the ends. Notice also the printed upper- and lowercase *b*s and *d*s at the top of the page, supplied by her teacher to help her correctly orient those letters in her writing. Clearly, Chrissy's attention at this point in her writing development was as much on form—the mechanics of writing—as on meaning.

Once the various mechanical aspects of writing become more familiar and comfortable, children are usually able to return to the production of longer messages with more elaboration. Chrissy produced the sample of writing in Figure 1.5 toward the end of kindergarten. It is titled "My Dog" and reads, "My dog is fourteen. She has arthritis. I feel bad. She doesn't walk good sometimes. I feel very, very bad!" It is notable that Chrissy had gained full mastery of word boundaries by the time she wrote this piece. Further, an analysis of her spelling revealed that she now used a mix of fully phonemic spellings (those that included most of the sounds in the words she wrote) and conventional spelling of common sight words. She even included a new punctuation mark, the exclamation point, which she used appropriately, even though she followed it with a period—an indication that this was still a relatively new discovery for her. Most important, the quality of her message was significantly improved, with more detail and clear voice that very directly expressed her feelings about her older pet.

From a social perspective, Chrissy's writing had evolved to the point that she could use her journal entry to initiate a conversation with her teacher and her friends about her concern for her aging dog. Many of her journal entries at this point also seemed to function as a means of sorting out her feelings about events in her life. Whereas her earliest writing had served the purpose of solidifying her role as a writer, with little emphasis on the meaning attached to her print, by the end of the year, meaning had become a primary focus.

These writing samples illustrate patterns of development typically seen in emergent writers. While some of the new knowledge demonstrated across the

Figure 1.5   Chrissy's Writing in Late Kindergarten

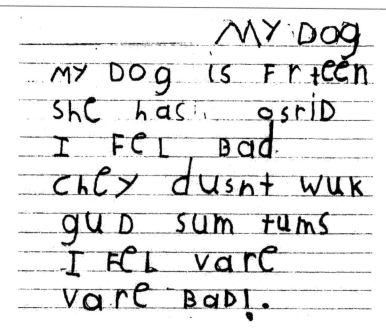

My Dog. My dog is fourteen. She has arthritis. I feel bad. She doesn't walk good sometimes. I feel very, very bad!

different pieces may have occurred naturally as Chrissy participated in the print environments that surrounded her both at home and at school, her development was not left to chance. Rather, her teacher carefully constructed multiple opportunities for Chrissy to experiment with print, and she provided helpful feedback and explicit instruction designed to foster her writing development.

Classroom Support for Emergent Writing

A primary goal for young writers is their development of facility with the process of writing, facility that enables them to communicate through writing as naturally and freely as they do through their drawings and their speech. Writing then becomes a natural means of sharing thoughts and ideas, one that has permanence and allows children to convey meaning beyond the scope of spoken language and drawings.

Children who write each day develop positive attitudes about writing and come to see it as an easy and instinctive means of expression. The children referred to in this chapter are all students in Room 2, a multiage kindergarten, first-, and second-grade classroom of one of the authors (Mary Beth Plauché). There are nine kindergarten children, eight first graders, and eight second graders in the independent school classroom. For these children, experiences with writing begin in their first days of kindergarten. Each child writes in a journal several times a week, starting the first week of school; although many kindergartners do not have a conventional understanding of writing this early in the year, they nevertheless quickly develop the sense of writing as communication, as evidenced in Chrissy's writing samples.

For young children, especially those just beginning to write, an essential part of the writing process occurs when they read what they have just written to an audience. This process strengthens the reading–writing connection and provides a basis for refinement of each child's storytelling and writing abilities. In Chrissy's earliest writing, she related stories that may or may not have been on her mind as she wrote the letters, but sharing her narrative nevertheless solidified for her the concept of writing as communication.

The teacher records the narrative the emergent writer "reads," using conventional spelling to retain the content the child relates, regardless of the letters on the page. A sticky note attached to the child's composition serves as a nonintrusive way to preserve the intended meaning. The teacher uses this translation to assess the child's developing composition skills (making meaning, organizing information, considering audience) and comprehension of the conventions of writing (letter formation, spelling, punctuation, grammar). It further serves as an ongoing record of the child's intentions and allows teachers to analyze children's progress over time. Once the writing develops into a more conventional and easily readable form, it stands on its own, without the need for translation by an adult. Reading the writing to an audience of peers and adults nevertheless remains an essential component of the writing process. Having students write in bound journals that are retained in the classroom gives the teacher and children a very clear indication of growth throughout the school year.

When kindergartners write, they usually begin by drawing a picture, often talking through the meaning they intend to create (Dyson, 1983). It is not unusual to see young children draw a little, write, return to their pictures to add more detail, then write again to include that detail in their text (Calkins, 1994; Dyson, 2001). Moving into writing a story is a natural progression as they describe what they've drawn, using whatever letters and sounds they already know. The teacher's role is to oversee the process, emphasizing that the goal is to share their thoughts. Spelling at this point is largely invented and, in the earliest writing, often bears little relationship to words the children say they are writing (Read, 1971; Richgels, 1995). As children become more familiar with phonic elements, the teacher gradually raises expectations of accurate sound-symbol correspondence, helping children to incorporate the phonics they are learning into their spelling. Handwriting (including the placement of spaces between words) is stressed only insofar as it affects meaning and legibility. Correct punctuation is introduced as the children develop the need for it in their own writing.

Supporting Early Phonics and Spelling Development

The development of phonemic awareness and the acquisition of phonics knowledge are essential adjuncts to young children's development of writing skills (Adams, Foorman, Lundberg, & Beeler, 1997; Richgels, 2001). The role of the teacher is to carefully guide students to apply the sounds they know to their spelling. In the context of writing, this is done individually as each child gains phonics knowledge from a variety of sources, including independent and teacher-directed word study. In the earliest writing, sound-symbol relationships are minimal, as seen in Chrissy's first pieces. As phonics knowledge grows and teachers help children connect phonics to writing, often through shared and interactive writing activities, spelling gradually becomes closer to conventional.

Spelling instruction that is organic, that proceeds from children's own developing abilities as applied in writing, is an effective means to move toward and learn conventional spelling (Snow, Burns, & Griffin, 1998). Children typically begin to demonstrate their understanding that specific letters represent specific sounds by writing the initial sound they hear to represent a word. For example, "The cat is black," might be written as "CSB." As writers become more proficient, they add ending sounds: "CTSBK." The teacher monitors each child's progress, offering suggestions for more precise spelling based on the child's phonics knowledge. A child who has internalized the short /a/ sound in reading might be asked what sound she hears in the middle of *cat*. The teacher would pronounce the word as "caaaat," stretching out and exaggerating the medial short /a/ sound; then the child would be encouraged to add that middle sound to her word. Another child who writes "KT" for *cat* might be asked what other letter makes the /k/ sound heard at the beginning of the word.

Sight words are likely to appear in children's writing from the time they first experiment with spelling. Certain sight words are tricky to sound out phonetically; for example, *the, when, they, was,* and *come* are used frequently by young writers but can't easily be spelled using phonemic strategies. Once children become comfortable with print and write freely using semiphonemic and phonemic spelling, they are ready to be given some of these sight words and told that they are words that are difficult to spell and that do not follow the normal spelling rules. Each individual child can be given short lists of often-used words to refer to when writing. As early as first grade, many children can be held accountable for checking to see that they have spelled these few words conventionally. Because the words selected are high-frequency words within the children's own writing, they will rapidly learn to spell them correctly. At that point, a few new words—or frequently used phrases like "once upon a time"—can be added to the children's personal lists. Those lists can be written in the back of journals, on a separate alphabetized "dictionary page," in personal dictionary notebooks, or on class word walls. These lists allow children to become more independent writers and encourage them to think about how they spell. Such resources also help children learn to rely on the visual information in words rather than exclusively on the sounds they hear. Helping children focus on spelling simple sight words conventionally will help them move from phonemic to transitional and then conventional spelling later on.

Spelling patterns are also addressed in the context of children's writing. Once a child begins to hear the vowel sound in *me*, he or she can be introduced to the conventional spelling of *he, we, she,* and *be* as well. The child who writes "LIK" for the word *like* can be taught the silent *e* rule and then encouraged to find words in his or her writing that might need a silent *e* to make the vowel sound long. Attention to spelling rules is likely to lead to their overgeneralization at first, with silent *es*, for example, decorating every other word on a page. But over time, and with more word study, children will gain a more refined understanding of the rules and will apply them more judiciously.

Other prompts to help emergent writers include visual cues for letter sounds. An alphabet frieze with pictures, such as an apple for short /a/, an ice cube for long /i/, and a thumb for the /th/ sound, will offer a resource children will readily use. Charts that list ways to write long vowel sounds, such as *ae, ai, ay,* and *eigh* for long /a/, will also provide spelling options for children. When children have a means to check for the appropriate letter(s) to represent a specific sound, they become more independent writers and more accurate spellers.

Supporting Handwriting and Punctuation

In Room 2, youngsters are routinely taught specific methods for writing individual letters with the goals of developing legibility, relative speed, and comfort. While this is a priority as children are learning to write, absolutely correct letter formation during the writing of narratives is developmental in the same way that spelling is. Children who see writing as communication need to have the freedom to get their words down on the page without being unduly concerned about their letter formation and handwriting. Poor letter formation should not mean that students do not write stories; rather, letter formation should be addressed separately and corrected in stories only when doing so does not interfere with the flow of the narrative, usually once the storytelling portion of the writing has been completed.

Spacing within and between words is one element of legibility that is actually related to much deeper understanding of words and print. Emergent writers typically do not recognize each word as a separate unit of meaning, even if they do recognize individual words in their reading. Only after they have read and written connected text for an extended length of time and have begun to recognize beginning, ending, and some middle sounds of words do they understand that they must put spaces between each word. When children do understand that each separate unit of meaning is represented by an individual word—the "concept of word" (Clay, 1975)—they are ready to place spaces between groups of letters that they intend to stand for words. The teacher determines how to best instruct each child based on his or her particular needs and skills. The teacher can help children to explore this concept of word boundaries by encouraging finger spacing, a process of placing a finger at the end of each word before writing the next one. Figure 1.6 shows Charlie, a kindergartner in Room 2, doing just that as he writes about castles in a journal about medieval times. Teachers should be aware, however, that when children first begin experimenting with spaces in their writing, they are likely to place spaces rather randomly, without regard for words as units of meaning.

Punctuation is another aspect of writing mechanics that can be addressed early in the writing process with young children. Routinely beginning narratives with capital letters and ending them with periods introduces children to these conventions of writing. As their narratives lengthen, the teacher helps them to listen to the natural rhythms as they read and to place ending punctuation in their writing when their voices come to a stop. At that point, they also add a capital letter to begin the following sentence. As writers progress and become more familiar with conventional writing, their teachers introduce them to other punctuation as it applies to their pieces. It is not uncommon to see even young children include commas in a series and quotation marks to signify speaking as their writing skills grow. And most emergent writers are especially taken with exclamation points as they recognize the usefulness of this punctuation mark for reflecting the excitement they want to share with their readers. For young

Figure 1.6   Charlie Demonstrates Finger Spacing

children, punctuation—often used creatively, as seen in Chrissy's writing in Figure 1.5—offers the best means of inserting voice into writing (Calkins, 1994).

Theme-Related Writing

While much of the instruction described above is carefully tailored to the development and needs of individual children as they learn to write, a comprehensive writing program should also include opportunities for children to use writing to learn (International Reading Association & National Association for the Education of Young Children, 1998). Writing across the curriculum, long recognized as an important activity for children in upper elementary grades (see Armbruster, McCarthey, & Cummins, this volume), is equally important for emergent writers. There are many natural opportunities for writing to occur in the early childhood classroom in addition to the routine of daily journaling. Young children are introduced to the power of reading and writing when writing is integrated into other content areas, such as science. Even the youngest children can research topics and record the information they find by examining artifacts, pictures, and informational text (Casbergue & Plauché, 2003). Learning about a concept and then sharing that information in writing, even if the writing is not conventional, gives young children a palpable reason to write. Observing the metamorphosis of a caterpillar into a butterfly and then writing down what occurs each day, as shown in Figure 1.7, makes writing part of a rich and exciting hands-on experience. Such expository writing prepares even very young children for the formalized writing they will encounter as they progress through school. While the amount of information they are able to include in their compositions will vary according to their writing development, any invitations to write about interesting content will entice children to explore topics more deeply and increase their knowledge of both the topic and expository writing conventions. (See also Copolla, Dawson, McPhillips, George, & McLean, this volume, who address ways to engage young second-language learners in nonfiction writing.)

Figure 1.7   A Sample of Early Expository Writing

Monarch Caterpillar. The caterpillar is on the milkweed. He, he's drinking the milkweed.

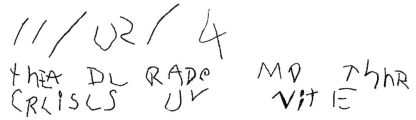

They already made their chryslis overnight.

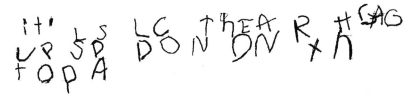

It looks like they are hanging upside down on the top.

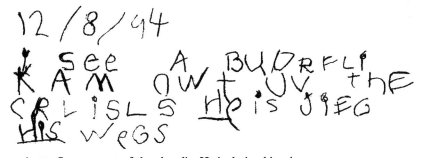

I see a butterfly came out of the chryslis. He is drying his wings.

From Casbergue, R.M. (1998). How do we foster young children's writing development? In S.B. Neuman & K.A. Roskos (Eds.), *Children achieving: Best practices in early literacy* (pp. 198–222). Newark, DE: International Reading Association.

Social studies is another content area that offers potent opportunities for writing. Children in Room 2 spent a year studying life in medieval times. They read books about castles and constructed their own from papier-mâché. They read and heard stories about the lives of both royalty and peasants in the Middle Ages and then wrote about what they had learned. For one ongoing writing activity, all of the children chose an occupation from that time, then made regular entries in a special journal about their lives as medieval artisans and merchants. The first entry in the journal was an introductory page. Figure 1.8 shows Jack's response to this activity, in which he simply says, "I am Michael the weaver." His illustration shows the weaver standing in front of his loom. Charlie's entry is more elaborate (Figure 1.9). He wrote, "My name is Durrell. I work for the carpenter and I hammer wood." Sara's introduction to her character (Figure 1.10) is very detailed and says, "I am Sara the carpenter. Today I made about 20 things. I live in Nightingale Glen. Today some merchants came to my shop, and some peasants. This day I got a lot of money. From customers. When I was walking about. I caught up with my friend Elise the goldsmith. We talked for a while. Then we went on our way."

These very different responses to the same activity reflect the varying developmental levels of the children in this K–2 classroom. While Jack's entry was extremely brief and written with invented spelling, it nonetheless demonstrated his awareness of a typical occupation of medieval times, and his drawing illustrated his knowledge of the major tool of the weaver's trade. Charlie's journal entry reflected his more advanced understanding of writing conventions and conventional spelling. His writing, too, reflected his knowledge of a common medieval job, and his statement also indicated his awareness of the role of apprentices, even though he did not use that term. Sara was clearly the most comfortable writing about her role, and her entry provided much more insight into

Figure 1.8   A Sample From Jack's Journal on Medieval Studies

I am Michael the weaver.

Figure 1.9   A Sample From Charlie's Journal on Medieval Studies

My name is Durrell. I work for the carpenter and I hammer wood.

medieval life. She made reference to both merchants and peasants, reflecting classroom discussions of the emerging merchant class. She also acknowledged another occupation, that of the goldsmith, as she described walking about the town.

It is significant that Sara's writing did not include a picture. The two younger children still needed to use drawing as a means of rehearsal to clarify their thoughts while writing. Older children like Sara, however, usually move beyond drawing as rehearsal and find that other means of organizing their writing are more effective. In fact, Sara used Inspiration software to construct a semantic web to summarize her knowledge about medieval carpenters (Figure 1.11) and began to write using ideas represented in her web. Later journal entries would include much more of the information included in the web as she returned to it again and again for ideas.

Figure 1.10   A Sample From Sara's Journal on Medieval Studies

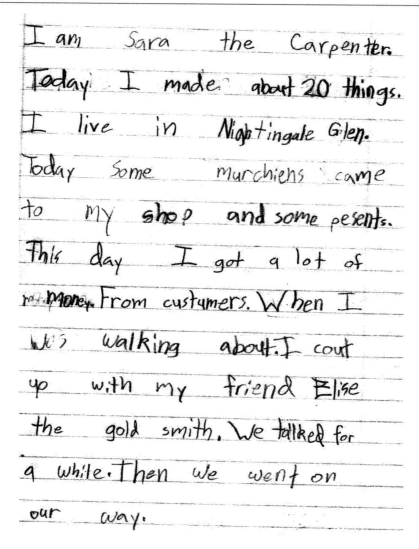

I am Sara the carpenter. Today I made about 20 things. I live in Nightingale Glen. Today some merchants came to my shop, and some peasants. This day I got a lot of money. From customers. When I was walking about. I caught up with my friend Elise the goldsmith. We talked for a while. Then we went on our way.

Additional Writing Opportunities

Daily journal writing routines and the theme-related writing described thus far represent only two of the many writing experiences enjoyed by the children in Room 2. These young writers are provided with a broad range of opportunities for composition. Some activities are structured and teacher directed, as when children

Figure 1.11   Sara's Semantic Web

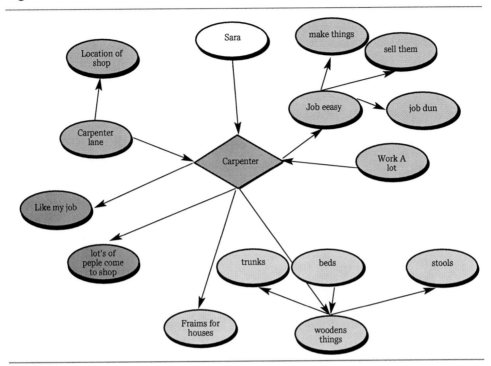

work to construct a carefully edited class book about a particular topic. Others are more casual and can be completed with little teacher intervention; for example, several children list ingredients for a cooking activity and sign up for items that they want to bring from home.

In a rich literacy environment, children who write easily and fluently do so throughout the school day as casually as they speak. For them, writing often serves very personal purposes, as when they make a sign asking that a block building not be knocked down, or when they write a note of apology to a friend, as did Olivia who produced the note displayed in Figure 1.12. It says, "Sorry, Noah. This will never happen again. I'm very sorry, Noah. So sorry. It will not happen again." Children like Olivia write with a lack of restraint and are concerned only with creating meaning, exchanging ideas, and accomplishing their goals. Sara's notes in her carpentry web could just as easily describe the perspective of children in Room 2 about writing for their own purposes: "Job eeasy/Job dun."

Putting Conventional Writing in Perspective

If young children are to feel free to engage so readily in writing, they must perceive that their classroom offers a risk-free environment. A question often arises about how and when young children's writing should be corrected. Although it is essential that children learn conventional spelling, grammar, punctuation, and

Figure 1.12   Olivia's Note of Apology to a Friend

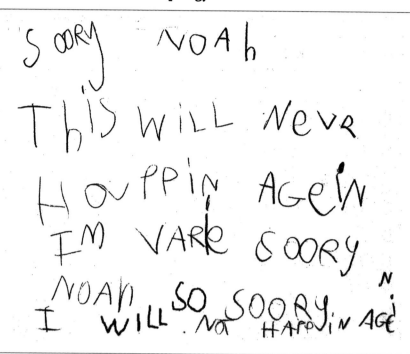

other elements of writing mechanics, it is not necessary for them to correct every piece of writing. In keeping with the principle of regarding each child as an individual, writing corrections take place at appropriate times for each child. Spelling corrections are gradually introduced as children are asked to correct words they can sound out, simple sight words, words that follow a pattern they have learned (word families), or words that can be looked up in their personal dictionaries. As spellers become more proficient, they are expected to find and correct misspelled words with increasing independence.

The same is true for other aspects of writing. However, emergent writers must be allowed to develop fluency as writers, to learn to use the words they want to when creating their narratives rather than resorting to using only words they believe they can write conventionally. Without the strictures of perfection for every piece of writing, emergent writers will feel free to express themselves and will view writing as communication. In acknowledgment of that philosophy, children's work is displayed in Room 2 both uncorrected and with final editing and corrections made. In either case, classroom displays are celebrations of all that young writers can accomplish when given both the freedom to write and appropriate support for their efforts.

REFERENCES

Adams, M., Foorman, B., Lundberg, L., & Beeler, T. (1997). *Phonetic awareness in young children: A classroom curriculum.* Baltimore, MD: Brookes.

Baghban, M. (1984). *Our daughter learns to read and write: A case study from birth to three.* Newark, DE: International Reading Association.

Bissex, G. (1980). *Gnys at wrk: A child learns to read and write.* Cambridge, MA: Harvard University Press.

Calkins, L. (1994). *The art of teaching writing.* Portsmouth, NH: Heinemann.

Casbergue, R. (1998). How do we foster young children's writing development? In S.B. Neuman & K.A. Roskos (Eds.), *Children achieving: Best practices in early literacy* (pp. 198-222). Newark, DE: International Reading Association.

Casbergue, R., & Plauché, M.B. (2003). Immersing children in nonfiction: Fostering emergent research and writing. In D. Barone & L. Morrow (Eds.), *Literacy and young children: Research-based practices* (pp. 243-260). New York: Guilford.

Clay, M. (1975). *What did I write?* London: Heinemann.

Duke, N., & Kays, J. (1998). "Can I say 'once upon a time'?" Kindergarten children developing knowledge of information book language. *Early Childhood Research Quarterly, 13*(2), 295-318.

Dyson, A. (1983). The role of oral language in early writing processes. *Research in the Teaching of English, 17*(1), 1-30.

Dyson, A. (2001). Writing and children's symbolic repertoires: Development unhinged. In S. Neuman & D. Dickenson (Eds.), *Handbook of early literacy research* (pp. 126-141). New York: Guilford.

Gardner, H. (1980). *Artful scribbles: The significance of children's drawings.* New York: Basic Books.

Inspiration 7.0 [Computer software]. (2000). Portland, OR: Inspiration Software.

International Reading Association & National Association for the Education of Young Children. (1998). *Learning to read and write: Developmentally appropriate practices for young children.* Newark, DE: Author; Washington, DC: Author.

Kamberelis, G. (1998). Relations between children's literacy diets and genre development: You write what you read. *Literacy Teaching and Learning, 3*(1), 7-53.

Kamberelis, G. (1999). Genre development and learning: Children writing stories, science reports and poems. *Research in the Teaching of English, 33*(4), 403-460.

McGee, L., & Richgels, D. (2000). *Literacy's beginnings: Supporting young readers and writers* (3rd ed.). Boston: Allyn & Bacon.

Pappas, C. (1991). Young children's strategies in learning the "book language" of information books. *Discourse Processes, 14*(2), 203-225.

Read, C. (1971). Pre-school children's knowledge of English phonology. *Harvard Educational Review, 41*(1), 1-34.

Richgels, D. (1995). Invented spelling ability and printed word learning in kindergarten. *Reading Research Quarterly, 30*(1), 96-109.

Richgels, D. (2001). Invented spelling, phonemic awareness, and reading and writing instruction. In S. Neuman & D. Dickenson (Eds.), *Handbook of early literacy research* (pp. 142-155). New York: Guilford.

Roskos, K., Tabors, P., & Lenhart, L. (2004). *Oral language and early literacy in preschool.* Newark, DE: International Reading Association.

Schickedanz, J. (1990). *Adam's righting revolutions: One child's literacy development from infancy through grade one.* Portsmouth, NH: Heinemann.

Schickedanz, J. (2003). Engaging preschoolers in code learning: Some thoughts about preschool teachers' concerns. In D. Barone & L. Morrow (Eds.), *Literacy and young children: Research-based practices* (pp. 121-139). New York: Guilford.

Schickedanz, J., & Casbergue, R. (2004). *Writing in preschool: Learning to orchestrate meaning and marks.* Newark, DE: International Reading Association.

Snow, C.E., Burns, M.S, & Griffin, P. (Eds.). (1998). *Preventing reading difficulties in young children.* Washington, DC: National Academy Press.

Snow, C.E., & Ninio, A. (1986). The contracts of literacy: What children learn from learning to read books. In W. Teale & E. Sulzby (Eds.), *Emergent literacy: Writing and reading* (pp. 116-137). Norwood, NJ: Ablex.

Chapter *2*

Writing in Primary Classrooms: A Teacher's Story

Nancy L. Roser and Katherine Bomer

*W*riting workshop, writing process, shared writing, interactive writing, scaffolded writing, composing, conferring, revising, editing, publishing— the concepts and labels related to writing that have seeped into the lexicon of primary teachers sound vastly different from the terms of just a few decades ago (Jensen, 2002). Not so long ago, "handwriting" and "creative writing" were the terms most frequently bandied when teachers talked about young children's writing. But changes in labels alone don't necessarily signal conceptual or instructional change. Even so, when it comes to writing instruction, we think these terms represent real shifts in thinking, organization, and classroom procedures.

Teachers are spending more time supporting children's routes toward written products than exclaiming over their best *r* in a trailing line. They've given more effort to helping children learn to find the topics they want to write about than they have to assigning compositions with titles like "My Three Wishes" or "The Funniest Thing." It seems to us that professional insights into writing and its development may have produced one of the last century's most significant changes in primary pedagogy.

To make the intricacies of terms and teaching seem both real and manageable, we focus on describing one multiage, primary classroom—a place/space where children write and write and write. We look closely at how the writing workshop seems to hum when a teacher has deep understandings of how young children's writing grows and knows what it means (cognitively, socially, and personally) for children to write (Bomer & Bomer, 2001). But depth of understanding doesn't necessarily imply ease of installing a writing workshop (Ray & Cleaveland, 2004; Ray & Laminack, 2001); neither does deep knowledge prevent rough spots, quandaries, and even the commission of seeming violations of an increasingly instantiated view of "the" writing process. That is, the steps often ascribed to a single process of writing have become prescriptive in many classrooms of writers (Hoffman, 1998). We offer the assumptions of just one classroom teacher, as well as the persistent questions that are a part of her attempts to build more (and more relevant) writing opportunities into the lives of children. Along the way, we, like Julie Jensen (2002), acknowledge the shoulders of the giants who have lifted our sights—the researchers and thinkers and teachers who have shared what they know about teaching to, and learning from, young writers.

Learning to Write, Writing to Learn: Theory and Research in Practice edited by Roselmina Indrisano and Jeanne R. Paratore.
Copyright © 2005 by the International Reading Association.

Into a Writing Place: Katherine Bomer's Classroom

Before you step across the threshold of Katherine's classroom, you can tell it will be a place where writers write. The walls and desks, the bound volumes and journals, the trays, folders, and cubbies can't contain the writing that has gone on inside, so writing snakes from the doorway and down the hall like the waving tentacles of an untamed beast. These hallways invite visitors to get to know Katherine's students through their words and the stories embedded in their artwork. Before you enter, you can "hear" children's voices in print:

"Wht I cok in mikrwa"

"3 waze to wrsh a dog"

"Dear Msr Bommer..."

"My Favrit Book"

Above the doorway, a sign scrawled in a child's shaky hand announces "Entrance" and, on the other side, "Exit." Jaime explains it this way: "Just like on doors at the store!" (See Figure 2.1 for a sign posted on the door when the class went on a field trip.)

Figure 2.1   Sign Posted on Door During Class Field Trip

We Are Going to a Carnival

Walk in. Use caution, though. Children nearest the door are likely to pounce—pressing their latest creations:

"Look, I'm writing about Pikachu!"

"Me too, only I'm changing his character a little bit so I won't be just copying the cartoon!"

Meander around the room. An astonishing amount of print surrounds you. Some of it is clearly teacher writing (charts and records that list features of learning), but most of it is kid writing: labels for areas of the room (Math Center, Art Center); directions for how to do things; examples of poetry, fiction, and nonfiction; and even a big sign labeling the hamster's cage: "Stuart Little, Our Hamstr." Hanging by the calendar is a book by Luis, explaining a calendar. (See Figure 2.2 for Luis's planning graphic.) None of it bears Katherine's markings, and much of it demonstrates approximations of conventional spelling (Figure 2.3). School has been in session for only nine weeks, yet writers are growing here.

If you have arrived on time, you can observe the minilesson that opens writing workshop. It is called a minilesson because it focuses briefly on an introduction or

Figure 2.2   Luis's Planning Graphic for a Book About Calendars

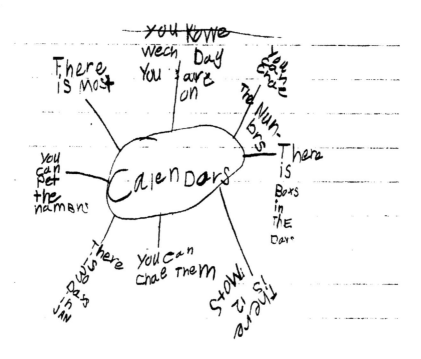

You know which day you are on. You can change the numbers. There is boxes in the days. There is 12 months. You can change them. There is 30 days in January. You can put the numbers. There is most.

Figure 2.3   Sample of Spelling Approximations in a Child's Guidelines for Health

I am drinking milk and I do not talk to strangers.

demonstration of some content, convention, or genre of writing. Writing time always begins promptly and at the same time each day because Katherine believes it is important that children learn to anticipate its arrival and come prepared to the meeting area ready to listen, think, and share—already planning for their writing that day. The minilesson happens in the meeting area of the room—a large rug with a chair for the teacher (or the classroom author), an easel with chart paper and markers, and baskets of books near the author's chair (Graves & Hansen, 1983) full of "touchstone" or "teaching" books. The meeting rug is wrapped on two sides by bookshelves lined with hundreds of books.

Katherine begins by recalling and linking with some ongoing focus of writing instruction. Today, she demonstrates writing powerful leads to nonfiction pieces by sharing a portion of her own writing, explaining to her children that she has tried a new beginning because she wanted to better pull in her audience. She shows them her first attempt that "sounds like a dictionary—kind of boring" and then her revised version, one that uses repetition, figurative language, and even a sense of mystery. "Which do you like better?" she asks, and their decision is both unanimous and aware. She asks the children to turn to a partner and talk about some ways they, too, might begin their writing by thinking about getting the attention of their readers. The volume rises as children happily chatter to each other. Katherine settles beside two boys, listening carefully:

"Today...I'm going to start my book with a question, like that book we read yesterday called *What Is the World Made Of?* [Zoehfeld, 1998]."

"I'm gonna say, 'Have you ever seen a shark? Well, I have, and I wasn't even scared!'"

"That's cool! Where'd ya see a shark?"

Katherine gently clears her throat, raises an eyebrow, and smiles questioningly at the second speaker. He understands this as code for "That's for later. Get back on track!"

"Oh yeah. OK. My book is gonna start...um...my book is all about my ferret, Hot Dog. His name is Hot Dog 'cause he looks like a hot dog, only he has hair!"

"Maybe you shouldn't say, 'My book is about...,' 'member, we said that's a boring thing to say? Make it more exciting. Like start with a question."

All around the meeting rug, writers are trying out possible beginnings for their nonfiction books (Figure 2.4). When Katherine beckons them back to attention,

Figure 2.4   **Draft Lead for a Nonfiction Book About the Tooth Fairy**

Tooth Fairy gives dollars. You get anything that you can buy, and if you put seven teeth under your pillow, you will get seven dollars.

she reminds them that their favorite writers think hard about how to begin their writing so that people will want to read it. And then she says: "Go write!"

Children move unusually calmly from the rug. Katherine has spent several weeks encouraging them to "slide like snakes" and "float like bubbles" through the room, and now they know how to get to favorite writing spots without mishap. Some children need to get a fresh piece of paper, so they move purposefully to a special bookshelf, raggedly labeled by a child: "Writing Center." On the top shelf, there are small, colorful baskets full of pencils and markers. There is a basket with sticky notes and another with erasers. There is a stapler and staple remover, a tape dispenser, a bucket of glue sticks, and an electric pencil sharpener.

On the second shelf there are two baskets from which children can choose, one labeled "Lined paper" and another "Unlined paper." On the third is a basketful of ready-to-write books (four to eight sheets of different sizes and shapes bound with construction paper or wallpaper), along with choices of multicolored scraps. Easily in reach are several children's dictionaries. Katherine's students are completely in control of their own supplies, and they use the tools that writers need, treating them with respect. At the beginning of the school year, Katherine teaches lots of lessons and provides demonstrations about writers' tools and how to use them, giving children many chances to practice.

Although some children need to choose fresh paper today, others have already settled into their writing spots with drafts they will be adding to or revising with their reconsidered leads. In this classroom, the children have been invited to find places where they will be able to keep the writing flowing. For some, this means returning to the rug, snugging their backs against a bookshelf, and using clipboards to hold their paper. For others, sitting at a table works better. One child loves to sit in the teacher's/author's comfy chair, and she turns on the floor lamp beside it. A few boys choose to write together today, and Katherine keeps a careful eye to ensure that their talk stays within a productive range and they keep their focus. If not, she will cross the room to speak to them, sometimes even asking them to make a different decision for their writing space.

All children retrieve their writing folders. These folders, stored in plastic bins, contain working drafts of children's writing pieces. Most of the children already have ongoing projects: stories, poems, picture books, nonfiction articles they are developing, and letters that will travel outside the classroom (Figure 2.5). Children choose what they wish to write about, with topics ranging from the personal—"My Dog," "My New Baby Sister," "What I Want for My Birthday"—to fantasy and science fiction topics involving characters from popular culture (currently Pokémon and Yu-Gi-Oh).

For the next few weeks in this writing classroom, Katherine's students will focus on learning the features and elements of nonfiction. Across the year, the class will study other genres and literary forms—and learn to write in those modes what they and others want to read. They are learning to read like writers and write as readers. Writing conferences and celebrations will be held. Some pieces will be taken to the computer for typing; others are ready for binding with covers, endpapers, and title page; still others can be posted directly on the wall. Related pieces will be grouped in volumes, books of child writing will be sent home to share, and a steady flow of production will continue. A writing workshop is in full operation.

Figure 2.5   Letter to the Art Teacher and Her Fiancé

Miss Green. You too, Mr. Mosely. I wish you good luck. I know you will be happy. Never forget that you made a vow.

Teacher Knowing/Teacher Doing

Instruction in Katherine's classroom is "as practical as a good theory" (a maxim often attributed to Kurt Lewin [refer to Marrow, 1969, p. ix]). What does she know about children and their writing that would have surprised early childhood and primary teachers of not so very long ago? While her precepts are many, we have chosen to highlight and describe six especially critical ones: (1) all children can write, (2) primary children's writing should be purpose filled (and all day), (3) writing develops readers, (4) writing is a social act in primary classrooms, (5) writers must be both fed and instructed, and (6) writers can be fragile beings.

All Children Can Write

Katherine knows that all children think. And as James Squire (1983) taught us, for most children, thinking involves language. Talk, text, and models of eloquent language support Katherine's writing curriculum. Further, she knows that children bring sets of unique experiences, expressions, and depths that feed their writing. The luckiest of them have been read to (Adams, 1990; Teale, 1986) and have been writers at home (Baghban, 1984; Bissex, 1980), but all of them have been living life, and those lives fuel the stories they have to write (González, Moll, & Amanti, 2005). Katherine understands that some children take longer than others to discover their voice, their flow, their resources, their confidence, and their skills, but her classroom (its organization, resources, expectations) testifies to her conviction that all children can write and that she is working to ensure they know it, too.

Primary Children's Writing Should Be Purpose Filled (and All Day)

In her book on the writing life, Julia Cameron (1998) waxes euphoric about what writing means to grownups:

> We should write because it is human nature to write. Writing is sensual,
> experiential, grounding. We should write because writing is good for the soul.
> (p. xvi)

But the purposes and satisfactions of writing in classrooms seem (on the surface) much more pragmatic: Children say they write to label their pictures, to record favorite foods, to tell others about something important, and to echo patterns inspired by other authors, such as Donald Crews or Denise Fleming. In purpose-filled writing classrooms like Katherine's, children write to say what they think or feel and what they are learning. When expert teachers insist that writing for children must be authentic, they mean that the writing tasks should make sense to children and that young writers should be involved in the same kinds of writing tasks that literate people perform outside classroom walls. Inside Katherine's room, there are few blanks to be filled in or rows of perfectly formed letters to complete. Instead, there is writing for a host of legitimate purposes. And even though there is time set aside for writing instruction and writing each morning, children write all day and all across the curriculum. From attendance ledgers to word problems; from queries to the librarian to loving letters to former teachers; from graphs, labels, and charts to playground and neighborhood social action projects, writing stitches the day together. Children may not all see the value of writing "to the soul," but they do see writing as a serious, sensible, and satisfying undertaking.

Writing Develops Readers

That writing feeds children's understanding of their written language system is not a new idea (Beers & Henderson, 1977; Ehri, 1989; Read, 1975), but it is a central one. Children working to encode their thoughts are also paying attention to the phonemes of their spoken language. As they attend, supported by instruction, they steadily record more sounds and retain more spelling patterns. From scribble-scrabble to letter strings to spelling approximations, writing grows, and, along the way, learning to write supports learning to read (at the beginning, even more directly than reading supports writing). Writing is also a way young children try out their understandings of print conventions (Clay, 1975; Holdaway, 1979)—how print travels across the page, how words are spaced, and how the mechanics of punctuation and capitalization can help their readers make meaning. Classroom writing, then, besides its function to ensure thoughtful response to literature, to record hypotheses and conjectures, to keep records, to communicate, and to learn, provides firm support for learning to read.

Katherine's students represent a mix of ethnicities, interests, and reading levels. In any one year, she receives children ranging from the beginning of the learning-to-read process to readers of chapter books. The same could be said of almost any teacher of any primary grade. Because writing, like reading, develops at different rates and often in different ways, Katherine believes her observations and logs of her children's development inform her teaching and ensure her children's growth. Based upon notes and records, Katherine decides what lessons need repeating and what additional demonstrations, coaching, and support she will need to provide. Katherine, as Yetta Goodman would describe it, is a skilled "kidwatcher" (Owocki & Goodman, 2002). She understands that assessments should have value and authenticity.

Writing Is a Social Act in Primary Classrooms

It almost seems clichéd to state that children's writing grows in the presence of a community of other writers. Peter Elbow (1973) describes the benefit of a community:

> Two heads are better than one because two heads can make conflicting material interact better than one head usually can.... I say something. You give a response and it constitutes some restructuring or reorienting of what I said. Then I see something new on the basis of your restructuring, and so I, in turn, can restructure what I first said. (pp. 49-50)

Writers building in confidence want readers. They share their journals; they sign for conferences; they applaud for others and receive applause in turn. They ask questions, add ideas, and borrow freely. They come to express what they think and how their ideas connect with others. They explore both together and individually (Dyson, 1989). Writing improves in classrooms as works in progress are shared and talked over. And writing is affected in profound ways when children's conversations about writing become more knowing and sophisticated—one of Katherine's instructional goals for writing workshop.

Writers Must Be Both Fed and Instructed

Katherine knows that better writing doesn't just happen. Her children are fed with examples from the best of authors—inside and outside the classroom. She relies on children's literature not just to motivate her children to read and write but to offer her children fine models of writing.

> "Listen to how Cynthia Rylant [*When I Was Young in the Mountains* (1982)] helps you feel what she feels about her mountain home."

> "Let's look at how Petra Mathers [cf. 1998, 2000] starts her stories with a character action to see what we can learn from that."

> "Here are two stories about lost toys [*Plaidypus Lost* (Stevens & Crummel, 2004) and *Where Are You, Blue Kangaroo?* (Clark, 2001)]. When we're finished, let's talk about how two authors wrote differently about the same topic."

Besides the models of books and peers, Katherine, like other expert teachers of writing (Ada & Campoy, 2004; Hindley, 1996), is a writer in her classroom. She writes in front of children, along with children, and shares her planning and revision processes, just as they do. Her reflection on her own intentions and changes makes sense to children and shows what Frank Smith (1981) calls the messy process of writing.

Writers Can Be Fragile Beings

Some of the checkpoints that most reveal young writers' fragility are in (a) selecting a topic, (b) knowing how to sustain and when to abandon a piece of writing, and (c) learning to talk with other authors about their work. From Katherine's point of view, these are all issues of providing support, determining how much and how frequently support is needed.

Selecting Topics. In Katherine's classroom, topic selection is a strategy that is taught. Like Donald Graves (1983, 1994), Katherine encourages children to generate ideas continuously for writing. But as beginners, they also generate a class chart of ideas, one they can turn to if they run dry on ideas for writing. Like Lucy Calkins and Shelley Harwayne (1991), Katherine invites children to move about the room to gather ideas from what others are writing. And to help children keep track of their productions and stimulate ideas, a chart with places for sticky-note postings of children's current topics is on the wall. (Figure 2.6 presents a sample topic chart.)

Figure 2.6   Sample Wall Chart

Name	Title or Topic
Nathan	Evil laugh story
Manuel	How I got my nickname
Tomas	Ferret Diary
Mavis	The Box

Sustaining and Abandoning Topics. Young writers can protest that they have nothing to write about, then write about their bicycle for week after week, followed by a sudden shift that results in a sheaf of superhero stories with a derring-do character and no story line. It's a test of Katherine's faith in the writer's development to know when to encourage, when to receive, when to gently steer, and when to stand by. Katherine is continuously asking herself questions about the challenges individual writers are taking on, the attention they are paying to their own writing, the interest they demonstrate in their audience (the act of revision as an act of civility), and the passion with which they adhere to topics.

Sharing Writing. Learning to talk meaningfully, kindly, and pointedly about your own and others' writing is another central and continuously shaping part of primary writing instruction. About a decade ago, we (Labbo, Roser, & Hoffman, 1995) labeled the author's chair in one primary classroom as a kind of "hot seat" on which young writers were being questioned too closely and shaped past their own intentions for their writing. The sharing of writing in the workshop, it seems, must be even more carefully planned than the distribution of materials—because there is more at stake. Sharing writing is an essential piece of a writing community; it can even help to build community. But if the sharing time is the only example of civil exchange that occurs in the day, it will not be successful. Katherine demonstrates for her young writers how to receive writing not only by her behaviors but also by her words: "Your words pleased my ears. In the sentence that began, 'Spiderman struggled with all his strength...,' I liked the ways the sounds repeated. Poets, too, sometimes use Matt's technique to please the ears of listeners. They call it alliteration." Important, too, Katherine demonstrates appropriate responses to the works of writers from outside the room—authors of children's literature: "What did you observe in Peggy Rathmann's story, *Officer Buckle and Gloria* [1995]? What did you like? What would you ask Ms. Rathmann about her writing if she were here?"

A Teacher's Ongoing Quandaries

Katie Wood Ray describes instituting a writing workshop as "all the hard parts" (Ray & Laminack, 2001). Katherine points to three areas that she continuously mulls, considers, and tweaks: (1) conferring, (2) revising, and (3) assessing.

Conferring

Much like Carl Anderson (2000), Katherine considers the conversations that occur over writing as central to her writing instruction. She believes that these conversations are not so much about perfecting a product as about teaching a writer. Because the writing is received and talked over in a genuine, companionable way, there are decisions to make about who takes the lead, how a writer's development can be provided for, how many topics to graze, and how pointedly to make a point. Katherine struggles with making those decisions on the fly. Each conference presents a new case, and each case must be handled carefully. She divides conferences, though, into two types: The first is the kind that many primary teachers don't count as "conferences." These are the times Katherine stoops beside a writer at work and waits quietly for a moment to see if he or she looks up, has a question, or wants to share. Sometimes the writer is too engaged to break focus, and Katherine moves away. But when either of them starts a conversation, for example, "What are you working on?" or "Listen to this," a conference has begun.

The second kind of conference is scheduled—the kind children indicate they are ready for—when the children sign up or report their intentions in the morning meeting. These are the pull-up-a-chair conversations, and Katherine carries a spiral notebook—the type with a divider for each child—to these. Like Joanne Hindley (1996), Katherine has already observed and taken notes about what amazes her about each child writer, but she begins these conference times with careful, intensive listening. She listens to the child describe what he or she is working on, asking questions to clarify the child's intentions or the piece of writing itself. She intends to take the conference to a teaching place in which she equips the writer with an idea or strategy for becoming an even better writer (e.g., choosing vivid words to describe). Yet even with structure, preparation, and direction, some conferences don't go as intended, slide off the mark, or wander. Conferring is a skill of teaching writing more easily talked about than done.

Revising

The notion of changing their writing is an idea that astonishes some beginning writers (as much as the idea of "repainting" their artwork). But revising is a subject Katherine considers seriously. Like Carol Avery (1993), Katherine attends to revision the very first time she sees someone erase. It's then she demonstrates that crossing out is a fine way to show you have changed your mind on paper. Although she often demonstrates her own rethinking when she models writing on the chart tablet, it's when young writers say "Oops, I forgot to..." or "I put too many letters there" that she considers the best teaching moment to remind them that all good writers rethink and cross out. The computer is also an intriguing revision tool in Katherine's classroom. Children in primary grades, preparing their writing for publication, sometimes choose the keyboard. And just as often, as they enter their stories and texts, they revise (Wolfer, 2001).

Even so, Katherine has some decided beliefs about revisions—born of experience with writers of all ages (see Fitzgerald, 1987, 1988, 1992). Substantively revisiting writing, to Katherine, is a sensitive, slowly developing process. When she taught fifth graders, many of whom were reluctant to write because of early frustrations, she came to see the students' earliest demonstrations of writing begun without protest as a spark to be fanned into flame. Just as for her early learners, she provided tiny, successful steps until writing came without groan. In a kind of instructional oxymoron, she was both waiting patiently and providing sufficient opportunities for writing fluency to develop. For Katherine, writing fluently means that pencils move across the page—the writer under the steam of his or her own ideas rather than burdened with untangling conventions. Fluency isn't a constant. Even good writers lose their fluency often (if not within every piece). Writing fluidly means that, for the most part, the writer has control of the process. When writers demonstrate fluency of thought on paper, they are signaling to Katherine that they are getting ready to think more carefully and critically about themselves as writers and the work they want to produce. It is then that her conferences can take up more thoughtful notions about the writer's efforts and what may be a next step. But conferring, for Katherine, is not a skill to be mastered, but rather strategies to be practiced.

Assessing

Assessing isn't a problem for Katherine. Like all good teachers (such as Bobbi Fisher, 1991), she is constantly sampling, monitoring, gathering data, registering, recording, planning—all the meatiest chunks of assessment. Over the course of the year(s) children reside in her classroom, Katherine amasses large amounts of data from conference notes and from the actual writing samples tucked into writing folders. The problem is not with assessment, which she is committed to, but with the vastly different stances on assessment held by classroom teachers who use richly detailed portraits of children's literacy to gauge their progress and inform instruction, and with the makers of policy who make decisions based on test scores.

In Katherine's schools (and she has taught in many), sooner or later demands for accountability on particular types of writing begin to take sway over the legitimate, authentic writing her students are doing. The demands for scores on benchmark assessments and standardized tests are evidence of distrust of teachers to achieve those scores without installing artificial practice materials and mandating days devoted to "benchmarking" students' progress. Those features of a writing curriculum based on children's understandings of why they write, what they want to say, how they want to say it, and to whom are sidelined by instruments with contrived tasks and invisible audiences. Keeping writing intentional and legitimate is a constant struggle for Katherine and teachers like her.

Conclusion

Writing in primary classrooms can mean both tentative squiggles and exquisite poetry, or the first movements toward meaning and substantial reports, all in the same classroom, all in the same week. Surely, one of the biggest challenges facing teachers of young children is how to support writers from wherever the children begin. Katherine Bomer is one of those teachers who grows writers. Through examining her organization, planning, goals, opportunities, instruction, and dilemmas, the authors have attempted to make one classroom tangible, one teacher's struggles transparent, and one teacher's linkages to the professional community of researchers and practitioners evident. Katherine's is a classroom that permits writers to find pen and topic, purpose and audience, fluency and voice—toward becoming increasingly capable readers and writers who take pleasure in both.

REFERENCES

Ada, A.F., & Compoy, F.I. (2004). *Authors in the classroom: A transformative education process.* Boston: Allyn & Bacon.

Adams, M. (1990). *Beginning to read: Thinking and learning about print.* Cambridge, MA: MIT Press.

Anderson, C. (2000). *How's it going? A practical guide to conferring with student writers.* Portsmouth, NH: Heinemann.

Avery, C. (1993). *And with a light touch: Learning about reading, writing, and teaching with first graders.* Portsmouth, NH: Heinemann.

Baghban, M. (1984). *Our daughter learns to read and write.* Newark, DE: International Reading Association.

Beers, J., & Henderson, E. (1977). A study of developing orthographic concepts among first grade children. *Research in the Teaching of English*, *11*(2), 133-148.

Bissex, G.L. (1980). *Gnys at wrk: A child learns to write and read*. Cambridge, MA: Harvard University Press.

Bomer, K., & Bomer, R. (2001). *For a better world: Reading and writing for social action*. Portsmouth, NH: Heinemann.

Calkins, L., & Harwayne, S. (1991). *Living between the lines*. Portsmouth, NH: Heinemann.

Cameron, J. (1998). *The right to write: An invitation and initiation into the writing life*. New York: Jeremy P. Tarcher/Putnam.

Clay, M.M. (1975). *What did I write?* London: Heinemann.

Dyson, A.H. (1989). *Multiple worlds of child writers: Friends learning to write*. New York: Teachers College Press.

Ehri, L. (1989). The development of spelling knowledge and its role in reading acquisition and reading disability. *Journal of Learning Disabilities*, *22*(6), 356-365.

Elbow, P. (1973). *Writing without teachers*. Oxford, UK: Oxford University Press.

Fisher, B. (1991). *Joyful learning: A whole language kindergarten*. Portsmouth, NH: Heinemann.

Fitzgerald, J. (1987). Research on revision in writing. *Review of Educational Research*, *57*(4), 481-506.

Fitzgerald, J. (1988). Helping young writers to revise: A brief review for teachers. *The Reading Teacher*, *42*(2), 124-129.

Fitzgerald, J. (1992). *Towards knowledge in writing: Illustrations from revision studies*. New York: Springer-Verlag.

González, N., Moll, L., & Amanti, C. (Eds.). (2005). *Funds of knowledge: Theorizing practices in households, communities, and classrooms*. Mahwah, NJ: Erlbaum.

Graves, D.H. (1983). *Writing: Teachers and children at work*. Exeter, NH: Heinemann.

Graves, D.H. (1994). *A fresh look at writing*. Portsmouth, NH: Heinemann.

Graves, D.H., & Hansen, J. (1983). The author's chair. *Language Arts*, *60*(2), 176-183.

Hindley, J. (1996). *In the company of children*. York, ME: Stenhouse.

Hoffman, J.V. (1998). When bad things happen to good ideas in literacy education: Professional dilemmas, personal decisions, and political traps. *The Reading Teacher*, *52*(2), 102-112.

Holdaway, D. (1979). *Foundations of literacy*. New York: Ashton Scholastic.

Jensen, J.M. (2002). Teaching writing on the shoulders of giants. *Language Arts*, *79* (4), 357-362.

Labbo, L., Roser, N., & Hoffman, J. (1995). Ways to unintentionally make writing difficult. *Language Arts*, *72* (3), 164-170.

Marrow, A.J. (1969). *The practical theorist: The life and work of Kurt Lewin*. New York: Basic Books.

Owocki, G., & Goodman, Y. (2002). *Kidwatching: Documenting children's literacy development*. Portsmouth, NH: Heinemann.

Ray, K.W., & Cleaveland, L. (2004). *About the authors: Writing workshop with our youngest authors*. Portsmouth, NH: Heinemann.

Ray, K.W., & Laminack, L. (2001). *The writing workshop: Working through the hard parts (and they're all hard parts)*. Urbana, IL: National Council of Teachers of English.

Read, C. (1975). *Children's categorization of speech sounds in English*. Urbana, IL: National Council of Teachers of English.

Smith, F. (1981). Myths of writing. *Language Arts*, *58*(7), 793-795.

Squire, J.R. (1983). Composing and comprehending: Two sides of the same basic process. *Language Arts*, *60*(5), 581-589.

Teale, W.H. (1986). Home background and young children's literacy development. In W.H. Teale & E. Sulzby (Eds.), *Emergent literacy: Writing and reading* (pp. 173-206). Norwood, NJ: Ablex.

Wolfer, P. (2001). My journey to create a writing workshop for first graders. In C. Pappas & L. Zecker (Eds.), *Teacher inquiries in literacy teaching-learning: Learning to collaborate in elementary urban classrooms*. Mahwah, NJ: Erlbaum.

LITERATURE CITED

Clark, E. (2001). *Where are you, Blue Kangaroo?* New York: Random House Children's Books.

Mathers, P. (1998). *Lottie's new beach towel*. New York: Atheneum Books for Young Readers.

Mathers, P. (2000). *A cake for Herbie*. New York: Atheneum Books for Young Readers.

Rathmann, P. (1995). *Officer Buckle and Gloria*. New York: Putnam.

Rylant, C. (1982). *When I was young in the mountains*. New York: Dutton.

Stevens, J., & Crummel, S. (2004). *Plaidypus lost*. New York: Holiday House.

Zoehfeld, K.W. (1998). *What is the world made of? All about solids, liquids, and gases* (Let's-Read-and-Find-Out Science, Stage 2). New York: HarperCollins.

Chapter 3

"In My Country, We Don't Write Stories, We Tell Our Stories": Writing With English-Language Learners in the Primary Grades

*Julie Coppola, Catherine J. Dawson, Susan McPhillips,
Joanne George, and Diane MacLean*

English-language learners (ELLs) from many different language and cultural backgrounds, with a wide range of oral and written English skills, represent the fastest growing population of students in America's classrooms (Kindler, 2002). As a group, these students achieve limited success in school. The results of the National Assessment of Educational Progress (NAEP, 2002) showed that the writing achievement of students identified as limited English proficient continues to lag substantially behind that of students whose first language is English (Persky, Daane, & Jin, 2003). The No Child Left Behind Act of 2001 requires that all students, including ELLs, meet high standards in writing and demonstrate their writing abilities through their participation in high-stakes writing assessments. Data indicate, however, that those students who are learning English as an additional language fare poorly on these tests. In the state of Massachusetts, where the work presented in this chapter was implemented, 32% of all fourth-grade students identified as limited English proficient received a failing score on the recent statewide English Language Arts assessment. Furthermore, test results showed a statewide, persistent achievement gap between limited English proficient students and their native–English-speaking peers (Massachusetts Department of Education, 2002–2004).

America's increasingly diverse student population presents a challenge for classroom teachers. Teachers must ensure that all their students, regardless of language background or level of English proficiency, become successful writers. Helping ELLs meet high standards in writing is a complex endeavor. It requires teachers who know about writing and effective writing instructional practices and who also are prepared to respond to the needs of children who are learning an additional language at the same time they are learning about literacy (Grant & Wong, 2003). Nationwide, however, there is an acute shortage of teachers prepared to teach ELLs. The majority of classroom teachers completed preservice teacher education programs in which little attention was paid to the educational needs of ELLs (Carrasquillo & Rodriguez, 2002). There is evidence that this trend of limited attention to learning about teaching ELLs persists during the inservice years. Results of a national survey of general education classroom teachers showed that professional development related to the teaching of ELLs was the area in which teachers were least likely to participate. Yet only 27% of all survey respondents reported that they were confident about their ability to teach ELLs (Parsad, Lewis, Farris, & Greene, 2001). Without appropriate training, teachers will not be able to help children such as Ilana, a recent immigrant from Africa and a student in Diane MacClean's third-grade classroom. Ilana told elaborate oral stories, but she struggled when she had to write a story that conformed to English narrative text structure. "In my country, we don't *write* stories," she announced, frustrated by a lack of progress on a story about her dog Zus, "we *tell* our stories."

This chapter describes one schoolwide effort to deepen teachers' knowledge about writing and to improve writing instruction for students from many different language and cultural backgrounds who are in general education classrooms. The context for this work was a yearlong, site-based professional development program with the goal to move writing instruction from a focus on writing skills and products to one that encompasses process, product, and attention to the needs of ELLs. We begin with a brief overview of the research in writing and writing instruction as it relates to ELLs. Next, we provide a description of the school and its students and the key components of the professional development plan. Then we turn our attention to the successes and challenges in teaching writing in three focal classrooms at Vine School.

What We Know About English-Language Learners and Writing

Writing is a complex cognitive process involving increasing control of many skills (Dyson & Freedman, 2003). Research with elementary-grade monolingual children (Graves, 1983) and secondary school monolingual students (Emig, 1971) reveals that writing is a recursive process that involves planning, drafting, revising, and editing. Most children demonstrate common developmental sequences as they move from the earliest stages of experimenting with print to full control of the writing process (see Casbergue & Plauché, this volume), yet others may follow a different route that is dependent upon their experiences with written language (Dyson & Freedman, 2003).

Research on writing instruction in English demonstrates that the most effective writing programs are those that use a process writing approach that includes frequent opportunities for children to plan, compose, revise, and edit their written pieces as they collaborate with their teachers and peers (Bromley, 2003; Farnan & Dahl, 2003). In addition, research indicates that isolating the teaching of grammatical and mechanical skills from this process does not significantly increase children's writing abilities (Hillocks, 1986).

Influenced by these understandings about writing in a first language, researchers have examined ELLs' composing processes and behaviors and their written products. Although the bulk of the research on second-language writing has been conducted with college-age subjects, there are a few studies that focus on young children and their early writing development (Matsuda & De Pew, 2002). The available evidence suggests that the developmental sequences and composing processes of young second-language writers are more similar to than different from those of first-language writers (Peregoy & Boyle, 2005). Both groups of young writers begin by drawing and scribbling, and their early efforts reflect their growing understandings about how print represents oral language. Research also demonstrates that ELLs can write in English long before they have complete command of the oral and written systems of their new language (Peyton, 1990). ELLs often use knowledge of their first language as they write in English, and opportunities to write in English promote the development of both oral and literate abilities in the second language (Hudelson, 1994).

Second-language researchers also have investigated ELLs' responses to process writing instruction. Results indicate that, similar to native-English speakers, ELLs benefit when they write for authentic purposes; observe teachers as they model writing; participate in repeated opportunities to draft, share, and revise their written pieces; and routinely interact with their peers and teachers about their writing (Hudelson, 1994; Urzua, 1987). Particular concerns for teaching writing to ELLs include attention to vocabulary development; consistent opportunities to hear, read, and write extended text to become familiar with English vocabulary, language structures, and text structures; and explicit instruction in the organization of English text structures and in the cohesive devices and language structures used to organize English texts (Wong-Fillmore & Snow, 2000). Also of importance for teaching writing to ELLs is the practice of using learning scaffolds, such as patterned writing, that provide a consistent model of predictable language and discourse patterns and allow students to participate in grade-level activities (Peregoy & Boyle, 2005).

Most experts agree that learning to write in a first or a second language proceeds best when children attend schools where (a) teachers provide sustained time to write, (b) teachers examine their understandings about the writing process and their teaching practices, and (c) best practices are evident in a school's writing program (Strickland et al., 2001). In the next section, we outline the plan we implemented to help teachers achieve these instructional conditions. We begin with a description of the school and its students. Then, we present the key components of our professional development plan.

Creating an Effective Context for Writing Instruction

Vine School, a small K–4 elementary school with two classrooms at each grade level, is one of 14 elementary schools in a large urban school district located 30 miles from Boston, Massachusetts. The district enrolled approximately 16,300 students during the 2002-2003 academic year, the year this project took place. Forty-four percent of the student population was Caucasian, 21% Hispanic, 30% Asian, and 5% African American. Districtwide, 47% percent of the students spoke a home language other than English, including Spanish, Portuguese, Khmer, Laotian, Vietnamese, Swahili, Urdu, and Gujarati. Sixty-one percent of all students qualified for free or reduced lunch. Overall, the district's students fared poorly on statewide literacy assessments. In spring 2002, 21% of all fourth-grade students earned a failing score on the statewide test of English Language Arts, while 62% of the fourth-grade students identified as limited English proficient earned a failing score (Massachusetts Department of Education, 2002-2004).

There were 261 students attending Vine School during the 2002–2003 school year. Eighty-four percent of the students' families lived at or below the poverty level. In 1999, the district designated Vine School as one of two schools that would serve children who spoke less commonly represented languages in the community. As a result, at the time of this project, 41% of the students spoke a home language other than English and 30% of the students were identified as limited English proficient. These students and their families were from Cameroon, China, Laos, Haiti, Kenya, India, Liberia, Malaysia, Nigeria, Pakistan, Taiwan, Uganda, and Vietnam.

In response to new classroom demographics and as part of a districtwide commitment to improve literacy instruction for children at risk for failure, in 1999 the Vine School faculty applied for and received a competitive state grant to support professional development in reading instruction. During the next two years, working with a university partner, teachers focused on establishing a two-hour literacy block and implementing research-based practices in reading instruction (National Institute of Child Health and Human Development, 2000; Snow, Burns, & Griffin, 1998).

Analysis of students' 2001 test scores demonstrated that students at Vine School made gains in statewide and local literacy assessments; however, overall the students continued to score below their peers in both their district and the state. In particular, teachers identified writing achievement and writing instruction as areas of concern. Although there was increasing congruence in reading instructional practices throughout the school, teachers noted that writing instructional practices, as well as time devoted to writing instruction, varied from classroom to classroom. Some teachers provided their students with opportunities to learn about the writing process. In these classrooms, students planned, drafted, revised, and edited their written pieces; however, teachers were concerned that they did not provide these opportunities frequently or systematically enough to help their students, particularly the ELLs, become competent writers. These teachers also expressed uncertainty about their ability to teach writing skills using a process approach to writing instruction.

Other teachers emphasized isolated grammar instruction and evaluated students' writing with limited attention to teaching the children the processes utilized by good writers. These teachers reported that they were uncertain about how to manage a process approach to writing instruction. In these classrooms, students most often wrote in response to teacher-provided prompts. It was evident that teachers at Vine School differed in their approaches to writing instruction. They were in agreement, however, that in every classroom they needed help to establish instructional conditions that supported teaching and learning about the writing process as well as grammar, spelling, and language conventions.

Teachers identified the delivery of language and literacy support services to the ELLs as another area of concern. With the addition of two English as a second language (ESL) specialists to the faculty in 2001, more time during the literacy block was devoted to pull-out ESL instruction for students identified as limited English proficient. In these pull-out sessions, instruction emphasized listening and speaking skills with less attention paid to reading and writing. As a result, teachers reported that there was increasing fragmentation of the students' instructional program. Although teachers were grateful for the extra support, they viewed student success as the responsibility of both the classroom teacher and the ESL specialists. Teachers noted that writing instruction was one area where the classroom teacher and the ESL specialists needed to work closely to ensure a coherent instructional program for the ELLs in their classrooms.

In the summer of 2002, Julie Coppola, a university professor, collaborated with the building principal and Catherine Dawson, the school literacy specialist, to establish a professional development plan that responded to teachers' desires to address writing instruction at Vine School. In the following section, we present our professional development plan.

Professional Development Plan

One way for teachers to learn about best practices in writing instruction is through a site-based, sustained form of professional development in which teachers have opportunities to (a) develop deep content knowledge; (b) learn about teaching and assessment strategies through demonstration, guided practice, and independent practice; (c) collaborate with other teachers; (d) analyze and reflect on their teaching practice; and (e) assess the effects of their teaching practices on student learning (Darling-Hammond, 1998). Thus, our professional development plan consisted of five major activities that occurred monthly from September to May:

1. Literacy conversations
2. Classroom demonstration lessons
3. Coteaching sessions
4. Classroom observations
5. Analysis of student work sessions

Literacy conversations provided opportunities for the teachers to develop deep content knowledge about writing and writing instruction, and to analyze and reflect on their teaching practices. These one-hour meetings were held before the beginning of the school day. Facilitated by Julie, the faculty discussed research and practice on writing and writing instruction with an emphasis on age- and grade-appropriate writing accomplishments for K–4 children, including ELLs. From September to January, literacy conversations addressed the following topics:

• Strengthening reading-writing connections
• Teaching narrative writing: Planning and drafting
• Responding to students' work: Conferencing
• Selecting and teaching minilessons: Revision
• Selecting and teaching minilessons: Editing

Starting in February, mindful of the need to prepare students to write a variety of forms for a variety of purposes and to increase students' exposure to informational texts (Duke, 2000), we turned our attention to the instruction and assessment of nonfiction writing. In doing so, we followed a similar sequence of topics. Literacy conversations continued through the end of May. As teachers developed more experience and understanding about the differences in narrative and nonfiction writing, the discussions often integrated both forms of writing.

Each literacy conversation was followed by classroom demonstration lessons in which Julie modeled the teaching of a writing strategy or skill related to the literacy conversation topic. These demonstration lessons were followed the next week by coteaching sessions in which Julie and a classroom teacher worked together in the classroom to teach the same or similar lesson modeled in the demonstration lesson. Classroom observations in which the classroom teacher took the lead in the lesson while Julie worked with small groups of students were scheduled for the third or fourth week of each monthly cycle. Taken together, this cycle of demonstration lessons, coteaching lessons, and classroom observations provided frequent opportunities for the teachers to learn through demonstration, guided practice, and independent practice. Debriefing meetings held after each lesson provided additional opportunities for teachers to analyze and reflect on their teaching practice. To ensure that ESL instruction supported ongoing classroom instruction, Julie also led this cycle of demonstration lesson, coteaching, and observation sessions, as well as debriefing meetings for the ESL specialists during their small-group, pull-out lessons.

Frequent opportunities for collaboration formed an important component of the professional development plan. Substitute teachers were used during the school day to release each grade-level team and the ESL specialists from teaching duties to participate in demonstration, coteaching, and classroom observation sessions. There were additional opportunities for collaboration during monthly after-school meetings that focused on analysis of student work. In these meetings, we worked to (a) establish schoolwide goals in writing in accordance with state standards, (b) gauge students' progress in writing, and (c) determine the next teaching steps. We discussed the criteria for good writing, and we developed rubrics to guide our analysis of student work. We continually revisited the state curriculum frameworks and writing standards to ensure that all students at Vine School received instructional opportunities to help them meet these standards.

During each component of our professional development plan, we focused on instructional practices that were not only essential to support ELLs but also known to benefit all children learning to write. These included (a) attention to the integration of reading, writing, and oral language instruction to support literacy development (Au, 1998); (b) frequent opportunities to read and write for authentic purposes; and (c) teachers' consistent attention to discussion of important narrative and nonfiction text structures and cohesive devices during both reading and writing instruction (Peregoy & Boyle, 2005). To develop students' oral language abilities, we were also mindful of the need to plan structured activities that promoted interaction between the native–English-speaking children and the ELLs (Pica, 1987; Wong-Fillmore, 1991) as they planned and composed their written pieces. For example, a typical instructional routine was to provide time after each minilesson for the children to talk in pairs or small groups about their writing plan for that day.

In addition, we studied children's literature to determine those titles that provided the best models for the text and language structures (Kamberelis & Bovino, 1999) and vocabulary that formed a lesson focus. For example, *Cat on the Mat* by Brian Wildsmith (1983/1986) and *Rosie's Walk* by Patricia Hutchins (1968) were selected for their simple language structures and clear narrative text structure. *Brave Irene* by William Steig (1986), *Owl Moon* by Jane Yolen (1987), and *One Hot Summer Day* by Nina Crews (1995) provided examples of descriptive language. As students began to write longer pieces, we chose *Charlotte's Web* by E.B. White (1952) as a model for topic sentences and well-formed paragraphs. *Weather Words and What They Mean* by Gail Gibbons (1990) was used as a model for informational text. *On the Go* by Ann Morris (1990) provided the necessary vocabulary to teach simple compare–contrast structures.

Finally, we critically examined the graphic organizers that teachers routinely used in their classrooms to ensure that each graphic organizer provided a guide that helped the students to learn about English text structures and organize their written pieces. For example, as the children began to write personal narratives, we noted that teachers routinely used semantic maps for two distinct purposes: as a way for students to record their ideas about what to write and as a tool to guide the students as they organized their ideas. To help the students organize their ideas, we provided a graphic organizer that guided the students to include a beginning, middle, and end in their personal narratives.

In the following section, we look at the implementation of writing instruction across the three focal classrooms. We begin with our successes; then we turn our attention to challenges and our continuing plans to respond to students' writing instructional needs.

A View Into Three Classrooms

To understand the effects of the professional development efforts on the writing of ELLs, we chose three classrooms that enrolled high numbers of children identified as limited English proficient as well as high numbers of children who spoke a home language other than English. The teachers in these classrooms, Susan McPhillips, Joanne George, and Diane MacLean, were experienced and successful classroom teachers who were highly regarded by school administrators, colleagues, and parents. However, like their peers, they were uncertain about their instruction of ELLs.

In Diane's third-grade classroom of 22 children, 16 children spoke a home language other than English. Eight of these 16 children were identified as limited English proficient. In Joanne's second-grade classroom of 24 children, 14 children spoke a home language other than English. Nine of these students were identified as limited English proficient. In Susan's first-grade classroom of 24 children, 16 children spoke a home language other English. Nine of these children were identified as limited English proficient. In each classroom, the children identified as limited English proficient received ESL support services in the form of pull-out sessions; however, these children spent the bulk of the school day in their general education classrooms. They relied on their classroom teacher and their native–English–speaking peers to help them make the necessary gains in oral and written English. In the next section, we share some of our successes. We focus on three major areas: (1) the organization of writing instruction, (2) the integration of reading and writing instruction, and (3) the ways teachers scaffolded instruction for student success.

Organization of Writing Instruction. In all three classrooms, teachers and students were accustomed to a sustained and uninterrupted two-hour block of time devoted to literacy instruction because of the teachers' previous work on improving reading instruction. To accommodate our increased attention to writing instruction, one half-hour was added to the literacy block, four days a week. Students worked in a print-rich environment, and they enjoyed easy access to resources to support young writers, such as word walls, dictionaries, paper, pencils, markers, crayons, children's literature used for read-alouds, and many bins of books organized by reading level or topic. Each teacher had set aside an area of the classroom where children could gather for whole-class lessons. There were easels and chart paper for teachers to use as they conducted their lessons. Classroom furniture and seating arrangements accommodated many different grouping arrangements.

Each teacher began the writing block by gathering the children on a rug in front of a large easel to participate in a minilesson. Teachers used the minilessons to model each phase of the writing process and to teach writing conventions and skills. Following each minilesson, children briefly shared their writing plan for the day with a partner or small group. Then children returned to their seats where they worked individually or in small groups to practice the skill or strategy taught in the minilesson. Teachers worked with small groups to reinforce the teaching of the focal skill or strategy, or they conferred with small groups or individual students. At the end of the writing block, students once again gathered on the rug to share their work.

Providing a consistent, sustained time to write four days a week was important for the ELLs in each classroom as they experimented with their new language and tackled the demands of writing (Watts-Taffe & Truscott, 2000). Many students spent the early weeks drawing and writing one-line or two-line sentences about their drawings. These early attempts reflected their growing understandings about sound–symbol correspondences and the new vocabulary and grammatical structures they were learning, important foundations for longer pieces that appeared as the school year progressed. Figure 3.1, composed by a first-grade ELL, is representative of the early attempts at writing among these children.

An additional benefit of the increased time for writing was the opportunity for the teachers to learn more about their students. Susan, Joanne, and Diane found

Figure 3.1   Writing Sample of a First-Grade English-Language Learner, September 2002

that the students' personal narratives helped them learn important information about students' early and home experiences as they adjusted to a new life in the United States. Topics as varied as a first-time visit to the dentist, an airplane trip to America, a description of a first cold New England winter, or the memory of an African festival reminded the teachers of the rich stores of background knowledge that each student brought to the classroom.

Integration of Reading and Writing Instruction. We also observed the integration of reading and writing instruction. We credited this to previously established reading instructional routines. Susan, Joanne, and Diane routinely pointed out narrative text structures and discussed beginning, middle, and end or setting, problem, solution, and consequence during reading instruction. They also introduced nonfiction text structures, such as simple listings and compare-contrast structures. They read aloud to the children every day; however, their increased attention to writing instruction influenced their choices of read-alouds. For example, when they taught the use of descriptive language as a revision strategy, Joanne and Diane began with a read-aloud of *Owl Moon* by Jane Yolen (1987). Susan chose *When Sophie Gets Angry—Really, Really Angry* by Molly Bang (1999). During this time, teachers discussed how the authors used descriptive language to let the readers see what was happening, and teachers generated lists of descriptive words with the children. As they began the writing block, teachers briefly revisited the sections of the book that best supported the writing lesson. They modeled how writers add descriptive words to their pieces, and they asked the children to try to do the same in their writing (Calkins, 1994).

To increase her students' exposure to children's literature during the writing block, Diane established a writing workshop bookshelf. Here she stored exemplar texts that she had read aloud to the children. Students had easy access to this bookshelf, and often they were observed retrieving a favorite title, such as Thomas Locker's *Water Dance* (1997), to refer to as they wrote.

The integration of reading and writing instruction provided the ELLs with repeated opportunities to hear and use the same language. Often, the vocabulary from a read-aloud appeared spontaneously in students' writing. For example, after several readings of *The Snowy Day* by E.J. Keats (1962/1996), one first-grade ELL picked up both the setting and vocabulary from the text to compose her next writing piece (Figure 3.2).

To prepare students to write nonfiction texts, teachers began by reading aloud texts, such as *From Tadpole to Frog* by Wendy Pfeffer (1994), that contained the features of nonfiction texts that they planned to teach. These included illustrations, labels, captions, and simple descriptions. We observed the children in all three classrooms selecting, reading, and talking about nonfiction texts during independent reading times. Joanne's and Susan's students responded eagerly during the writing block as they researched, talked, and wrote about topics such as snakes, butterflies, frogs, and lizards, and then deliberately integrated the ideas they learned into their writing pieces (Figure 3.3).

Diane commented that increased attention to nonfiction text structures and text features contributed to students' success as they read their social studies and science textbooks. Nonfiction writing during the writing block also contributed to vocabulary development as the ELLs had repeated opportunities to hear and use

Figure 3.2   Writing Sample of a First-Grade English-Language Learner, January 2003

Figure 3.3   An Excerpt From Melvin's Butterfly Report

content vocabulary at different times throughout the school day, an important factor in vocabulary learning (Scott, 2004).

Scaffolding Instruction. In all three classrooms, teachers perceived graphic organizers and other written scaffolds as being very important in the writing success of the ELLs. Although the teachers commented that letting go of commercially prepared graphic organizers was difficult, they observed that their students wrote more, and their pieces better reflected English text structures when the teachers first analyzed the writing task and then provided the students with a graphic organizer that matched the targeted text structure. They provided different levels of support depending upon students' abilities to accomplish writing tasks independently. In all three classrooms, we found that the children with the lowest levels of English proficiency benefited when the teachers provided them with a three-page booklet for their personal narratives (Fletcher & Portalupi, 1998). The teachers first drew pictures on each page of the booklet to represent the beginning, middle, and end of their stories. Next, the teachers modeled writing a one-sentence beginning of the story on the first page, a one-sentence middle of the story on the second page, and a one-sentence end of the story on the last page. With repeated practice, the children grasped the organizational pattern. Then they abandoned this three-page template and moved on to the use of graphic organizers that helped them organize their stories.

As Joanne's students began to write personal narratives that contained a multiple-event structure, she provided a corresponding graphic organizer (Figure 3.4) that guided the students to sequence the events.

The teachers also provided graphic organizers that included vocabulary that may not yet be part of students' spontaneous oral language structures but are commonly used to organize texts. For example, when Joanne taught a series of how-to writing lessons, she used a graphic organizer that contained the signal words *first, second, next, then,* and *finally.* As children demonstrated the ability to initiate these signal words on their own, Joanne removed them from the graphic organizer.

For a multiparagraph report on Inuit life as one part of a social studies unit, Joanne provided written scaffolds in the form of topic and concluding sentences for each paragraph for students who needed that support. Students then proceeded to complete their paragraphs with the facts they had gathered about Inuit life (Figure 3.5).

Diane had several students in her classroom who were orally proficient in English. They struggled, however, when they were expected to compose stories that reflected English narrative text structure. Over time, the added support of well-constructed graphic organizers benefited the students in all three classrooms as they learned about school-based English writing practices.

Finally, like others (e.g., Fitzgerald & Noblit, 1999), we found that limited oral English skills did not prevent children from participating successfully in writing activities. Susan observed that in her first-grade classroom, the ELLs often were more willing than their native–English-speaking peers to take risks in their writing. Susan commented that they appeared less afraid of making mistakes as they tried to make sense of new sound–symbol correspondences, new vocabulary, and even new ways of organizing stories. She made particular note of one child who, although she rarely talked in the classroom, took risks in writing and thrived as a writer.

Figure 3.4   Jessenia's Plan for a Multiple-Event Narrative

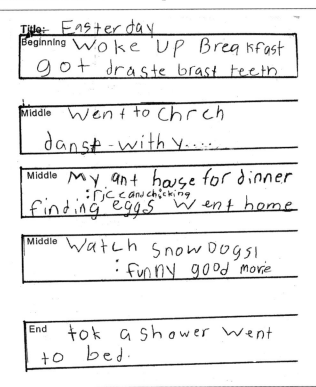

Title: Easter day

Beginning: Woke UP Breakfast got draste brast teeth

Middle: Went to chrch danst-with y....

Middle: My ant hause for dinner
: ric c and chicking
finding eggs Went home

Middle: Watch snow Dogsl
: funny good movie

End: tok a shower Went to bed.

Figure 3.5   Sample of Student Inuit Report

The Inuits attire is important for their survival. The Inuits wear animal skins. They wear fur jackets called parkas. They wear mukluks to keep their feet warm in the winter. They wear mittens to keep their hands warm. They hunt animals for clothing. The Inuits need to keep warm for their survival.

Despite these successes, there were, of course, significant challenges. In the next section, we discuss some of these. We describe our responses, including the teachers' long-range plans to continue their work in this area.

Some Stumbling Blocks and Our Responses

The challenges teachers confronted were of four types: (1) meeting the individual needs of all the children, (2) managing the amount of writing children were now producing, (3) providing appropriate books as writing models, and (4) supporting teachers' ongoing need to deepen their understanding of writing instruction.

Meeting Individual Needs. Although teachers had created excellent and supportive classroom writing environments, we saw little evidence that the students routinely made effective use of the resources that were available to them. Instead, students most often turned to a peer or the teacher for assistance. All three teachers found that their classroom word walls did not provide enough support for the ELLs. These students often needed assistance on words that were already known to their first-language peers and thus were not displayed on the word wall. In response, Joanne and Diane added individual word books for the ELLs. Susan decided to try individual word lists and made individual folders that students kept at their tables in a basket for easy access. They found that these additional supports were helpful for teachers and students as students were observed consulting these resources instead of interrupting the teachers or their classmates.

Although this solution helped children to become increasingly self-directed during independent reading time, it did not address children's varied instructional needs. To meet this challenge, teachers took several steps. First, they extended the flexible grouping model (Paratore, 2000) already in use during the reading block to the organization of the writing block. At the same time, Catherine, the literacy specialist, reorganized the schedules of the two schoolwide literacy specialists so that there was additional support in the classroom during several of the weekly writing instructional periods. With these two modifications in place, a typical lesson sequence began with a whole-group lesson on a writing strategy or skill, followed by two small needs-based groups, one of which was led by the classroom teacher and the other by a literacy specialist.

Next, the teachers sought ways to provide the ELLs with additional opportunities throughout the day to read and talk about books at their independent reading levels that contained the text or language structures that were addressed during the writing lessons. For example, when learning about the beginning, middle, and end, the ELLs in Joanne's classroom read and reread Brian Wildsmith's (1986) *Cat on the Mat* or their favorite, *Trashy Town*, by Andrea Zimmerman and David Clemesha (1999). Susan used *Little Cloud* by Eric Carle (1996) in her classroom. We also found that when teachers employed consistent classroom management routines as well as consistent language routines to talk about classroom events, the children learned the routines and became increasingly independent. This also allowed teachers to meet more often with children individually or in small groups for additional practice in writing skills and strategies after each whole-group minilesson.

In addition, the ESL specialists worked to strengthen connections between their pull-out ESL sessions and ongoing classroom writing instruction. A typical ESL lesson began with a rereading of the classroom read-aloud or a related text with a similar text structure or language structure that was the focus of the classroom minilesson. This reiteration provided even more opportunities for the children to practice the necessary oral and written English they needed for success in grade-level activities. For example, after repeated readings of *Rosie's Walk* by Patricia Hutchins (1968), the ESL specialist guided a small group of ELLs from Joanne's classroom to write their own "walk" stories that contained a beginning, middle, and end.

Managing the Amount of Writing. We were excited when the children in Diane's third-grade classroom began writing longer and longer pieces. This, however, presented a somewhat daunting management problem. Diane and the children were frustrated by the length of time it took to arrive at a published piece. Diane responded to this in two ways. First, she worked with the children to help them select one or two pieces per month to bring to the final publishing stage. She guided children to choose a favorite piece or a piece that showed their best work. Next, she enlisted the help of a parent who was herself acquiring English to type the final pieces. This particular arrangement was pleasantly (and somewhat accidentally) reciprocal: Diane and the children received the publishing support they needed and wanted, and the parent viewed her work in the classroom as an opportunity to learn more English and to learn about classroom life in the United States.

Finding Appropriate Books. In every classroom, despite a districtwide initiative to provide more literacy instructional materials, we struggled to find enough books that were exemplars of the text or language structures we were teaching. Nonfiction texts written at the students' independent reading levels were also in scarce supply. We responded to this problem in several ways. First, Susan organized several meetings before school, during which she and her colleagues examined existing titles in the school library and book room. They made lists of books that supported their teaching goals. Mindful that many of their students spoke languages with syntax that differed from that of English, they looked for texts with strong picture-text match and simple subject-verb–object sentence structure, such as *My Five Senses* by Aliki (1962/1989) so that students would have opportunities to learn both English vocabulary and sentence structure. Teachers also enlisted the help of the school librarian, who was able to locate specific titles at other schools in the district. Next, when ordering instructional materials, all teachers actively worked with Catherine to change their focus from one of simply increasing reading materials to selectively purchasing materials that best supported the reading and writing needs of their students.

Providing Ongoing Professional Development. As teachers responded to the array of organizational and instructional challenges, they were reminded of the need to continue their conversations about effective practice. During literacy conversations, they typically discovered that they were confronting common challenges, and they worked together to solve their problems. Each of the focal teachers credited the opportunity to work with their peers as an important resource in their quest to improve their teaching effectiveness. During the period of this study, we observed two particular issues that were resolved because of the opportunity for teachers to study and learn together. One occurred when Diane raised a concern that children were most often talking about everything but their writing. In Joanne's and Susan's classrooms, peer editing was also an issue because so many children were struggling with basic skills that they were at times simply unable to help each other. In response, teachers renewed their attention to modeling during minilessons. Our observations indicated that, over time, teachers had retreated to an "assignment" mode and were talking more about what to do and providing students with fewer demonstrations and models. The need for ongoing modeling and demonstration was important not only because of the evidence that suggests children need ongoing support but also because of the particular classroom demographics: In each classroom teachers continued to receive new students who arrived with limited English skills. The numbers of children who were at various stages of learning in their second language dictated that teachers pay close attention to modeling and talking about the steps to complete a strategy or skill. In every classroom, children were more successful when they had an opportunity to observe teachers modeling and talking about an aspect of the writing process, including how to talk about a written piece with a peer, before the children went off to write. As a result of the literacy conversation, teachers renewed their attention to demonstration and modeling and vowed to monitor their routine implementation of this stage of the instructional model.

The second issue related to the development of editing checklists. Teachers had agreed that commercially available editing checklists were not well matched to the skills and strategies they were teaching, but developing their own seemed overwhelming for individual teachers. Instead, they agreed to work together (and with their students) to construct editing checklists. These shared checklists became familiar from classroom to classroom.

Next Steps

The teachers at Vine School improved writing instruction in many ways; however, we recognized that sustained change in instructional practices and, consequently, meaningful increases in student achievement take time. At the end of the year, the faculty met to plan for continuing study in writing and writing instruction and assessment. Despite the fact that funding for the university–school collaboration had been exhausted, teachers agreed to maintain their study of writing and writing instruction through a teacher study group. They planned to examine other writing genres, especially poetry. In addition, each grade-level team generated a month-to-month plan to ensure that all students would have opportunities to write a variety of forms for a variety of purposes. They believed that they needed to continue their commitment to provide coordinated instruction between classroom and ESL teachers, and they planned to continue to explore ways to strengthen this connection.

What We Learned About Teaching Writing to Young English-Language Learners

There is a critical need for teachers who can teach ELLs, yet most teachers report that they are not prepared to meet the needs of these students. Failure to help all children, including ELLs, reach higher levels of literacy will result in dismal consequences for both students and schools. We believe that our experiences learning about writing instruction with ELLs at Vine School are informative for two reasons. First, at Vine School, we found support for Linda Darling-Hammond's (1998) conclusion that "teachers learn best by studying, doing, and reflecting; by collaborating with other teachers; by looking closely at students and their work; and by sharing what they see" (p. 8). Second, we found that ELLs have opportunities to learn about oral and written English when they are in classrooms with teachers who are allowed to work together in this way. Laurie Lewis et al. (1999) identified teacher expertise as the single most important component of a student's success. We share our experiences in the hope that they shed light on the kinds of teacher training practices that can lead to teacher and student success in the increasingly diverse classrooms in America's schools.

REFERENCES

Au, K. (1998). Social constructivism and the school literacy learning of students of diverse backgrounds. *Journal of Literacy Research, 30*(2), 297-319.

Bromley, K. (2003). Building a sound writing program. In L. Morrow, L. Gambrell, & M. Pressley (Eds.), *Best practices in literacy instruction* (2nd ed., pp. 143-166). New York: Guilford.

Calkins, L. (1994). *The art of teaching writing.* Portsmouth, NH: Heinemann.

Carrasquillo, A., & Rodriguez, V. (2002). *Language minority students in the mainstream classroom* (2nd ed.). Clevedon, UK: Multilingual Matters.

Darling-Hammond, L. (1998). Teacher learning that supports student learning. *Educational Leadership, 55*(5), 6-11.

Duke, N. (2000). 3.6 minutes per day: The scarcity of informational texts in first grade. *Reading Research Quarterly, 35*, 202-224.

Dyson, A., & Freedman, S. (2003). Writing. In J. Flood, D. Lapp, J.R. Squire, & J.M. Jensen (Eds.), *Handbook of research on teaching the English language arts* (2nd ed., pp. 967-992). Mahwah, NJ: Erlbaum.

Emig, J. (1971). *The composing processes of twelfth graders* (Research Report No. 13). Urbana, IL: National Council of Teachers of English.

Farnan, N., & Dahl, K. (2003). Children's writing: Research and practice. In J. Flood, D. Lapp, J. Squire, & J. Jensen (Eds.), *Handbook of research on teaching the English language arts* (2nd ed., pp. 993-1007). Mahwah, NJ: Erlbaum.

Fitzgerald, J., & Noblit, G. (1999). About hopes, aspirations, and uncertainty: First-grade English-language learners' emergent reading. *Journal of Literacy Research, 31*(2), 133-182.

Fletcher, R., & Portalupi, J. (1998). *Craft lessons: Teaching writing K-8.* York, ME: Stenhouse.

Grant, R., & Wong, S. (2003). Barriers to literacy for language-minority learners: An argument for change in the literacy education profession. *Journal of Adolescent & Adult Literacy, 46,* 386-394.

Graves, D.H. (1983). *Writing: Teachers and children at work.* Exeter, NH: Heinemann.

Hillocks, G. (1986). *Research on written composition: New directions for teaching.* Urbana, IL: National Conference on Research in English.

Hudelson, S. (1994). Literacy development of second language children. In F. Genesee (Ed.), *Educating second language children: The whole child, the whole curriculum, the whole community* (pp. 129-158). New York: Cambridge University Press.

Kamberelis, G., & Bovino, T. (1999). Cultural artifacts as scaffolds for genre development. *Reading Research Quarterly, 34,* 138-170.

Kindler, A.L. (2002). *Survey of the states' limited English proficient students and available educational programs and services, 2000-2001 summary report.* Washington, DC: U.S. Department of Education, National Clearinghouse for English Language Acquisition; Language Instruction Educational Programs.

Lewis, L., Parsad, B., Carey, N., Bartfai, N., Farris, E., & Smerdon, B. (1999). *Teacher quality: A report on the preparation and qualifications of public school teachers.* Washington, DC: U.S. Department of Education, Office of Educational Research and Improvement.

Massachusetts Department of Education. (2002-2004). *Massachusetts Comprehensive Assessment System: Results.* Retrieved January 12, 2005, from http:www.doe.mass.edu/mcas/results.html

Matsuda, P., & De Pew, K. (2002). Early second language writing: An introduction. *Journal of Second Language Writing, 11*(4), 261-268.

National Institute of Child Health and Human Development. (2000). *Report of the National Reading Panel. Teaching children to read: An evidence-based assessment of the scientific research literature on reading and its implications for reading instruction* (NIH Publication No. 00-4769). Washington, DC: U.S. Government Printing Office.

No Child Left Behind Act of 2001, Pub. L. No. 107-110, 115 Stat. 1425 (2002).

Paratore, J.R. (2000). Grouping for instruction in literacy: What we've learned about what's working and what's not. *The California Reader, 33*(4), 2-10.

Parsad, B., Lewis, L., Farris, E., & Greene, B. (2001). *Teacher preparation and professional development, 2000* (NCES 2001-088). Washington, DC: U.S. Department of Education, Office of Educational Research and Improvement. Retrieved September 15, 2004, from http://nces.ed.gov/pubs2001/2001088.pdf

Peregoy, S., & Boyle, O. (2005). *Reading, writing, and learning in ESL: A resource book for K-12 teachers* (4th ed.). Boston: Pearson/Allyn & Bacon.

Persky, H.R., Daane, M.C., & Jin, Y. (2003). *The nation's report card: Writing 2002* (NCES 2003-549). Washington, DC: U.S. Department of Education, Institute of Education Sciences, National Center for Education Statistics.

Peyton, J. (1990). Beginning at the beginning: First-grade ESL students learn to write. In A. Padilla, H. Fairchild, C. Valadez (Eds.), *Bilingual education: Issues and strategies* (pp. 195-218). Newbury Park, CA: Sage.

Pica, T. (1987). Second language acquisition, social interaction, and the classroom. *Applied Linguistics, 8*(1), 3-21.

Scott, J.A. (2004). Scaffolding vocabulary learning: Ideas for equity in urban settings. In D. Lapp, C.C. Block, E.J. Cooper, J. Flood, N. Roser, & J.V. Tinajero (Eds.), *Teaching all the children: Strategies for developing literacy in an urban setting* (pp. 275-293). New York: Guilford.

Snow, C., Burns, M., Griffin, P. (Eds.). (1998). *Preventing reading difficulties in young children.* Washington, DC: National Academy Press.

Strickland, D., Bodino, A., Buchan, K., Jones, K.M., Nelson, A., & Rosen, M. (2001). Teaching writing in a time of reform. *The Elementary School Journal, 101*(4), 385-397.

Urzua, C. (1987). "You stopped too soon": Second language children composing and revising. *TESOL Quarterly, 21*(2), 279-304.

Watts-Taffe, S., & Truscott, D.M. (2000). Using what we know about language and literacy development for ESL students in the mainstream classroom. *Language Arts, 77*(3), 258-265.

Wong-Fillmore, L. (1991). Second language learning in children: A model of language learning in social context. In E. Bialystok (Ed.), *Language processing in bilingual children* (pp. 49-69). Cambridge, UK: Cambridge University Press.

Wong-Fillmore, L., & Snow. C. (2000). *What teachers need to know about language.* Washington, DC: Center for Applied Linguistics.

LITERATURE CITED

Aliki. (1989). *My five senses.* New York, NY: Crowell. (Original work published 1962)

Bang, M. (1999). *When Sophie gets angry—really, really angry.* New York: Blue Sky.

Carle, E. (1996). *Little cloud.* New York: Philomel.

Crews, N. (1995). *One hot summer day.* New York: Greenwillow.

Gibbons, G. (1990). *Weather words and what they mean.* New York: Holiday House.

Hutchins. P. (1968). *Rosie's walk.* New York: Macmillan.

Keats, E.J. (1996). *The snowy day.* New York: Viking Press. (Original work published 1962)

Locker, T., (1997). *Water dance.* New York: Harcourt Brace.

Morris, A. (1990). *On the go.* New York: Lothrop, Lee & Shephard.

Pfeffer, W. (1994). *From tadpole to frog.* New York: HarperTrophy

Steig, W. (1986). *Brave Irene.* New York: Farrar, Straus, Giroux.

White, E.B. (1952). *Charlotte's web.* New York: HarperCollins.

Wildsmith, B. (1986). *Cat on the mat.* New York: HarperCollins.

Yolen, J. (1987). *Owl moon.* New York: Philomel.

Zimmerman, A., & Clemesha, D. (1999). *Trashy Town.* New York: HarperCollins.

Chapter 4

Writing and Poetry in the Elementary Grades

Roselmina Indrisano, Jennifer Hauck Bryson, and Merri Jones

In the particular physical presence of memorable language we can find a reminder of our ability to know and retain knowledge itself, the "brightness wherein all things come to see." —Robert Pinsky (1998, p. 116)

R obert Pinsky was named poet laureate of the United States in 1997. Believing that poetry is vital to more people in the country than had been assumed, Pinsky initiated a one-year call to the general population for the submission of a favorite poem. In that period, 18,000 Americans spanning every state and age group responded to his call. These submissions led to the creation of the Favorite Poem Project for the purpose of "celebrating, documenting, and promoting poetry's role in Americans' lives" (Favorite Poem Project: Welcome, n.d.). Ultimately, the project yielded a website, four anthologies, a video series, a book based on Pinsky's Tanner Lectures at Princeton University, and three summer institutes for teachers and administrators. The summer institutes and their effects on teachers, administrators, students, and their schools and communities are the focus of this chapter.

The Principles

The theoretical foundation of the Favorite Poem Project, as described by Pinsky in his writing and teaching, are the principles of autonomy and physicality. Autonomy can be described as granting the right of selection to the reader to assure ownership of the poem. If readers, young and older, are encouraged to choose the poems that resonate with their own lives, they will be better able to gain the benefits that the printed word affords—an understanding of other people, other times, and other places. In his message to teachers on the Favorite Poem Project website, Pinsky writes,

> We need to communicate not only with our peers but our ancestors and descendants, and the arts of poetry, writing, print, digital media serve that communication. As the oldest of these arts, poetry in a deep-going way calls upon

Learning to Write, Writing to Learn: Theory and Research in Practice edited by Roselmina Indrisano and Jeanne R. Paratore.

the very nature of human society, our interdependence upon one another not only in space but in time. We need the comfort and stimulation that this vital part of us gets from this ancient art. (Favorite Poem Project: Revitalizing Poetry in the Classroom, n.d.)

The second principle, physicality, is based on the understanding that the poet writes for the human voice, and that meaning is derived not only from the words but also from the cadences and nuances that can only be gained by a vocal rendition of a poem. In his description of the principles of the Favorite Poem Project, Pinsky writes, "If a poem is written well, it was written with a poet's voice and for a voice" (Favorite Poem Project: Giving Voice to the American Audience for Poetry, n.d.).

As we set out to review the research related to the instruction of poetry in general and the principles of autonomy and physicality in particular, we found no empirical studies. It is interesting to note that in the most recent edition of the *Handbook of Research on Teaching the English Language Arts* (Flood, Lapp, Squire, & Jensen, 2003), a remarkably comprehensive work, there is no chapter devoted to poetry and only a single entry on the topic in the index. However, despite the absence of scientific research, there is a strong theoretical foundation for grounding instruction in Pinsky's principles. In the following sections, we will present the work of scholars in the field of literacy that is reflective of Pinsky's guiding principles of autonomy and physicality.

The Literature

Autonomy

The principle of autonomy is resonant in the decades-long scholarly work of Louise Rosenblatt who, as early as 1938, introduced the process she named "transaction," defined as the essential interaction between the individual reader and a text. In her seminal work, *Literature as Exploration* (1938), Rosenblatt writes,

> There is no such thing as a generic reader or a generic literary work; there are only the potential millions of individual readers of the millions of individual literary works. A novel or poem or play remains merely inkblots on paper until a reader transforms them into a set of meaningful symbols. (p. 25)

More than 60 years later, Rosenblatt (2004) again wrote of the centrality of the individual reader in the process of transaction: "The evocation of meaning in transaction with a text is indeed interpretation in the sense of performance, and the transactional theory merges with the idea of interpretation as individual construal" (p. 1378).

Consistent with the theme of this chapter, we recall that one of Rosenblatt's most inspired works is *The Reader, the Text, the Poem* (1978), in which she suggests that the response of an individual reader to a chosen text is, itself, a poem.

> "The poem" comes into being in the live circuit set up between the reader and "the text". As with the elements of an electric circuit, each component of the reading process functions by virtue of the presence of the others. A specific reader and a specific text at a specific time and place; change any of these, and there occurs a different circuit, a different event—a different poem. (p. 14)

Indeed, the reasons readers give for selecting their favorite poems in the anthologies edited by Robert Pinsky and Maggie Dietz embody Rosenblatt's concept of response as poem. In the most recent volume, *An Invitation to Poetry: A New Favorite Poem Project Anthology* (2004), Yina Liang, a 16-year old student from Atlanta, Georgia, offers her thoughts on Emily Dickinson's poem "I'm Nobody! Who Are You?"

> I discovered this poem in seventh grade when one of my English teachers showed
> it to me. And then eighth grade came and ninth grade, and every year as life gets
> busier the poem keeps on coming back to me...so much better every time, that I
> think in time it discovered me. (p. 59)

Physicality

The second principle, physicality, was a central theme in the work of Bill Martin Jr. who introduced the Sounds of Language series in 1972 with the expressed purpose of giving voice to the words children read from the earliest stage of reading development. Martin relied on the sounds of the language, particularly the language of the poem, to introduce young readers to the texture and the beauty of the printed word. Earlier, Martin wrote a pamphlet in the form of a poetic dialogue between teachers and administrators. Titled *The Human Connection: Language and Literature* (1967), this text offers numerous examples of the power of poetry on the individual child and concludes with a series of basic premises for teaching, including the following:

> The goal of language instruction
> is not to develop language skill in and of itself,
> but to help children claim their humanity
> through the use of language. (p. 39)

Glenna Davis Sloan (2003), an advocate for the use of quality literature to afford students opportunities for thoughtful response, writes of the child's natural physicality and inclination to sound:

> Primitive poetry is linked to movement, to the basic bodily rhythms involved in
> singing, dancing, marching. Children are kinesthetic creatures who delight in
> moving to rhythmic chants of words that take their fancy. Polysyllabic mouthfuls
> become rhythmic background for table-beating and pan-pounding. Children
> know how language and movement relate. They bounce balls and skip rope in
> time to chanted words; they tease in taunting rhythmic rhymes. They call on the
> magical powers of incantation. (p. 99)

In his summary of the research in reader response, James R. Squire affirms the wisdom of these teacher scholars. Squire (1994) cites as a critical conclusion of the research, "The sounds of words are often as important as their sense" (p. 645). He suggests that a neglected aspect of the literary experience for students is reading and hearing text read aloud. Poems, plays, and stories written for the human voice are particularly amenable to enhanced response when experienced orally.

We present, now, a description of the poetry institutes that were inspired by the Favorite Poem Project and informed by the principles of autonomy and physicality.

The Poetry Institutes

Following the completion of his unprecedented three-year term as poet laureate, Pinsky, a faculty member at Boston University, and his associate, Maggie Dietz, met with Roselmina Indrisano and Stephan Ellenwood, faculty members at the School of Education, to extend the focus of the Favorite Poem Project to educators and their students, schools, and communities. Together, they planned three summer institutes to be held in the following years for the purposes of introducing the participants to the principles and resources of the Favorite Poem Project, affording the participants opportunities to work with distinguished poets, and providing the participants opportunities to create lessons and plans for implementation in their classrooms, schools, and communities, guided by experienced teachers of poetry.

In 2001, the first Poetry Institute for Educators in New England was held, and the pattern for subsequent summers was set. Twenty-five teacher–administrator teams, a total of 50 participants from public and private schools in New England, attended the weeklong institute. The decision to recruit teacher–administrator teams was made to assure the maximum opportunity for implementation by educating the decision makers as well as the teachers.

On the first day, participants were given a notebook that included the poems to be discussed, a bibliography of poetry anthologies, and the outline for the lesson plans they would create during the week. Participants also received the video and one of the poetry anthologies that resulted from the Favorite Poem Project. A library of poetry anthologies was available to the participants as well.

Each day's program followed the same schedule, a pattern that received such positive feedback from the participants of the first institute that it was repeated in subsequent years. In the morning, participants viewed the Favorite Poem Project videos and participated in seminars with visiting poets. The videos present a series of poetry readings by individuals selected from the original 18,000 submissions received by Pinsky in response to his call at the beginning of his first term as poet laureate. In addition to a reading of the poem, each individual tells the reason for choosing this particular poem. The themes are resonant of the universals of the human experience: memory, grief, joy, and discovery, made particular by the circumstances of the individual life. A remarkable feature of the videos is the use of a setting for each presentation that offers insight into the person and to the connection between the life and the art, rather than a background for the poem.

The institute's seminars were conducted by distinguished poets in the manner of a graduate course on poetry. In addition to Pinsky, participants of the three institutes were privileged to work with Mark Doty, Carol Muske-Dukes, David Ferry, Gail Mazur, Heather McHugh, Rosanna Warren, and Louise Glück. Later in the day, the visiting poets presented readings attended by institute participants and faculty, and open to the general public.

In the afternoon, participants met in grade-level groups, each led by an experienced teacher who had been successful in teaching poetry in a classroom setting. These groups had a single purpose: to apply what the participants had learned from the seminars and videos to the creation of lessons for use in classrooms, schools, and communities. The classroom lessons included the sources of the poems for the lesson; teachers' reflections; teaching ideas; and teaching connections to other topics, subjects, and projects. In addition, teachers planned activities for school and community poetry events. At the conclusion of the institute, the lesson plans were edited and sent to the participants in time for the opening of schools in September.

Each institute concluded with a favorite poetry reading by the participants. Representatives from each group read a poem and offered insights into their reasons for choosing the selection. The audience responded often with laughter or tears, in the latter case, evidence of the trust that had been developed during the institute. Many of the participants offered, as well, their own poetry, some created with or by their former students.

The responses of participants in the institutes have affirmed the wisdom of the principles that guided their design and conduct. A statement in the evaluation completed by one of the participants is reflective of many others. A high school teacher wrote,

> We, as teachers have shared so much information here through this program that the contributions seem endless. Specifically, however, the concepts of physicality and autonomy have seemed to jump out at me as necessities for next year. (Favorite Poem Project: Feedback From Teachers, n.d.)

In the next section, we present a description of the ways two classroom teachers, Jennifer Hauck Bryson and Merri Jones, with the support of their principal, Nancy Birmingham, and their Title I director, Sheila Garnick, implemented the work of the institutes in their urban school district. All four professionals have attended one of the poetry institutes, and Jennifer Hauck Bryson and Sheila Garnick have served as teacher leaders. Here we present, as well, the ways the principles and the lessons designed to guide the reading of poetry have been applied to writing.

The Implementation

The setting for the implementation of the Favorite Poem Project is an elementary school in a small city located north of Boston, Massachusetts, and which, for many generations, has been home to immigrant families. The school is one of four in an elementary complex that shares a central library. Data reported by the district indicate that during the 2001–2002 school year, of the 475 students, 70% were Hispanic, 18% white, 6% Asian, and 8% black. The home languages spoken by 72% of the children included Spanish, Khmer, Portuguese, Serbo-Croatian, Vietnamese, Somali, Filipino, Farsi, Luganda, and Haitian Creole. The principal and the faculty are committed to helping the students and their families realize their aspirations by providing a high-quality education for the children and respectful collaboration with the families.

In the following sections, third-grade teachers Jennifer Hauck Bryson and Merri Jones describe the initiatives they introduced as a result of their attendance at the Poetry Institute, from the first steps taken within the confines of the classrooms to the districtwide projects adopted later. These initiatives were implemented over the course of two years (2001–2003) and are continuously being improved to represent the principles of the Poetry Institute and to meet the needs of the students. Jennifer and Merri also describe their goals for the initiatives in the near future.

The Classroom

We are committed to the diverse community our school serves, and we wish to ensure that all the students benefit from the project. Our initial goal was to provide poetry to the students and, guided by the principles of autonomy and physicality, to give them more opportunities to choose poems, to perform them, and to respond in oral and written forms of language.

Before our attendance at the Poetry Institute, our students kept notebooks of all of the poems learned during the daily morning meeting or as part of the literacy curriculum. The poems came from many sources but were most often selected by the teacher. After attending the institute, we began to consider the ways the principle of autonomy could guide our future efforts. Our first step was to replace the notebook of poems selected by the teacher with a personal anthology of poems chosen by the individual student from anthologies that they read during classroom reading time, school and classroom library visits, or at home. When a student found a favorite poem, a sticky note was placed in the text and brought to the teacher for copying and placement in the anthology. The children had absolute freedom to choose poems they liked. If a child chose a poem that was too difficult to be read independently, we ensured that the student had an opportunity to read it with someone who could help. As part of our literacy curriculum, the children were given opportunities to share their anthologies with the class during the one period per week known as Poetry Anthology Time.

In addition, students frequently chose to read their poetry anthologies during our reading workshop. Reading workshop is a time when students choose what they read, and it was during this time, as well, when students added to their anthologies poems that had a personal meaning or were marked by a particular rhythm. The results of our commitment to the principle of autonomy were evident very early as we saw many of the children giving the anthologies a permanent place in their book bags. They enjoyed sharing them daily with their friends and families. It was remarkable to hear the words of Robert Frost and Emily Dickinson whispered throughout the room. Furthermore, students were encouraged to keep their anthologies from year to year as an ongoing personal collection of poetry anthologies.

The student response to this change from poetry notebook to personal anthologies has been dramatic. Our students now view poems as belonging to them, and for many, Poetry Anthology Time is the favorite period of the week. They also have become far more articulate when discussing why they like or dislike particular poems and are not reluctant on occasion to respectfully disagree with their teachers. Merri once taught her class a poem about Alaska and invited the children to recite the poem as a class during the morning meeting. At the end, one of the students raised her hand and asked if she could recite another poem instead because she felt the one Merri had chosen "did not sound good out loud." Many other students agreed, so a new poem was chosen. Similarly, during Poetry Anthology Time in Jennifer's room, two students were sharing their anthologies when at the conclusion of a reading of Eloise Greenfield's "Honey, I Love" (1978), the other student replied, "I think it is supposed to sound more like this..." and read the poem aloud with a liveliness and appreciation for the voice heard in the poem. During the reading, the student added hand motions and facial expressions to deliver a dramatic reading that left all of us stunned. The principle of physicality was at work.

Having established the principles of autonomy and physicality as children selected their favorite poems, read, and responded to them, we have begun to seek ways to have the children begin to write their responses to their chosen poems and to those chosen by their classmates. In the next section, we describe the steps that we took to involve parents in our work with poetry.

The Home

Once our poetry anthology routines were established, we searched for a way to bring more poetry into our students' homes and to encourage parental involvement. As a result, we began a home-poetry project. Poetry homework provides opportunities to extend curricular themes and to support family reading and discussion of poetry.

During the first open house of the year, we introduced the poetry project and discussed the institute with teachers, parents, and students. We promised parents that at least one poem would be sent home each week as part of homework. A letter was sent home with the initial poem to inform those parents who had not attended the open house. We made a great effort to include poems written in other languages, with English translations. Parents were encouraged to read and talk about the poem with their children and to write a response in their home language. About one month into the initial year, many parents began including their own responses to the poems. Following their lead, we began to include a place for adult responses on the homework. We assured parents who wrote in their home languages that we would find a translator to share the response with the class. These responses were brought to the classroom where many were posted with copies of the poems.

Although parents' responses were not mandatory, nearly three-quarters of them responded regularly, an impressive number. Parents have also informed us during meetings or conferences that this poetry addition is their favorite part of the homework each week. They have stated that they enjoy reading the poems with their entire families and discussing them together. Many children have said that their parents often dramatize the poems or try to memorize them. Some of the parents have sent their favorite poems to the class. As a result of these shared experiences, students have included these "home" poems and the written responses in their poetry anthologies. The children also enjoyed sharing their parents' poems and the family responses to all the poems they read together. Parents were invited to the classroom during Poetry Anthology Time to join in class discussions and to share their favorite poems and their responses.

We have been most pleased with this project because it allows us to serve both the students and their families in a community where many cultures enrich our collection of favorite poems. The responses we have received from both parents and students have been insightful and moving. In response to "The Dream Keeper" by Langston Hughes (1932/1994), many parents expressed their worry and concern for their children in this harsh world, as well as their enthusiasm and support for their children's dreams.

Throughout the years we have conducted this part of the project, our students' responses have shown an increased level of sophistication when responding to poems, both in class and at home. Their responses have evolved from simply retelling the poem to making both personal and literary associations. (See Figure 4.1 for examples of a child's and a parent's responses.)

As a result of the enriched discussions that began in the home, our classroom discussions have changed. In the beginning, the prompts we provided to elicit responses were open-ended questions, such as What did you like about this poem? How did this poem make you feel? As our students progressed in responding to poetry, we have refined the prompts to focus on a particular poem and to invite more elaborate responses. The cooperation of the school and the home has benefited the children and their families in countless ways and has contributed to our aspirations for a community of learners.

We have observed that our students are using poetry to enhance their voices in all of their writing. Poems such as "The Dream Keeper" were used to teach the craft of voice and served as excellent models and inspiration to our student poets. Poetry has also been used to teach simile, metaphor, alliteration, and repetition. Although students are encouraged to write poetry, reading and responding to poetry is taught months before we expect our students to write. During the early part of the year, a poetry study was conducted during the writing workshop. Students read a wide variety of poetry and wrote responses to the poems they read. These experiences were the first step in writing poetry. (See Figure 4.2 for poetry written by Jennifer's third-grade students who were inspired by "The Dream Keeper.")

Figure 4.1   A Child's and a Parent's Responses to "The Dream Keeper" by Langston Hughes

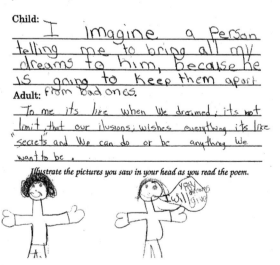

Read the Langston Hughes poem *The Dream Keeper* with an adult at home. Then talk about what the poem means to you. What was your favorite part and did you see any pictures in your head? Both you and the adult may write a few sentences describing your favorite part and your discussion at home. Then illustrate the poem.

Child:
I imagine a person telling me to bring all my dreams to him, because he is going to keep them apart from bad ones.

Adult:
To me its like when we dreamed; its not limit, that our ilusions; wishes everything its like "secrets" and we can do or be anything we want to be.

Illustrate the pictures you saw in your head as you read the poem.

**Figure 4.2   Poems by Third-Grade Students Inspired
by "The Dream Keeper"**

<u>*Dreams*</u>
Dreams are like wishes that you can depend on.
Dreams are nice to think about.
Dreams will be with you.
*Do not give up on your dream because dreams will
come true.*
What ever you want to be just follow your dream.
Like a teacher...
that is what I want to be when I grow up.

By Elizabeth Rodriguez

<u>Dreams</u>
Dreams are scary like rollercoasters.
Dreams are funny like comedians.
Dreams are full of thoughts like
daydreams.
By Juan Pagan

<u>My Dream</u>
I dream to be a baseball player.
Or maybe a football player.
It's hard to choose, so I'll just be myself.
By Carlos Figueroa

The School

Following our attendance at the Poetry Institute, Nancy Birmingham, our principal and a former institute participant, gave us the opportunity to introduce the Favorite Poem Project to the entire faculty at an early September meeting. We described the highlights of the institute, presented the notebook of lesson plans, and showed selections from the video collection. We conducted a series of staff development sessions in which we shared the lessons with our colleagues and used the videos to initiate discussions of poetry. In *The Sounds of Poetry* (1998), Pinsky states, "poetry is just as physical or bodily an art as dancing" (p. 8). The videos were most helpful in illustrating to our colleagues what is meant by the principles of autonomy and physicality, and the value of the individual's response to a poem.

Throughout these staff development sessions, our goal was to convey the primary focus of the Favorite Poem Project. This is not to say that poetry was not being performed in the elementary classroom; most, if not all, of our colleagues read poems to and with their students every day. It was the application of the principles of autonomy and physicality, and the act of responding—the oral and written dialogue between the reader and the poet—that was missing.

Inspired by our seminars with Pinsky and other notable poets during the institutes, we set an initial goal for the first year to increase the poetry collection in the elementary classrooms to include fewer poets who write exclusively for children and more classic and contemporary poets who write for readers of all ages. Our principal, who understood and supported our goal, quickly helped us to achieve it by ordering a series of classic poetry anthologies for every classroom library.

In the next year of our poetry initiative, we created a poetry corner in an alcove in a central location in the school. The corner was filled with beanbag seating and a variety of poetry books, including anthologies written by individual students and whole classes. On the bulletin board opposite the corner, a showcase of famous poets and their work was posted, along with copies of their poems for children to take with them when they returned to their classrooms.

Students were invited to visit the corner during the daily half-hour independent reading period that is a part of the literacy curriculum. Although teachers schedule and structure this time in different ways, they encouraged children to read poetry in the poetry corner or in the classroom during this period. Because the independent reading time occurs at different times during the day, crowding was not a problem, but students were reminded to return to their classrooms if the corner was fully occupied when they visited. A timer was given to the students when they left the classroom to assure their prompt return at the end of the independent reading period. Students also visited the poetry corner during indoor recess time when inclement weather prevented them from playing outside. The teachers monitored the students in the poetry corner according to their availability.

During our weekly school assembly, students were invited to share talents and favorite books and poems. Sharing poems continues to be the request received most frequently by our principal. Students read poems individually, with partners, and even groups comprised of whole classes. In the manner of the original Favorite Poem Project Readings, the students were invited to tell why they chose their favorite poem. (See Figure 4.3 for introductions to favorite poems offered by two fourth graders who were previously members of Merri's class in second and third grades.)

We saw the results of these expanded opportunities to read and respond to poetry demonstrated in many ways. A study of the circulation of books in the school library, which is used by three other elementary schools in our complex, found that the circulation of poetry books increased by 38% in the year following our attendance at the Poetry Institute and 92% in the second year, when the other schools joined in our poetry project.

At the same time, our school implemented the writing workshop model to better develop students' writing abilities. Although we never intended the two initiatives to intersect, we found that the reading of poetry provided inspiration to

Figure 4.3   Introductions to Favorite Poems

I like the poem Honey, I Love because it tells people all about the things that she likes and places that she likes to go. I also like how she says I love a lot of things a whole lot of things. I like how she expresses herself with her words in this poem. I also like this poem because it reminds me of things I like and places I like to go and things I like to do with my family and my friends. The picture in my mind is me playing and doing things with my friends and places I like to go like a vacation. This is my favorite poem by Eloise Greenfield and always will be.

Shandalee Colon

I like a poem named Dreams by Longston Hughes. My favorite lines are Hold fast to dreams for if dreams die life is a broken-winged bird that cannot fly. Hold fast to dreams for if dreams go life is a barren field frozen with snow. The poem Dreams reminds me of dreams I want to dream again. It feels like my soul is that girl in the poem. I get a picture in my mind of the little girl sleeping in her bed and then her dreams just flowing away from her mind and never coming back.

Veronica Martinez

teachers and students, both for the teaching of the craft and for making models of good writing accessible.

The culmination of our efforts to share with our school community what we learned at the Poetry Institute was a family poetry night. Our principal gathered a group of teachers and led the group in planning every aspect of the event. The evening began with a welcome by the school principal and a favorite poem reading by several community members. The variety of poems exemplified the principle of autonomy as the superintendent of schools read "Fog" by Carl Sandburg (1916/1992), a custodian read "The Children's Hour" by Henry Wadsworth Longfellow (Schoonmaker, 1998), a school nurse read "Sick" by Shel Silverstein (1974), and a member of the school district read a poem he had written as a young boy.

Following the favorite poem reading, families visited six poetry stations created by the teachers. The station-centered model of our poetry event was inspired by our school's consistently successful science family night. Instead of offering science experiments, these stations were places where families could read or write poems and participate in accompanying activities. The themes of the stations were mathematics, science, art, music, and physical education. A faculty volunteer was available at each station, where there were three different poems and three activities. For example, the teacher at the science station read a poem about plants with the families, then helped the children to plant seeds in small cups. An activity at the physical education station involved students jumping rope while reading jump-rope rhymes posted on large charts. Children were given personal copies of the poems at all of the stations. Our goal was to introduce a wide variety of poems while providing an atmosphere where autonomy and physicality were encouraged.

The District

In the summer of 2002, Sheila Garnick, our Title I director, who had been a lead teacher in the institute, invited us to coordinate a summer workshop for educators interested in learning more about the Favorite Poem Project. Teachers from the four elementary schools in our district were invited to attend this five-day workshop. This workshop comprised two parts: exposure to the Favorite Poem Project and the development of a K–4 districtwide poetry homework binder. Each day began with a viewing of the Favorite Poem Project videos, followed by a discussion of the principles and practices we had learned in the institute and the ways these ideas can be implemented in the elementary school classroom. In the second half of the day, groups of teachers read, collected, and discussed poetry and developed response sheets consistent with the instructional themes of the curriculum. The poems and response sheets were discussed in the larger group, final decisions were made, and a binder was created for each of the four elementary schools in the hope that all elementary classrooms would begin to participate in this project in the next school year. Although representatives from each school attended the workshop, we also presented this project at each school at a September staff meeting. Our presentation of the binder and our own family responses from the previous year led to great excitement across the elementary schools and a quick adoption of the home-poetry project. Today, classrooms throughout the elementary complex actively engage their students and families in the home-poetry project.

The Professional Community

We have had opportunities to make presentations to the participants in the two poetry institutes that followed our initial attendance. At these events, we have described many of the initiatives presented in this chapter and, as a result, have been invited by some of the participants to present professional development sessions in their school districts. During the first year of the implementation of the poetry project our school was named a Compass School by the Massachusetts Department of Education. Both Nancy Birmingham and Sheila Garnick believe that the poetry initiatives were instrumental in our success in literacy. We made presentations at two Title I conferences to audiences that included educators from many school districts in the state.

Next Steps

The genesis of the implementation described in this chapter is the direct result of our (Jennifer and Merri's) attendance at the Poetry Institute. Our ideas about how and when to teach poetry were changed. We were reminded of our own love of poetry and affirmed what we knew to be true, that many methods of teaching poetry in primary and secondary schools generally have the effect of muting the voices of the poet and the reader in the midst of exhaustive studies of syntax and meter. We encourage university departments of literature and education to join in replicating Boston University's Summer Poetry Institute for Educators in their areas. We can think of no better way to encourage broad changes in the way poetry is taught in schools and to convince educators that giving poetry its rightful place in the curriculum will not result in a negative effect on high-stakes testing.

Our goals for the near future are to continue to refine the initiatives we have in place and to encourage more family involvement. We hope to invite parents to come to school each week to participate in Poetry Anthology Time and to host regular Favorite Poem Readings throughout the year. In light of the recent study by the National Endowment for the Arts (Bradshaw & Nichols, 2004) that finds that the reading of literature has declined dramatically, we hope to reverse that trend by giving our students and their families a forum in which to read and respond to their favorite poems. Our efforts to nurture and teach the next generation of poets will continue as well.

REFERENCES

Bradshaw, T., & Nichols, B. (2004). *Reading at risk: A survey of literary reading in America*. Washington, DC: National Endowment for the Arts.

Favorite Poem Project: Feedback From Teachers. (n.d). Retrieved August 16, 2004, from http://www.favoritepoem.org/forteachers/index.html

Favorite Poem Project: Giving Voice to the American Audience for Poetry. (n.d). Retrieved August 16, 2004, from http://www.favoritepoem.org/theproject/principles.html

Favorite Poem Project: Revitalizing Poetry in the Classroom. (n.d). Retrieved August 16, 2004, from http://www.favoritepoem.org/forteachers/index.html

Favorite Poem Project: Welcome. (n.d). Retrieved August 16, 2004, from http://www.favoritepoem.org/theproject/index.html

Flood, J., Lapp, D., Squire, J.R., & Jensen, J.M. (2003). *Handbook of research on teaching the English language arts* (2nd ed.). Mahwah, NJ: Erlbaum.

Martin, B., Jr. (1967). *The human connection: Language and literature*. Washington, DC: Department of Elementary-Kindergarten-Nursery Education, National Education Association of the United States.

Martin, B., Jr. (with P. Brogan). (1972). *Sounds of language readers*. New York: Holt, Rhinehart and Winston.

Pinsky, R. (1998). *The sounds of poetry: A brief guide*. New York: Farrar, Straus, and Giroux.

Pinsky, R., & Dietz, M. (2004). *An invitation to poetry: A new Favorite Poem Project anthology*. New York: W.W. Norton.

Rosenblatt, L.M. (1938). *Literature as exploration*. New York: Appleton-Century.

Rosenblatt, L.M. (1978). *The reader, the text, the poem: The transactional theory of the literary work.* Carbondale: Southern Illinois University Press.

Rosenblatt, L.M. (2004). The transactional theory of reading and writing. In R.B. Ruddell & N.J. Unrau (Eds.), *Theoretical models and processes of reading* (5th ed., pp. 1363–1398). Newark, DE: International Reading Association.

Sloan, G.D. (2003). *The child as critic: Developing literacy through literature, K-8* (4th ed.). New York: Teachers College Press.

Squire, J.R. (1994). Research in reader response: Naturally interdisciplinary. In R.B. Ruddell, M.R. Ruddell, & H. Singer (Eds.), *Theoretical models and processes of reading* (4th ed., pp. 637–652). Newark, DE: International Reading Association.

LITERATURE CITED

Greenfield, E. (1978). *Honey I Love and other poems.* New York: Crowell.

Hughes, L. (1994). *The Dream Keeper and other poems.* New York: Scholastic. (Original work published 1932)

Sandburg, C. (1992). *Chicago poems.* Urbana: University of Illinois Press. (Original work published 1916)

Schoonmaker, F. (Ed.). (1998). *Poetry for young people: Henry Wadsworth Longfellow.* New York: Sterling.

Silverstein, S. (1974). *Where the Sidewalk Ends: The poems and drawings of Shel Silverstein.* New York: Harper & Row.

Chapter 5

Writing to Learn in Elementary Classrooms

Bonnie B. Armbruster, Sarah J. McCarthey, and Sunday Cummins

We begin this chapter with a definition of "writing to learn" and a discussion of its purported benefits. We then present a brief review of research on writing and learning in elementary classrooms. The main focus of the chapter, however, is on practice—how publications for teachers promote writing to help children learn and how elementary teachers use writing to enhance learning in their classrooms.

The connection between writing and learning is referred to as "writing to learn," "writing in the content areas," or "writing across the curriculum." Writing to learn is the term we will use in this chapter. Writing to learn has been an area of increasing interest to both researchers and practitioners over the past two decades.

Interest in writing to learn is based on the assumption that the act of composing promotes thinking and learning. Writing has been advocated as a "mode of learning" (Emig, 1977, p. 122) and "a powerful tool for the enhancement of thinking and learning" (Tierney & Shanahan, 1996, p. 272). Claims have been made that students can use writing as a tool to develop concepts and generalizations, promote critical thinking and problem solving, analyze and reflect on their thinking and understanding, gain new insights, and contribute to learning and remembering content information.

Consistent with the constructivist view that meaningful, lasting learning is constructed and "owned" by the student, writing to learn purportedly helps students use language to make meaning of new information in light of what they already know about the topic, thus acquiring a personal ownership of ideas. In this way, writing to learn helps students to not only acquire content information but also to transform knowledge and to generate new knowledge (Beyer, 1982; Connolly, 1995). Thus, writing can play a powerful role in the production, as well as the presentation, of knowledge (Connolly, 1995). As Morrow, Pressley, Smith, and Smith (1997) put it, "writing changes the development and shape of ideas" (p. 57).

Writing as a tool to help children think about and learn content is the major focus of the writing-to-learn movement. Writing to learn, however, can also help students learn to become better writers. "The research on writing instruction is clear on one important point: children do not learn to write by working exclusively on exercises in grammar texts; they primarily learn to write by writing" (Templeton,

Learning to Write, Writing to Learn: Theory and Research in Practice edited by Roselmina Indrisano and Jeanne R. Paratore. Copyright © 2005 by the International Reading Association.

1997, p. 230). Or as Moore, Moore, Cunningham, and Cunningham (2003) put it, "Students who read and write much tend to improve their reading and writing" (p. 19). In other words, as children write to learn, they are gaining additional practice writing. Even when the main purpose of writing is to enhance content learning, children may also be learning how to write, or at least improving their writing.

In addition to the direct benefits for students in learning content and learning how to write, writing in the content areas also has been identified as an important means for teachers to assess student understanding and learning. By examining students' written products, teachers can determine the effectiveness of their own teaching and decide what must be retaught or approached in a different way. As Jenkinson (1988) states, "Thus, writing can be as important a mode of learning for the teacher as it is for the student" (p. 717).

Although the benefits of writing to learn are often claimed, there is relatively little supporting research. Some research supports the benefit of writing for learning content at the middle school, high school, and college levels (for reviews, see Armbruster, 2000; Tierney & Shanahan, 1996). There is less research on writing to learn at the elementary level. We turn now to a brief review of that research.

Review of Research

A study by Armbruster, Anderson, and Ostertag (1987) investigated whether instruction in a conventional expository text structure (problem–solution) would facilitate fifth graders' learning from social studies text that had a problem-solution structure. Over 11 days, students in the structure-training group received direct instruction in recognizing and writing summaries of several social studies passages that had a problem–solution structure, while control-group students read and discussed answers to questions about the same passages. (Although writing was not the only aspect of structure training in this study, it was an important component of the instruction.) On an essay test on the main idea of a problem–solution passage, structure-trained students recalled about 50% more information, and more important information, than control-group students; however, structure training did not facilitate learning as measured by an objective test. In addition, the structure-trained students wrote higher quality summaries than the control group.

Konopak, Martin, and Martin (1990) studied the effect of a writing strategy to enhance sixth graders' learning of a history topic. Over a four-day period, the experimental group completed writing tasks in addition to reading and discussion, while the control group completed more traditional identification and short-answer comprehension tasks. Although there was no difference between the groups on a multiple-choice test on the content, the experimental group generated more new ideas and higher quality ideas on a posttest requiring them to write about their knowledge of the topic. In addition, the experimental group improved in writing ability over the four-day period. The authors concluded that the writing strategy not only facilitated learning but also improved the students' writing.

Davis, Rooze, and Runnels (1992) investigated the effect of journal writing on fourth graders' learning of social studies content and writing fluency. Students in the experimental group wrote in journals in response to prompts for 10 minutes twice a week for nine weeks. Objective tests of social studies knowledge were administered immediately after the treatment and two weeks later. Although there was no difference between experimental and control groups on the immediate test, students in the experimental group scored significantly higher than control-group students on the delayed test. The study suggests that journal writing can facilitate learning retention of fourth-grade social studies content.

Bristor (1994) briefly describes a five-year research project that studied the effects of an integrated curriculum strategy (reading, writing, and science) on the achievement, attitudes, and self-confidence of fourth- and fifth-grade students. In the experimental group, students received integrated instruction in science and reading and writing, while the control group received their regular science and basal reading programs separately. For at least the first four years of the study (the fifth year's data had not yet been analyzed at the time of publication), the students in the experimental group outperformed the control-group students in both reading and science; they also had more positive attitudes and greater self-confidence toward science and reading. Although science and reading were the main curricula of interest in this research, writing played a prominent role. For example, students kept learning logs, paraphrased or summarized their science learning, wrote pieces applying science content to their personal lives, constructed an alphabet book on weather, and wrote riddles about science content. Unfortunately, no results for writing achievement were reported.

In a study by Rudnitsky, Etheredge, Freeman, and Gilbert (1995), over a 16-day period, third and fourth graders were taught addition and subtraction story problem types through discussion and student writing of word, or "story," problems. Compared to students who simply practiced solving problems and students in a control group, students who had authored their own story problems scored higher on both immediate and delayed tests of ability to solve addition and subtraction word problems.

Writing to learn has also been a component of some large-scale instructional interventions for elementary students. For example, Morrow et al. (1997) investigated the effect of a literature-based program integrated into literacy and science instruction on achievement, attitudes, and use of literature. Over the course of a school year, six third-grade classrooms were assigned to either a control condition or two experimental conditions. In one experimental condition, science instruction remained as usual, but literacy instruction included the use of trade book literature along with the basal reading program. In the second experimental condition, literature was integrated with the science curriculum: Students read science informational books and wrote about what they were reading. Classrooms using the integrated literature–science program scored significantly higher statistically on two of three measures of science content and on writing ability (as well as other literacy measures).

Another example of a large-scale intervention is the Concept-Oriented Reading Instruction (CORI) program (e.g., Guthrie et al., 1996; Guthrie et al., 1998; Guthrie & Ozgungor, 2002). CORI is a yearlong instructional intervention designed to increase upper elementary students' engagement in reading, writing, and science. One of the four phases of the program is Communicate to Others, in which students are taught to present the answers to questions they are researching in many forms, including journals, written reports, class-authored books, and informational stories. Participation in CORI has resulted in many positive outcomes for students, including greater conceptual learning (Guthrie et al., 1998). Because CORI so far has been studied as a complete composite program, however, it is impossible to determine the relative contribution of "communicating to others" (writing) to the outcomes, including learning.

Although research on the effect of writing on learning at the elementary level is certainly insufficient, enough positive support apparently exists so that writing to learn has become a recommended practice for elementary teachers. For example, a recent publication makes the assertion, "The value of linking classroom reading and writing experiences has been well established. Combining reading and writing improves achievement" (Moss, 2003, p. 132). We were curious about how the recommendation to use writing to improve learning and achievement is affecting elementary classroom instruction. Therefore, we turn now to the main focus of this chapter—writing to learn in practice.

Writing to Learn in Practice

Although the benefits of using writing to enhance learning are often claimed, and some research supports those benefits, teachers infrequently use writing to promote learning (Rosaen, 1990). Writing in the content areas often consists primarily of "knowledge telling"—students answering questions at the ends of chapters or on worksheets; writing traditional reports; and recording what they know, what they want to know, and what they learned using the popular Know-Want-Learn (K-W-L) strategy (Ogle, 1986). There does, however, appear to be an increasing focus on using writing to promote learning by helping students reformulate and extend knowledge of topics.

In this section, we will first examine the push for writing to learn in publications for teachers—books and magazines or journals targeted for teachers. Then, we will share what we learned from observing, interviewing, and (in the case of the third author, Sunday Cummins) working with some elementary teachers in local school districts.

Writing to Learn in Books

Education publishers are offering increasing numbers of books written for preservice or inservice teachers that advocate writing to learn or closely related topics such as reading-writing connections, reading and writing in the content areas, or incorporating language arts across the curriculum. These books typically present a rationale for writing across the curriculum, including the idea that writing enhances thinking and learning; the books then present many ideas on how to implement writing to learn in the classroom, sometimes including examples of how real teachers have used writing to learn. Table 5.1 presents a small sample of recent books related to writing to learn. This list is not exhaustive, and the presence or absence of any title does not reflect on the quality or value of the work. We've assembled this list simply as an indication of growing interest in the field.

In addition to whole books addressing the topic of writing to learn, general language arts methods textbooks often also contain chapters or sections on this topic, bearing titles such as "Reading and Writing in the Content Areas" (Tompkins, 2003), "Reading and Writing in the Content Areas and Study Skills" (Gunning, 2005), and "Writing Across the Curriculum" (Alvermann & Phelps, 2002).

Table 5.1   A Sample of Books Related to Writing to Learn

Alvermann, D.E., Swafford, J., & Montero, M.K. (2004). *Content area literacy instruction for the elementary grades*. Boston, MA: Pearson/Allyn & Bacon.

Buss, K., & Karnowski, L. (2002). *Reading and writing nonfiction genres*. Newark, DE: International Reading Association

Cohle, D.M., & Towle, W. (2001). *Connecting reading and writing in the intermediate grades: A workshop approach*. Newark, DE: International Reading Association.

Duke, N.K., & Bennett-Armistead, V.S. (2003). *Reading & writing informational text in the primary grades: Research-based practices*. New York: Scholastic.

McMackin, M., & Siegel, B. (2002). *Knowing how: Researching and writing nonfiction 3–8*. Portland, ME: Stenhouse.

Portalupi, J., & Fletcher, R. (2001). *Nonfiction craft lessons: Teaching information writing K–8*. Portland, ME: Stenhouse.

Rasinski, T.V., Padak, N.D., Church, B.W., Fawcett, G., Hendershot, J., Henry, J.M., et al. (Eds.). (2000). *Developing reading–writing connections: Strategies from* The Reading Teacher. Newark, DE: International Reading Association.

Stead, T. (2002). *Is that a fact? Teaching nonfiction writing K–3*. Portland, ME: Stenhouse.

Stephens, E.C., & Brown, J.E. (2000). *A handbook of content literacy strategies: 75 practical reading and writing ideas*. Norwood, MA: Christopher-Gordon.

Writing to Learn in Magazines and Journals

Over the past two decades, several articles on writing to learn have appeared in teacher-oriented magazines and journals, often specific to particular content areas such as science, mathematics, and social studies. Typically, these articles describe how teachers have used writing to learn successfully in their classrooms. The following are just a few examples, organized by content area.

Science. Kronholm and Ramsey (1991) report on the use of an extended case study (ECS) approach to help fifth graders learn about issues related to the Wisconsin Timber Wolf Recovery Plan. As part of the project, students engaged in many types of writing activities, including writing a survey and cover letter to solicit the local residents' attitudes about the Timber Wolf Recovery Plan. Once the students had established their views on the issue, they wrote poems and songs, prepared skits, and wrote reports. The authors believe that the students had developed a sense of ownership of the issue by immersing themselves in it; this immersion created many opportunities for writing.

In their article, Reif and Rauch (1994) discuss students at various grade levels writing their own books about science content. These books can take the form of alphabet books, concept books, or science narratives. One kind of alphabet book focuses on relatively broad topics, such as animals, the oceans, or space, with each page representing topic-related words from A to Z. Another kind of alphabet book has pages describing in depth a specific subject, such as a particular animal or scientist/inventor. A concept book is written to answer a specific science-related question or describe a particular concept. In a science narrative, students report on field trips or other events that can be told as a story. Reif and Rauch claim great benefits from student-produced books, including developing science concepts, making science relevant to students' lives, integrating science with other subjects, fostering communication skills, promoting a sense of pride and accomplishment, and enhancing motivation to read and learn science.

In response to student aversion to the traditional "research-and-write-about-a-scientist assignment," Hoofman (1994) developed creative alternative writing assignments for her sixth-grade students. After students have read at least two biographies, an autobiography (if available), and other resources, Hoofman has them choose from a number of alternative writing assignments, based on the idea that they are somehow personally involved in the scientist's life. For example, students may pretend they work for the scientist during summer vacation and write letters home telling about their experience, host a party for several different scientists and record their interactions and conversations, or interview the scientist for a television talk show or newspaper article. Excerpts from students' papers are presented throughout the article.

Di Biase (1998) recommends that students write letters to real scientists to get answers to questions about science. The activity requires students to generate a science question, identify an appropriate scientist, and draft and send a letter. The author reports on the experience of second graders writing to an astronomer.

Yockey (2001) presents a simple "key word" writing technique that helps students communicate their understanding of important science concepts. In this method, students select key words or concepts about a topic they have explored in hands-on activities and then use these key words (e.g., *cohesion*, *vibration*, *gases*, *liquids*) in constructing sentences and paragraphs that reflect their understanding of the concepts. The key words can also form the basis for longer writing projects, such as stories, essays, and research papers. The author claims that students who used science key words as the basis for their writing remembered the content better and were more easily able to communicate their content knowledge on tests.

Mathematics. Zanger (1998) reports on a schoolwide effort to get parents involved in their children's mathematics learning. Teachers enlisted parents to help their children create mathematical story problems, which were published in a school mathematics storybook along with story problems created by students and staff; the storybook was then distributed to the entire school community. Because the family-created stories reflected the children's culture, community, and personal interests, they strengthened the connection between mathematics and the children's daily lives. Benefits of the math storybook included "students' mathematics empowerment" (p. 101), increased student motivation and interest in mathematics, and greater involvement of parents.

Nationally known mathematics educator Marilyn Burns writes frequently about the importance of writing in learning math. In a 1995 article, Burns states, "Now I can't imagine teaching math without making writing an integral part of it" (p. 40). She claims that writing supports learning because students must organize, clarify, and reflect on their thinking in order to record their ideas on paper. The article is full of practical advice to teachers about how to use writing in math classes: math and writing strategies, answers to common questions, math activities that lead to writing, and various math writing assignments. In particular, Burns suggests four types of writing assignments: writing in journals or logs that provide an ongoing record of what students do in math class, writing and explaining solutions to math problems, writing essays explaining math concepts (e.g., explain what *equally likely* means and give an example), and writing about more general learning processes or activities in math class.

In a later article, Burns and Silbey (2001) claim that math journals are one of the most effective ways of introducing writing into math classes. They describe four ways to motivate students to write in journals: problem solving, process prompts, language experience, and class discussion. In problem solving, students write their thoughts about how to solve a specific problem prior to engaging in a class discussion about possible solutions. To help students reflect on their learning, teachers can use process prompts such as "Today I learned _____," "What I know about _____ so far is _____," or "What I'm still not sure about is _____." Language experience involves having the students orally explain a difficulty they are having and then write down their explanation. Next, the teacher asks the students to elaborate on what they have written, thus helping them to clarify their ideas. In class discussion, students first write a description of the process they used to solve a problem. They share their descriptions with the rest of the class, and their classmates provide feedback on the clarity or completeness of the descriptions and offer suggestions for how to make the description more complete. Finally, students revise their descriptions. The authors claim that "the math journal thus becomes a great learning tool" (p. 18).

Social Studies. We found two articles in the area of social studies that advocate writing poetry to enhance learning. For example, fifth-grade teacher Carney-Dalton (1994) believes that children must be involved personally in history in order to learn it. One way she involves her students in learning about injustices in American history is to invite them to write poetry to express their feelings about a troubling historical situation. She states, "In training my fifth graders to see society through a poet's eyes, I hope to encourage them to look at issues critically and with insight" (p. 239). Examples of children's poetry about issues such as slavery, forced relocation of Native Americans, and child labor are included in the article.

Like Carney-Dalton, Maxim (1998) believes that "one of the most powerful methods for encouraging creative writing in the social studies is to involve children in poetry" (p. 208). He writes about using cinquains (structured five-line poems) in a fourth-grade thematic unit on the southwestern United States, focusing on the topic of *vaqueros*. Starting with a brainstormed word bank of "describing words," "doing words," and "*Vaqueros* things," the class composed a cinquain that reflected their knowledge of *vaqueros*. Maxim's article includes a suggested sequence of instruction for introducing cinquains as a form of creative writing, which he believes should be "a treasured tool for pleasurable learning" (p. 210).

Across the Curriculum. In addition to articles about writing to learn in specific content areas, some articles for teachers more generally address writing across the curriculum. For example, Cudd and Roberts (1989) present a specific strategy, "paragraph frames," to help primary-grade students write about what they are learning in the content areas. Paragraph frames provide sentence starters that include specific signal words or phrases representing common organizational structures of expository text (e.g., chronological sequence, enumeration, comparison–contrast). Students then complete the paragraph frames by filling in information from the particular content they are studying. For example, a paragraph frame for a unit on frogs might consist of an initial sentence, "Before a frog is grown, it goes through many changes. First, the mother frog _____. Next, _____. Then, _____. Finally, _____. Now they _____" (p. 393). The authors claim, "Expository paragraph frames provide children with a structured way of using writing as a learning tool. Writing facilitates understanding and retention of material" (p. 403).

McClure and Zitlow (1991) discuss the importance of aesthetic responses (personal feelings, ideas, and attitudes) when reading nonfiction. Believing that the aesthetic dimension is neglected in the content areas, the authors claim that the aesthetic written responses "can help students look beyond the facts to discover the beauty and richness that lies within a subject" (p. 28), thus making learning more meaningful. According to McClure and Zitlow, one of the easiest ways to foster aesthetic response in the classroom is to encourage children to write poetry about the content they are studying. As evidence, they offer many intriguing examples of poems written by children in grades 4, 5, and 6 in response to science and social studies content.

All of these publications provide a plethora of ideas for how to incorporate various types of writing into the content areas in order to enhance learning. The suggestions include writings that range in length from single paragraphs to research papers; they encompass journals, logs, explanations, essays, story problems, and poetry. However, given that research suggests that teachers infrequently use writing to promote learning (Rosaen, 1990), we wanted to see what some of our local teachers were thinking and doing about writing to learn.

Writing to Learn in Classrooms: Observations and Interviews

We identified several local elementary teachers who were either currently employing writing-to-learn strategies or who were interested in offering more writing-to-learn opportunities in their classrooms. Two teachers, Michael and Marcy, were integrating writing-to-learn opportunities within the context of inquiry projects throughout the school day. Two other teachers, Ann and Matt, were working to implement focused writing-to-learn projects with a former district literacy coach, Sunday Cummins. Another teacher, Patricia, invited Sunday to observe lessons related to her writing-to-learn instruction. In addition, we interviewed two other teachers, Anna and Pat, who wanted to share their perspectives on reading and writing informational texts in their classrooms. We begin by highlighting the practices of Michael and Marcy, using writing to learn within inquiry projects. We then present vignettes of the three teachers who were working on extending writing to learn for their students. We end this section by presenting the perspectives of the teachers we observed and/or interviewed.

Writing to Learn in Inquiry Projects: A Grade K–1 Classroom. Michael Marks is
the K-1 teacher at a school that uses a project approach as part of its early childhood curriculum. The project approach derives from the progressive education movement and is based on the philosophy that students should be involved in constructive and purposeful activity to develop independence and responsibility (Dewey, 1938; Kilpatrick, 1918). Currently it is defined as a set of teaching strategies intended to guide children through in-depth studies of real-world topics. Learning environments are structured to be responsive to individual

student differences and interests and to involve students in their own learning. Curriculum integration, including continuity across subjects and opportunities to relate home and school, is a feature of the approach. Students are expected to work cooperatively on open-ended tasks through several phases from recalling experiences, to pursuing questions, to culminating activities (Katz & Chard, 1989).

Michael's school is affiliated with the local university and serves a population of students from diverse ethnic backgrounds. Michael uses writing to learn in his semester-long study of insects and arachnids that integrates language arts with science. The project developed from the students' interest in discovering that the playground was filled with caterpillars. Students collected, observed, and studied the caterpillars, discussing life cycles and other features of caterpillars. The initial writing experiences included students observing insects in their environment and then drawing and labeling what they observed. Figure 5.1 shows a student's observation of praying mantises' relative sizes. She has labeled the male and female as well as their body parts. Her observation says, "In this picture it shows that a male is smaller than the female."

Students then began bringing insects they found to school and adding them to the Insect Zoo. Each day, the teacher wrote a question related to insects on the board for students' responses. Initially, Michael took a survey to find out how many students thought spiders were insects. When all responses were recorded, he read information from a book that explained differences between spiders and insects.

Figure 5.1   Student Observation of Praying Mantises' Sizes

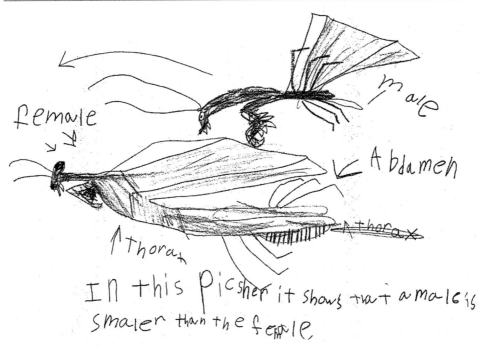

In this picture it shows that a male is smaller than the female.

Other questions such as "What insects that are pests have you had experience with?" initiated discussions and further observations.

Other activities related to the unit included the following:

- Students performed *The Very Hungry Caterpillar* by Eric Carle (1969) for an audience of younger students and parents.
- Students built and painted models of insects.
- Students made observational drawings of insects they had examined under the microscope.

Students had learned to make slides using the Digital Blue microscope that magnifies parts of the insect up to 200 times. After students made the observational drawings, they then created slide shows that involved labeling the slides and writing directions for using the computer-based slide show.

Figure 5.2 shows a list of the items presented in the student's slide show. For example, the first slide is a dragonfly's wing. In Figure 5.3, the student has written directions for using the digital microscope. She wrote, "Instructions for the Digital Blue. 1. Pick a insect in a petri dish. 2. Bring it to the Digital Blue. 3. We'll put it on the special moving dish and show it to you!" In a previous reflection, she had written, "The Digital Blue is a very new microscope and it is hooked to a computer" and "You can change the magnification but 200X is too much!"

Figure 5.2 List of Items Presented in a Student's Slide Show

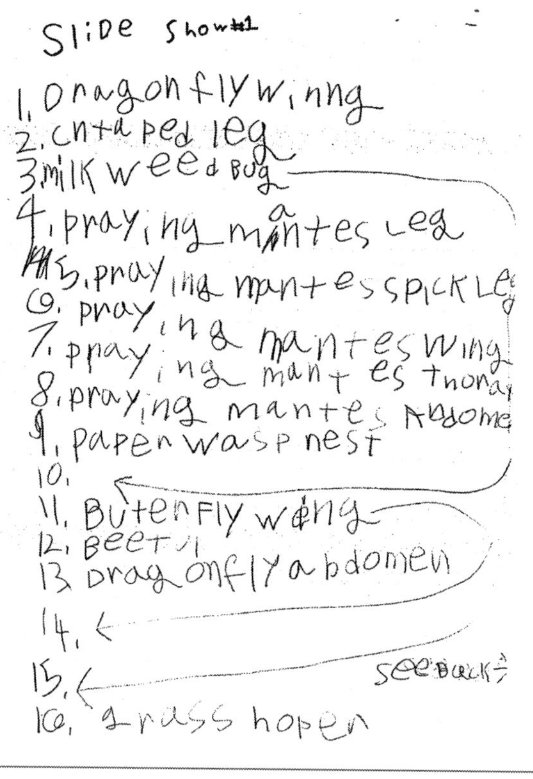
Slide Show#1
1, Dragonfly winng
2. cntaped leg
3.milk weed Bug
4. praying mantes leg
5. praying mantes spickle leg
6. praying mantes wing
7. praying mantes thoray
8. praying mantes Abdome
9. papen wasp nest
10.
11. Butenfly wing
12. Beetl
13 Dragonfly abdomen
14.
15.
see back
16. grass hopen

Figure 5.3   Student Directions for Using a Digital Microscope

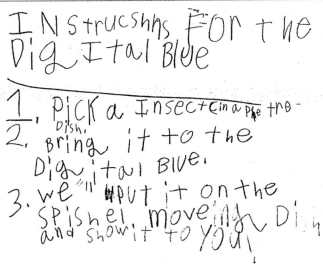

Instructions for the Digital Blue. 1. Pick an insect in a petri dish. 2. Bring it to the Digital Blue. 3. We'll put it on the special moving dish and show it to you!

Figures 5.1, 5.2, and 5.3 demonstrate different ways in which a student can use writing to learn within an inquiry project.

The culminating activity for the investigation, titled "Insect Extravaganza," involved an open house in which parents interacted with the student experts about their projects. At the Insect Safari, students had drawn different types of insects from their observations and labeled them. Students developed questions such as "How many legs does an insect have?" and "Does a boy mosquito bite?" for the parents to answer. Another group of students wrote "true or false flip books" (Tompkins, 2004, p. 327), in which students posed questions about pests, parents replied "true" or "false," and then the students revealed the answer with the explanation they had written. Two students had written books to teach others about the differences between insects and arachnids. Others wrote about their experiences finding a chrysalis and figuring out what it was. All of the projects incorporated observations of insects with reading and writing.

Almost every day, Michael read an informational book related to the insect project, and students were encouraged to remember facts from the reading. Throughout the day, students chose from the wide variety of books about insects and spiders that were available throughout the room. Michael wanted students to question and think about the information they were receiving, to consider whether the information was accurate or how it might conflict with information they found from another source. Students presented information from their observations and reading in both oral and written forms. The initial focus was on finding new facts that the audience may not know and communicating information effectively.

As part of the emphasis on informational text, Michael taught specific lessons about differences between fiction and nonfiction books to small groups. He began by asking students why they read different types of books. Students gave answers such as "for entertainment" and "to find out information." He distributed different genres of books to students and asked them to look at them carefully, asking whether the books were fiction or fact and why. After students responded, he probed them to find out whether the characteristics they had identified distinguished the genres from one another. To help students understand the characteristics of each type of text, Michael drew a Venn diagram to represent fiction and nonfiction genres. As students provided features of text, he placed them within the diagram. For example, descriptions such as "made-up stories" and "made-up illustrations" were written within the fiction part of the diagram, while "captions," "diagrams," "true information," and "index" were included within nonfiction. Ideas such as "boring," "interesting," and "dedication" went within the intersection of the Venn diagram. Each time students gave responses, Michael asked them to consider whether their statements held true for books other than the one they were currently examining. For example, some students had Eric Carle books about insects that contained factual information at the beginning, end, or embedded within the text. Michael dispelled some common myths about genres. For example, he helped his students understand that sometimes fiction books contain factual information and even nonfiction books use descriptive language that is interesting to the reader.

Once students were able to identify features of information texts and distinguish between fictional and informational texts, Michael began a writing-to-learn project to help students organize and share information they learned. His goal was to move them from rote memorization of the facts they read to interpreting the information. The project involved helping students to create graphic organizers using the computer software Kidspiration. This software contains tree diagrams and other types of organizers that students can use to select and organize information. The students were to write reports or use the information for other types of written or oral presentations.

Writing to Learn in Inquiry Projects: A Grade 2–3 Classroom. A teacher for 28 years, Marcy was one of the first in the area to be awarded a National Board Certification. She is currently teaching a split grade 2-3 class, but her teaching experience spans kindergarten through grade 4, much of it in multiage classrooms. She teaches in a K-5 elementary school that has 41% underrepresented minority students (African American and Latino) and where 58% of students qualify for free or reduced-cost lunch.

Marcy's instruction is unique. Spurning traditional curricula and programs, she has created her own inquiry- and theme-based integrated curriculum. That is, she chooses a theme, which often involves simulated travel (for example, to destinations such as London, Hawaii, or Africa) or time travel (for example, a theme of "Before I Was Born" time travel through history). Within these themes, Marcy cleverly interweaves reading, writing, science, social studies, math, and the arts, mostly using materials she has personally written or designed. Although she has an extensive classroom library (unusual because of its size and its heavy emphasis on nonfiction), Marcy has also authored literally thousands of her own nonfiction booklets to support the themes she uses.

Besides reading a considerable amount of nonfiction in Marcy's classroom, students write extensively to support their learning. Following are just a few examples of the many different kinds of writing Marcy's primary-grade students do.

Figure 5.4   Third-Grade Student's "Queen's Speech"

Queen Speech

As a queen I think there shall not be any more wars. There shall be more schools and shelters for our darling children. There shall be more canned good for people. There shall be more bobbies for London. Please don't take more than what you need.

As a queen this city should be cleaner than what it is. This city should have more tubes. There shall be more hotels. Lower down taxes so more people will visit London There shall be more guards standing me and my precious palace.

Love Queen

Thank you for listening

In the simulated trip-to-London unit, students visit the London Zoo, where they research various insects at the Insect House, and the Natural History Museum, where they research reptiles. Students complete science journal entries about their investigations. Students also write a "Queen's Speech." For this assignment, students pretend they are the Queen of England delivering the annual "Queen's Speech," in which they lay out their plans and ideas for England's future, based on what they have learned in class. (See Figure 5.4 for an example of a third-grade student's "Queen's Speech.")

In the "Before I Was Born" simulated time-travel unit, students write a journal or diary from the perspective of a settler in Plimouth Plantation, do a report on author Faith Ringgold, complete a Colonial Jobs Research book, and write a small book on "Exploring Leaves and Trees." For the Colonial Jobs Research book, the directions stated, "We will soon be choosing jobs for the Colonial Job Fair in Room 12. On the pages of this book, research three jobs that you might have liked to have in colonial times. Make sure to first tell what the job is, then what the person did and the tools they used, and why you would have liked that job." For "Exploring Leaves and Trees," students also write a small book, which contains information on a type of tree they have researched and an animal that lives in the rain forests. Then they respond to the question "What are some things that you think we could do to help protect our trees and forests?"

In addition to science and social studies journals, students also keep math journals. In these journals, they explain their thinking as they solve problems or make up story problems. For example, within the Hawaii simulated-travel unit, students use Hawaiian menus to construct word problems.

Students write a class newsletter (*The Room 12 News*) as well as letters home to parents.

The students themselves initiate other writing activities: "Children help decide what are the things they're going to write about," explains Marcy. "We kind of construct together, 'Okay, what is this particular book going to look like?'" At the time of the interview, the class had decided to do a book about "Rock Families," which would include pages on igneous, metamorphic, and sedimentary rocks; minerals; and a particular rock of each author's choice. These books also contained tables of contents, glossaries, and illustrations.

The preceding two examples of extensive inquiry projects incorporate many varied examples of writing to learn. We turn now to three focused vignettes in classrooms of teachers who are exploring writing to learn.

Writing to Learn: Three Teaching Vignettes

For the past three years, Sunday was a literacy coach in a local school district. In this role, she visited teachers' classrooms and led model lessons or cotaught with teachers for a series of lessons. Sunday has stayed in touch with several of the teachers in the district about their instructional practice, and she visits classes regularly as well. These vignettes come from lessons that Sunday observed in Patricia's classroom and cotaught in Ann's and Matt's classrooms.

Second-Grade Gifted Classroom. Teacher Patricia Plaut was reading aloud the book *Children of the Dust Bowl: The True Story of the School at Weedpatch Camp* by Jerry Stanley (1992). It is an expository narrative about a school that was opened for the poor dirt-farming families that migrated from Oklahoma, Texas, Arkansas, and Missouri to California looking for work during the Depression.

Patricia chose this book because she believes it is important "to find issues that kids can grapple with and that they have strong feelings about. I talk about *Children of the Dust Bowl* being a book that talks about discrimination...here's white poor against white less poor."

Each day after Patricia read aloud from a new section of the book, the students wrote short summaries of the events in their composition books. She facilitated their comprehension by writing key words on the board "that would enable the other children who didn't remember certain parts to remember just by looking at those key words."

After finishing her reading of the book, Patricia photocopied some of the photographs from the book to create a photo essay for display in the hallway. She asked the students to reread their summaries and mark one or two sentences that included fascinating details; she also encouraged them to add their own feelings about what they had selected. Then, Patricia shared with the class model sentences she wrote about the book:

"The Okies had to go to California in their jalopy stuffed with all they could take."

"I was really sad when we found out that the Okies had to drink dirty creek water as they drove to California."

Before releasing the students to begin their work, Patricia clearly outlined the steps they needed to take to complete the task. The following day, the students finished writing the final draft of their sentences. Patricia started the session by reminding the students of the steps involved in completing the task and by sharing some examples of sentences students wrote for the photo essay on the previous day:

"I was surprised when the girls were taught how to make makeup. I wish I could make makeup."

"The dust bowl is a blood-red storm. It is red because the soil is red. I wonder when the storm died out?"

Patricia highlighted the personal responses some of the students included in their writing and encouraged the other students to do the same. Patricia closed the minilesson by modeling for students how to reread their work "to make sure it makes sense." Patricia read aloud a sample sentence of her own with an error, and the students quickly identified her mistake. She asked the students to try rereading their own work for errors before turning it in.

Patricia found that students learned a tremendous amount and had very strong feelings about the book. In the beginning of the book Patricia had reported, "It's really depressing and the kids are just horrified by what state of lives they [children in the book] had," and then at the end where the characters get to go to a very good school, "the kids are just like 'Whoa! Whoa! Yeah! Yeah! Yeah!'" Many of the final entries of the photo essay included writing that reflected a clear understanding of the events and strong emotions. The following examples are as the children wrote them:

In Oklahoma there was no rain and once a wind began to blow and it got harder evry day. The red soil went wild as if it war alive until soon many okiys died. When okiys slept they would sleep in wet cloth it relly made me sad.

Because of the dust storms, the Okies had to go to another city. They picked California. They just stuff up what they could and drove off with their jalopy. They couldn't wait to get there.

One of the okies at a frost bit orange, and he got a disese, and went to the hospetle, and the people that worked there would'nt let him come in and he died. I was very sad!

The Oikes went to a camp called Weedpatch camp it was no pairadis but it was much better to the oikes than living on the streets of California.

Mr. Leo Hart was a superintendent. He tried to get the okies into other schools. But they didn't want the okies ether. So Leo had an idea he was going to bild a beter school wear only okies could go.

Leo Hart bought a C46 airplane for 200 Dollars! He let okie kids that got 90 or more on their test to ride in the C46 airplane. I feel happy for the okie kids because it would be a lot of fun to be riding back and forth down the runway!

Fifth-Grade Classroom. Ann Quackenbush was the teacher and Sunday Cummins was the coach. On the first of two days of instruction, 25 fifth graders listened intently as Sunday read aloud from a book about meat-eating plants titled *Strange Plants*, by Howard Halpern (2002):

> Of the hundreds of different kinds of plants in our world, only about 40 eat meat. Most of these plants grow in wet places like swamps, marshes, or bogs. The soil in these places is poor. It doesn't have enough minerals to keep plants healthy. So, these meat-eating plants have adapted over time. They get the minerals they need by eating animals.
>
> Meat-eating plants are too small to eat large animals. Most of them eat insects. But a few eat mice, frogs, and even small birds.
>
> All meat-eating plants do some things in the same ways. They offer a special treat, or bait, to attract animals. They catch the animals in some kind of trap. Then, they dissolve the animals into a kind of soup. Finally, they digest the soup. (p. 6)

The students were studying plants and plant classification in science, and Sunday planned a lesson on writing poetry in response to the related nonfiction texts they were reading. She chose this read-aloud because of its fascinating topic and interesting details. After the read-aloud, Sunday asked the students to turn and talk with a partner about a new fact they learned about the meat-eating plants. The students talked enthusiastically, and after a few minutes Sunday had to interrupt them to continue the lesson.

Sunday discussed with the students the importance of remembering details they have read in nonfiction texts and suggested that one way for them to recall facts was to complete a quick-write. She explained that during a quick-write students write as many details about the text as they can remember in just a few minutes. Sunday turned on the overhead and led a shared writing of a quick-write about the text she had just read aloud. Different students raised their hands and shared sentences aloud to be added to the quick-write. Sunday wrote each student's sentence on the overhead as part of a paragraph summarizing the text. The class participated in a shared reading of the class text afterward:

> These are some things I remember about strange, meat-eating plants. We can find them in swamps or other wet places. They eat frogs and birds and other animals and insects. They eat these things because the soil around them is not rich enough to support them. They cannot eat things that are too big. They don't eat 5th graders!

During this minilesson, Sunday modeled reading nonfiction text, provided an opportunity for students to think aloud about what they recalled from the text, and modeled writing facts the class learned from the text and their related thoughts. After the minilesson, she handed out excerpts from the book about specific meat-eating plants to pairs of students and asked them to follow the same steps: read, think aloud with a partner, and write independently in response to their reading.

The students worked in pairs or small groups as Sunday and Ann walked around, answering questions and prompting students to follow the steps. Following is an example of one student's quick-write:

I'm writing about stinging nettles. Stinging nettles have sharp needles that have asid in it, and, if you get a needle in you, you will get a read warm rash that stings and hurts very, very, very, badly. It will sting for 2 hours or, if its very bad, it will last for a day or even more. I would hate to run into that plant because I've gotton poked by a needle really hard, and it hurts!

Sunday closed the lesson by reminding the students about what they had done as good readers that day. They took the time to read a text carefully, think aloud with someone else about specific details in the text, and write in response to the text.

On the second day, Sunday began the lesson by reminding the students of the steps they took yesterday to remember details from the texts about meat-eating plants, including thinking aloud about the text with a partner and completing a quick-write. The students participated in a shared reading of the quick-write they wrote as a class yesterday. Sunday introduced the idea of writing poetry as another strategy for remembering the most important details in a text and for responding to a text in a creative format.

Sunday then led the students through rereading the paragraph on meat-eating plants and underlining the most important words in the quick-write. She asked them to identify the words or phrases in the quick-write that might be used to write a free verse poem.

These are some things I remember about <u>strange, meat-eating plants</u>. We can find them in <u>swamps</u> or other <u>wet places</u>. They eat <u>frogs</u> and <u>birds</u> and other animals and <u>insects</u>. They eat these things because the <u>soil</u> around them <u>is not rich</u> enough to support them. They cannot eat things that are too big. <u>They don't eat 5th graders!</u>

Afterward, Sunday led the class in a shared writing (on the overhead) of a free verse poem about the meat-eating plants. As the class composed the poem, different students gave Sunday advice about how to space or phrase words and when to capitalize letters, use particular punctuation, and write certain words in bold to emphasize their points.

Strange,

Meat-eating plant.

Swamps and wet places.

They **EAT**

FROGS

   INSECTS

     BIRDS!

The soil is

Not rich enough

For them.

I'm **glad** they don't eat

   5th GRADERS!!

After the class read aloud the poem they composed, Sunday asked the students to take the same steps to write their own poems. Sunday and Ann conferred with students as they wrote. (See Figure 5.5 for examples of the students' poems.)

Figure 5.5   Fifth-Grade Students' Poems in Response to Expository Text

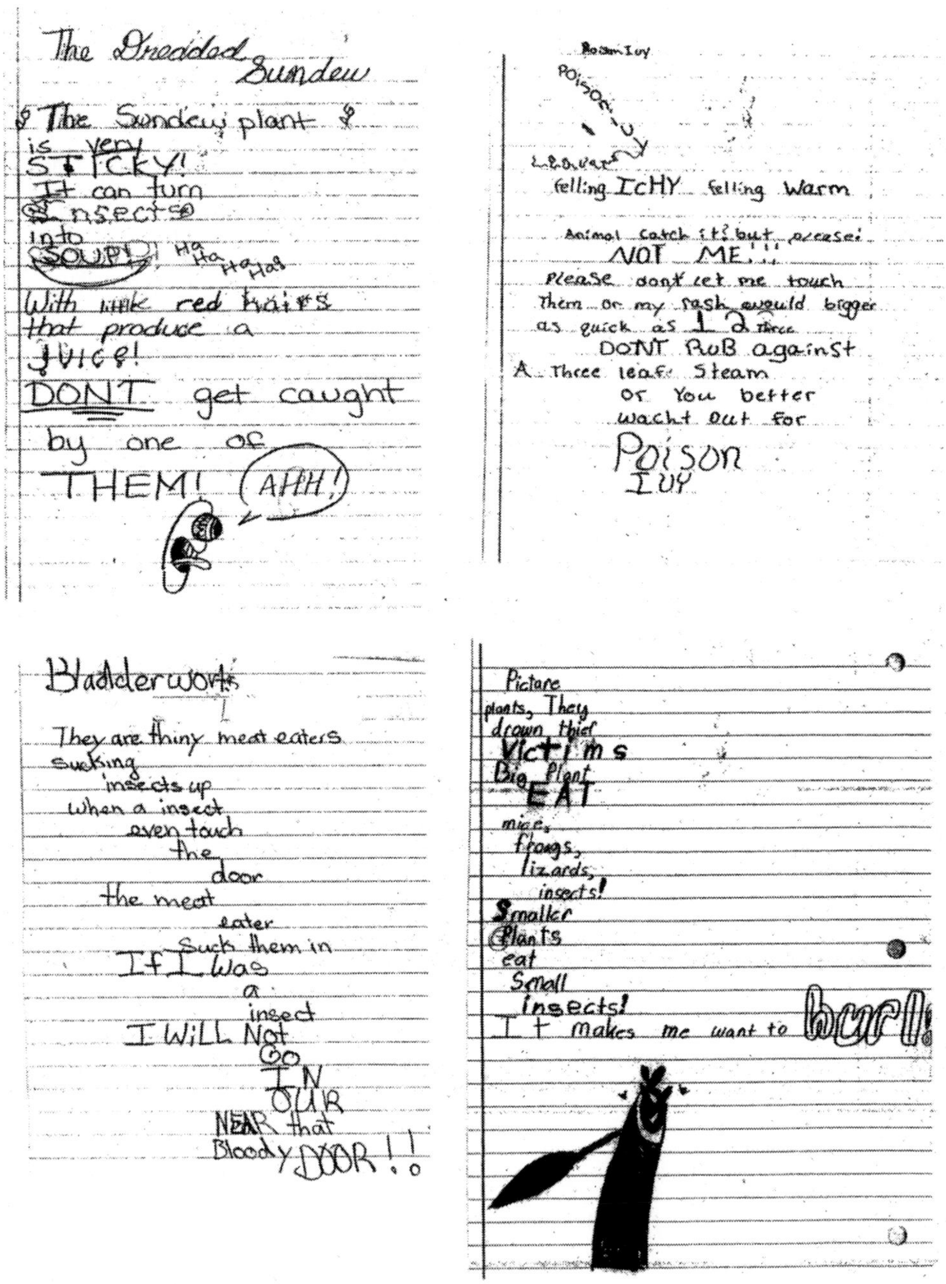

Prior to this lesson, Ann shared that the class had experienced different types of writing with the goal of helping students "make connections...between what they're reading and what their experience has been." They had written personal narratives, so they had practiced focusing on specific details. They had read articles about natural medicine and written expository responses to them. Earlier in the year, they had read a lot of poetry and written their own poems, so they were familiar with the poet's craft. The students, then, had many experiences writing in different genres before they responded to expository text in poetic form. Ann believed that these experiences laid the groundwork for the students "so they really took off with it. It [writing poems] was a lot of fun."

Fourth-Grade Classroom. Matt Nilles was the teacher and Sunday Cummins was the coach. The students sat in groups of three and four on the floor of their fourth-grade classroom. As part of their current science unit, the students had been studying animal adaptations. During this lesson, Sunday began by asking individual students to share their understanding of this concept with the whole class. Then she read aloud an excerpt from *Amazing Animals* by K.B. Jerome (2002) about a chameleon's adaptations and asked the students to turn and talk in their small groups about the different adaptations described by the author of the text.

After the read-aloud and brief discussion, the students in each group were given the opportunity to browse through a stack of books and magazines that included information about different animal adaptations. Their objective was to look for new information and share their new understanding with members of their group. The materials were colorful and attractive, and the texts were written at several reading levels.

After five minutes of discussion, Sunday interrupted the groups to begin a minilesson on the different features of nonfiction text and why it is important for readers to pay attention to these features. She explained that the features of nonfiction text help readers enrich their understanding of the main ideas the author is writing about. Sunday and the students brainstormed different features, and Sunday started a list on the overhead. As they created the list, they began to discuss why each of those features is important and looked for examples of those features in the stack of texts each group was looking through earlier. For example, a caption is important because it gives the reader more information about the picture, and bold words indicate special vocabulary or important ideas that are worthy of greater attention.

After drafting a list of important features, Sunday shared a model of a page from a handbook she was preparing on the features of nonfiction text. The model page defined a table of contents in Sunday's own words, shared an example of part of a table of contents from a nonfiction book, and included Sunday's thoughts about how a table of contents helps her as a reader. Sunday asked the students to begin completing pages on the different features in their own handbooks. The students returned to their desks with a nonfiction book to look through for examples and tackled the task of their first entry. Sunday and Matt, the students' classroom teacher, conferred with individual students about their work as the students worked steadily for the rest of the period.

In an interview, Matt reported that students had produced 8- to 10-page handbooks with a different element of nonfiction texts on each page. According to Matt, students' understanding of the components of nonfiction was evident in

Figure 5.6   Text Features From Fourth-Grade Students' Handbooks

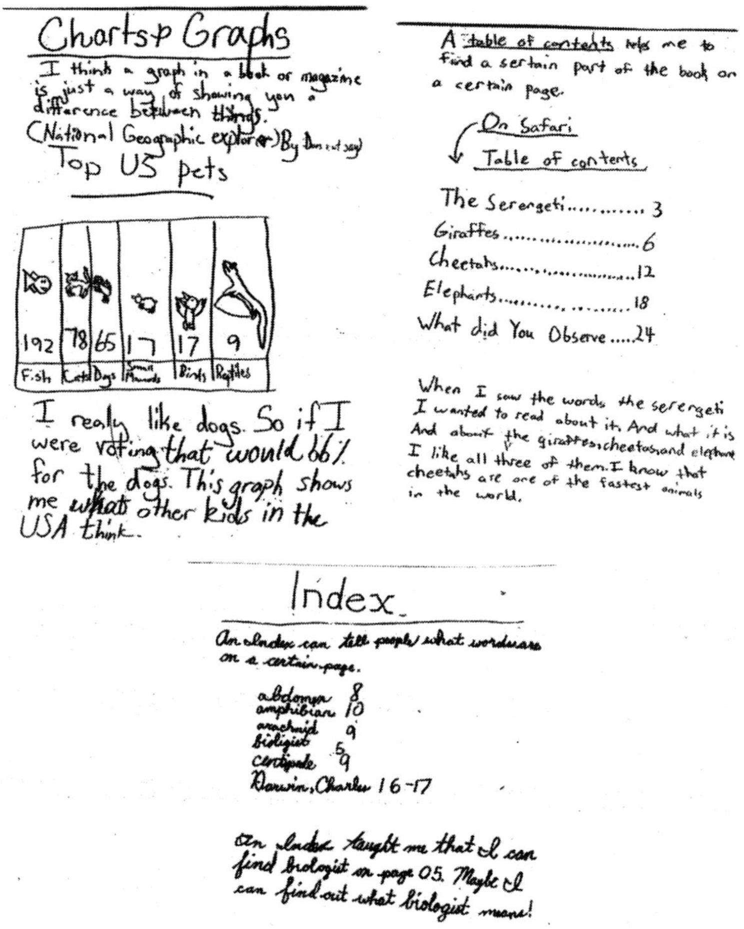

Charts & Graphs

I think a graph in a book or magazine is just a way of showing you a difference between things.
(National Geographic explorer) (By dm ...d say)

Top US pets

| 192 | 78 | 65 | 17 | 17 | 9 |
| Fish | Cats/Dogs | | Birds | Reptiles |

I really like dogs. So if I were voting that would be for the dogs. This graph shows me what other kids in the USA think.

A table of contents helps me to find a certain part of the book on a certain page.

On Safari

Table of contents

The Serengeti............ 3
Giraffes........................6
Cheetahs........................12
Elephants........................18
What did You Observe.....24

When I saw the words the serengeti I wanted to read about it. And what it is And about the giraffes,cheetas,and elephants I like all three of them. I know that cheetahs are one of the fastest animals in the world.

Index

An index can tell people what words are on a certain page.

abdomen 8
amphibian 10
arachnid 9
biologist 5
centipede 9
Darwin, Charles 16-17

An index taught me that I can find biologist on page 05. Maybe I can find out what biologist means!

The first is one student's graph illustrating children's preferences for pets; the second, a student's table of contents; and the third, a student's index.

their handbooks. Matt had then reinforced his students' understanding by helping them use sticky notes to identify the features of a variety of other informational texts available in the classroom. Figure 5.6 provides examples from students' handbooks. The first is one student's graph illustrating children's preferences for pets; the second, a student's table of contents; and the third, a student's index.

Teachers' Perspectives on Writing to Learn

We asked several local teachers to share their perspectives on teaching students to write for the purposes of learning. We were interested in both the reasons they provided for having students write to learn and the challenges they faced when teaching students to write informational texts. Several teachers also commented on the links they saw between reading informational texts and writing to learn.

Benefits of Writing to Learn

When they were asked about the importance of writing to learn, teachers offered benefits that closely paralleled those we identified in the beginning of this chapter: enhancing content learning, facilitating learning to write, and helping teachers assess learning.

Several teachers commented that writing enhanced their students' learning of content. Believing that writing about science experiments provides students with the opportunity to reflect and summarize their understanding, Ann used herself as a model to indicate how writing helps to facilitate memory:

> I know that when I write things down, or if there's a question that I have or something that I'm not sure about,...or if I'm even writing to someone else and...by the end of it I've figured it out. So, I think it can be like that for students, too. I think that just the act of writing something down triggers something in their memory. I know I'm a really visual person, so if I write something down or see it in print, I'm much more apt to remember it than if someone just tells me something. I think it can work for students that way, too.

Marcy suggested that writing allowed students to make representations of their learning:

> I just think it's so critically important for students from the beginning of their schooling, the beginning of their learning, and I'm talking about when they're 2 or 3—you know, you draw pictures about something you saw and you write something with it, and you begin to start to show representation of what's up here, what you're thinking. I think that is incredibly powerful.

Some teachers viewed writing to learn as a way for students to grapple with important issues, to synthesize material, and to learn critical thinking skills. Pat expressed the importance of writing to learn in this way:

> I see writing as part of their learning. It enhances everything we do in the classroom, what they're learning from the book, from the historical fiction, from all the genres that we're drawing in. They're formulating their own ideas and hopefully we're seeing some synthesis of the material through the writing...I have critical thinking up here on my board (she motions to a poster of thinking skills), and we go through all these. It's all important, and I think that writing helps us travel to these new levels of thinking.

Matt remarked that writing informational text helped students form and express their opinions: "They're taking a position on issues and current events, and I'm pushing them to do that so they're forming opinions." Patricia observed that writing aided in organizing ideas. Commenting on her own writing, Patricia noted, "Writing is a way to be able to organize my ideas. It's a way to be able to express myself so that the reader can get a good sense of what I'm trying to communicate."

Some teachers also commented that writing to learn enhances learning by helping students make connections between what they are reading and their prior knowledge and experiences. According to Ann, "So [it's] really trying to make connections for them between what they're reading and what their experience has been." Matt commented that through writing, students gain wider exposure to world events and become increasingly motivated to find information about a variety of topics.

Besides the immediate cognitive benefit of writing to learn, a couple of teachers recognized related affective benefits. Marcy found that writing provides a record of learning for students to treasure in years to come:

> It's also a record of what they know at this point. It's a record of their work in the classroom. This year it will be a London book that all of these journals and many other kinds of writing that they do will be put in this book, and then they take this home. I've had students from 28 years ago who made books and still have them, and I still hear from them. And I still hear from their parents. They're also memories; it's a way to document years from their childhood.

Patricia identified an additional affective benefit. She believes that when children find information and write about it, they feel more confident in their own abilities to learn in the future. By writing to learn, students come to "know that you can master your environment and...you can find information if you want to learn about it."

Although using writing to learn content was the major focus of teachers' responses, they also found other values for students' learning and their own teaching. Several teachers focused on the positive effect of writing to learn on writing, or as they put it, on communication in general. Anna suggested:

> By sharing your knowledge and writing in a clear, coherent manner, you're able to communicate. It [writing to learn] makes a great impact because it's a means of communicating to your audience...[Students] have to be able to have those main ideas and supporting details and get that very clear. Otherwise, you can lose your reader...I believe that students should develop their skills and be able to communicate. You have different purposes, not only to share, but also you want to inform someone. And if you're trying to persuade your mom for doing something, well, you'd better be prepared with some information so that you can really persuade her.

Pat agreed that communication was important, saying, "I see us as a society communicating more with the written word than we have in the past.... We're communicating with the written word, so I think it's important that it's included in schools."

Finally, one teacher commented that writing informational texts provides her with an assessment tool to understand students' thinking and to help her know where to go next in the curriculum. Marcy stated, "So, lots of times, particularly in science, it helps me understand where their thinking is right at this moment and then what I might do next."

Challenges of Writing to Learn

Although the teachers we interviewed were mostly enthusiastic about teaching students to use writing for learning, they also identified several challenges. First, several teachers noted the problem of lack of time in the school day to fit in writing to learn. One teacher stated that the district already required too much of teachers and that teaching more writing would require even more time. Pat struggled with the multiple expectations from the state: "The main problem is that we as educators don't have enough time to really grasp what the state wants us to do all at once." Ann pointed out that she was struggling to achieve all she wanted to do in light of the state tests. She was trying to balance teaching the structure of expository writing with helping students learn the craft of writing:

> I want them to write one good, focused paragraph in 5 sentences...but we're also working on other writer's craft things, like using good descriptions, and avoiding words like "stuff" and "things," also focusing on a small point in time instead of writing about something that's too broad or too general. It's interesting to try to balance those two things. The structure, I think, is very easy, and I can teach kids very easily how to write in that very structured way that the state is looking for. But then, using good craft to make it interesting and to make it come alive and have voice is a totally different thing. It's been kind of interesting to have to kind of mesh those two things.

Ann also noted other constraints that appear to influence her teaching less informational writing than she wanted; these challenges included the time it took to look at students' work and provide them with feedback and to organize the products of their learning. Pat also believes she needs to score all of the students' writing using rubrics, which takes significant time: "That's a lot of writing and a lot of scoring."

Another challenge that several teachers mentioned was overcoming the relative primacy of narrative texts over informational texts as reading materials, which may, in turn, affect writing in the classroom. With regard to the prevalence of fiction in reading materials, Ann believes that there are fewer informational texts available at libraries and bookstores, and that many of those are less accessible to struggling readers. She also feels that families tend to promote fiction, and as a result, students prefer series and other fiction books to nonfiction text.

Several informants also suggested that teachers prefer using fiction and narrative writing to informational or expository writing because of their own experiences, background knowledge, and teacher training. Matt, for example, suggested, "if all they read is fiction—and I read primarily fiction, so I'm kind of in that group, maybe they're less inclined to try it [writing to learn] in their classroom." Marcy thought that her colleagues were less willing for their students to write informational text because they believed that writing informational text was more difficult (or less "natural") than writing narratives:

> I also think that lots of times people have a thought process of "Oh, but when children start writing, it's natural to write stories." I've heard this over and over. "It's natural to write about what you know." I'm always puzzled because I would say it varies per child whether you've had more story influence so that maybe stories are natural for you to write or whether you have more knowledge that you want to get out. But I would say the kindergartners [want] to write about facts—their families, their pets, and so on. But I certainly think there's this sense of..."persuasive is very difficult, and expository—well, that's much too difficult for kids to write."

Links Between Reading and Writing

As suggested in the last challenge discussed above, many of the teachers expressed a strong connection between reading informational texts and writing to learn.

Those teachers who emphasized reading informational texts also offered many opportunities to write to learn content. For example, when Marcy first began teaching, she found a dearth of informational text and thus began to write informational texts herself:

> So when I started teaching, it seemed to me that [given] the importance of informational text in the direction that students take in school and the expectations they have, it was critical to spend time really learning to unpack them, to look at them. So I began writing my own texts.

Patricia finds few challenges with using informational text to read or write because she is such an enthusiast herself. She has an extensive background in science and brings this to the curriculum she teaches. She has found that her own enthusiasm encourages her students:

> I use it [informational text] all the time. I use it more often that I use fiction. And I use it more often than fiction because my background is science, and I happen to love science. I also have found that kids at this young age prefer informational texts, especially if you help them through it.... I happen to love it, and I find that the more I read, the more they tend to go to it if they're not already there.

Patricia likes to select texts that challenge and inform children. She thoroughly enjoys using informational texts and expresses it this way:

> My main goal is to give them something to chew on, something to think about, something to wrestle with...my main goal for these informational books is to teach information, because I love information, and these kids love it too. But by teaching the information, I can also teach the science, the social studies, the strategies.

For these teachers, bringing nonfiction texts into their classrooms was an essential component of their classroom instruction. The nonfiction texts provided important models and resources for students to use in their own writing. Thus, the teachers who informed this chapter have emphasized the importance of linking reading and writing. (See chapter 6, this volume, for additional discussion related to reading and writing connections.)

Conclusion

Writing to learn is a growing trend in elementary classrooms. Although research demonstrating the effectiveness of writing on learning for elementary students is still relatively sparse, advocacy for writing to learn remains strong. In publications targeted for elementary teachers—from books to journal and magazine articles— writing to learn is currently a popular topic. These publications encourage teachers to use a wide variety of writing assignments in all content areas in order to accomplish a number of purposes, including enhancing student thinking, promoting content learning, fostering writing abilities, and providing teachers with valuable assessment data.

We were interested to discover whether the push for writing to learn was influencing practice in local elementary classrooms. Although our investigation was neither intensive nor extensive, we found some interesting examples of writing to learn, and we heard several teachers' views about writing to learn.

The examples of writing to learn that we found went beyond the traditional knowledge-telling assignments of answering questions, writing summaries and reports, or recording information on a K-W-L chart. Instead, we found a variety of types of responses in several different forms of writing, ranging from journals to books, and from speeches to poetry.

The teachers we spoke with were enthusiastic about writing to learn, but they also mentioned some barriers. Among the problems they identified were lack of time (exacerbated by increasing demands from the state and district levels) and the bias of parents and teachers in favor of reading and writing fiction over nonfiction. The teachers' comments suggested the need for more professional development, at both the preservice and inservice levels, to help teachers efficiently and effectively incorporate writing into the content areas.

Of course, more research is needed. We need to know more about the effect of writing on both learning and teaching. We need to know what kinds of writing are most helpful with which subject matter areas and which students. We need to know how to prepare teachers to use writing to learn in their classrooms, and we need to continue to study how writing to learn is implemented in real classrooms.

As William Zinsser wrote, "we write to find out what we know and what we want to say" (1988, p. viii). In writing this chapter, we found out what we know and, especially, what we don't know about writing to learn. And we found we have a lot we want to say about it.

REFERENCES

Alvermann, D.E., & Phelps, S.F. (2002). *Content reading and literacy: Succeeding in today's diverse classrooms*. Boston: Allyn & Bacon.

Armbruster, B.B. (2000). Responding to informative prose. In R. Indrisano & J.R. Squire (Eds.), *Perspectives on writing: Research, theory, and practice* (pp. 140-160). Newark, DE: International Reading Association.

Armbruster, B.B., Anderson, T.H., & Ostertag, J. (1987). Does text structure/summarization instruction facilitate learning from expository text? *Reading Research Quarterly, 22*, 331-346.

Beyer, B.K. (1982). Using writing to learn social studies. *Social Studies, 73*(3), 100-105.

Bristor, V.J. (1994). Combining reading and writing with science to enhance content area achievement and attitudes. *Reading Horizons, 35*(1), 30-43.

Burns, M. (1995). Writing in math class? Absolutely! *Instructor, 104*(7), 40-47.

Burns, M., & Silbey, R. (2001). Math journals boost real learning. *Instructor, 110*(7), 18-20.

Carney-Dalton, P. (1994). Reflecting on American history through poetry: Classroom teacher's idea notebook. *Social Education, 58*(4), 238-239.

Connolly, P. (1995). Writing and the ecology of learning. In P. Connolly and T. Vilardi (Eds.), *Writing to learn mathematics and science* (pp. 1-14). New York: Teachers College Press.

Cudd, E.T., & Roberts, L. (1989). Using writing to enhance content area learning in the primary grades. *The Reading Teacher, 42*, 392-404.

Davis, B.H., Rooze, G.E., & Runnels, M.K.T. (1992). Writing-to-learn in elementary social studies. *Social Education, 56*(7), 393-397.

Dewey, J. (1938). *Experience and education*. New York: Macmillan.

Di Biase, W.J. (1998). Writing a letter...to a scientist. *Science & Children, 35*(6), 14-17.

Emig, J. (1977). Writing as a model of learning. *College Composition & Communication, 28*(2), 122-128.

Gunning, T.G. (2005). *Creating literacy instruction for all students* (5th ed.). Boston: Pearson/Allyn & Bacon.

Guthrie, J.T., & Ozgungor, S. (2002). Instructional contexts for reading engagement. In C.C. Block & M. Pressley (Eds.), *Comprehension instruction: Research-based best practices* (pp. 275-288). New York: Guilford.

Guthrie, J.T., Van Meter, P., Hancock, G.R., McCann, A., Anderson, E., & Alao, S. (1998). Does Concept-Oriented Reading Instruction increase strategy use and conceptual learning from text? *Journal of Educational Psychology, 90*(2), 261-278.

Guthrie, J.T., Van Meter, P., McCann, A.D., Wigfield, A., Bennett, L., Poundstone, C.C., et al. (1996). Growth of literacy engagement: Changes in motivations and strategies during Concept-Oriented Reading Instruction. *Reading Research Quarterly, 31*, 306-332.

Hoofman, J. (1994). "My summer with Leonardo" and other wonderful experiences. *Science & Children, 31*(6), 22-24.

Jenkinson, E.B. (1988). Learning to write/writing to learn. *Phi Delta Kappan, 69*(10), 712-717.

Katz, L.G., & Chard, S.C. (1989). *Engaging children's minds: The project approach.* Norwood, NJ: Ablex.

Kidspiration [Computer software]. (1992-2004). Portland, OR: Inspiration Software.

Kilpatrick, W.H. (1918). The project method. *Teachers College Record, 19*, 319-335.

Konopak, B.C., Martin, S.H., & Martin, M.A. (1990). Using a writing strategy to enhance sixth-grade students' comprehension of content material. *Journal of Reading Behavior, 22*(1), 19-37.

Kronholm, M., & Ramsey, J. (1991). Issues and analysis: A teaching strategy for the real world. *Science & Children, 29*(2), 20-23.

Maxim, G. (1998). Writing poetry in the elementary social studies classroom. *Social Education, 62*(4), 207-211.

McClure, A.A., & Zitlow, C.S. (1991). Not just the facts: Aesthetic response in elementary content area studies. *Language Arts, 68*(1), 27-33.

Moore, D.W., Moore, S.A., Cunningham, P.M., & Cunningham, J.W. (2003). *Developing readers and writers in the content areas K-12* (4th ed.). Boston: Allyn & Bacon.

Morrow, L.M., Pressley, M., Smith, J.K., & Smith, M. (1997). The effect of a literature-based program integrated into literacy and science instruction with children from diverse backgrounds. *Reading Research Quarterly, 32*, 54-76.

Moss, B. (2003). *Exploring the literature of fact: Children's nonfiction trade books in the elementary classroom.* New York: Guilford.

Ogle, D.M. (1986). K-W-L: A teaching model that develops active reading of expository text. *The Reading Teacher, 39*, 564-571.

Reif, R.J., & Rauch, K. (1994). Science in their own words. *Science & Children, 31*(4), 31-33.

Rosaen, C.L. (1990). Improving writing opportunities in elementary classrooms. *The Elementary School Journal, 90*(4), 419-434.

Rudnitsky, A., Etheredge, S., Freeman, S.J.M., & Gilbert, T. (1995). Learning to solve addition and subtraction word problems through structure-plus-writing approach. *Journal for Research in Mathematics Education, 26*(5), 467-486.

Templeton, S. (1997). *Teaching the integrated language arts* (2nd ed.). Boston: Houghton Mifflin.

Tierney, R.J., & Shanahan, T. (1996). Research on the reading-writing relationship: Interactions, transactions, and outcomes. In R. Barr, M.L. Kamil, P. Mosenthal, & P.D. Pearson (Eds.), *Handbook of reading research* (Vol. 2, pp. 246-280). New York: Longman.

Tompkins, G.E. (2003). *Literacy for the 21st century* (3rd ed.). Upper Saddle River, NJ: Merrill Prentice Hall.

Tompkins, G.E. (2004). *Teaching writing: Balancing process and product* (4th ed.). Upper Saddle River, NJ: Pearson Education.

Yockey, J. (2001). A key to science learning. *Science & Children, 38*(7), 36-41.

Zanger, V.V. (1998). Math storybooks. *Teaching Children Mathematics, 5*(2), 98-102.

Zinsser, W. (1988). *Writing to learn.* New York: Harper & Row.

LITERATURE CITED

Carle, E. (1969). *The very hungry caterpillar.* New York: Philomel.

Halpern, H. (2002). *Strange plants* (Windows on Literacy Series). Washington, DC: National Geographic School Publishing.

Jerome, K.B. (2002). *Amazing animals* (Reading Expeditions Series: Life Science). Washington, DC: National Geographic School Publishing.

Stanley, J. (1992). *Children of the Dust Bowl: The true story of the School at Weedpatch Camp.* New York: Crown.

Chapter 6

Writing in Immigrant Families: Parents and Children Writing at Home

Jeanne R. Paratore, Barbara Krol-Sinclair, Ana María Chacón, and Soledad Concha Banados

*U*nlike the other chapters in this book, the context for the work in this chapter is writing in homes rather than writing in classrooms. We base our work on the premise that a deeper understanding of the forms and functions of writing within families has the potential to inform and improve the teaching of writing in classrooms. We begin with an explanation of this fundamental premise.

In 1983, in a book that is often heralded as the first meaningful inquiry into the practice of family literacy, Denny Taylor explained in the preface that she had set out "to develop systematic ways of looking at reading and writing as activities that have consequences in and are affected by family life." Two decades have passed since Taylor laid the foundation for this field of study, and in that time, much has been studied and even more has been written about family literacies. Yet as an area of practice, it remains a field that is poorly understood and one that resists simple explanation. Repeatedly, investigators have underscored the inherent complexity in describing and coming to understand the ways families use reading and writing in their daily lives (Gadsden, 2000; Yaden & Paratore, 2002). As explained by Maurice Taylor and Adrian Blunt (2001), understanding literate practice requires a focus on "situatedness" (p. 82) and a change in the unit of analysis from "the individual learner to the structures and dynamics of the sociocultural setting in which the learning occurs" (p. 82).

Although simply stated, this is, in fact, a very difficult task. In any community, accurately depicting the sociocultural setting in which learning occurs presents a significant investigative challenge. But in the context of the ever-changing and ever-widening diversity of families in the United States, setting out to understand the "structures and dynamics" (Taylor & Blunt, 2001, p. 82) that influence family literacy practices and routines in the community seems at first overwhelming, perhaps even foolhardy. Which family or families might one choose to represent what is typical within a community? We embarked on this work with a goal far less lofty than that. Our purpose was not to find out what was typical but rather, in a

Learning to Write, Writing to Learn: Theory and Research in Practice edited by Roselmina Indrisano and Jeanne R. Paratore. Copyright © 2005 by the International Reading Association.

sense, to find out what was possible—to examine the range of writing practices that occurred across one group of families so that we could begin to understand the forms and functions of writing in the out-of-school lives of family members.

This study, in particular, and our work in family literacy in general (e.g., Paratore, 1993; Paratore et al., 1995; Paratore, Melzi, & Krol-Sinclair, 2003) have been deeply influenced by two findings that have emerged from related research. First, studies by Shirley Brice Heath (1983), Victoria Purcell-Gates (1995), William Teale (1986), and Catherine Compton-Lilly (2003), among others, support a finding that most families—whatever their educational experiences, social class, or cultural heritage—embed some form of literate traditions within their daily routines. Second, studies by Courtney Cazden (2001), Sarah McCarthey (1997), and Denny Taylor and Catherine Dorsey-Gaines (1988), among others, indicate that when family literacy practices go unnoticed by classroom teachers, potentially valuable opportunities to build on previous knowledge and experience are missed, and as a consequence, opportunities to optimize learning by adults and children are diminished.

For the most part, educators who have responded to these findings have emphasized the congruence of home and school reading routines (e.g., Ada, 1988; De Temple & Tabors, 1995; Edwards, 1991; Goldenberg, 1989; Straub, 2003). However, far less attention has been placed on coming to understand out-of-school writing routines and contexts in the lives of immigrant families and any implications these may have for instruction of children and adults in classrooms. We found that literature related to out-of-school writing could be categorized as three types: studies of young children's emergent writing (e.g., Baghban, 1984; Bissex, 1980; Ferreiro & Teberosky, 1982; Schickedanz, 1990); reports of practices that will involve parents and children in writing (e.g., Akroyd, 1995; Quintero & Huerta-Macîas, 1990; Reutzel & Fawson, 1990); and reports of ways to use adults' writing as a foundation for learning in adult education programs (e.g., Palmer, Alexander, & Olson-Dinges, 1999; Rhoder & French, 1995; Zakaluk & Wynes, 1995). We found only four studies that examined the nature of elementary-age children's or adults' writing outside of school. Two of these (Heath, 1983; Taylor & Dorsey-Gaines, 1988) examined the writing routines of families whose members were born and raised in the United States. These are instructive but may not fully represent the writing behaviors of immigrant adults and children. The other two investigations (Rogers, 2004; Volk & de Acosta, 2003) reported a general finding that writing outside of school is governed largely by social purposes but did not provide a detailed analysis of the types of writing engaged in by parents and children.

Given the paucity of information related specifically to what and why immigrant adults and children write at home, we embarked on our own exploration. Our specific purpose was to document the writing routines that commonly occur in families in which adults and children are both acquiring English as a second language and in which adults have relatively few years of formal education. In this chapter, we first report the outcomes of our study of writing in immigrant families, and then we describe how we applied the findings to instructional routines in a family literacy project.

The Learning Community

The 8 families we studied reside within a small urban city in the northeastern United States. The community is densely populated, with few single-family homes and many two-bedroom apartments inhabited by two or more families. It is also economically impoverished; nearly 80% of school-age children receive free or reduced-price school lunches. For more than a century, the community has served as a gateway for new immigrants. Currently, more than 75% of the school-age population speaks a first language other than English, and in many homes, a language other than English is the spoken language. And yet this is not a community in which English is not important. When walking the streets, what one hears from the children playing in parks and playgrounds is not their home language, but their common language—English. The predominant cultural groups are Latino and the predominant language is Spanish, but children from more than 30 countries are enrolled in the public schools.

Ten years ago, the newest school building in the community was 90 years old, but since 1996, three new school complexes have been constructed and the remaining schools in use have been renovated. The 5,300 students now attend classes in modern school buildings with expansive libraries and computer labs. Until the year that the study took place (2003–2004), newly arrived immigrant students were typically enrolled in Transitional Bilingual Education (TBE) classrooms, but a change in the law eliminated TBE. Now, all students are instructed only in mainstreamed or sheltered English classes (with the exception of a two-way Spanish–English bilingual program that serves one classroom at each elementary grade level).

Like the families in our study, most of the people in this city came to the United States in search of the American dream, a dream that is most readily understood by those from the American working class. Many of the families in the community live at or near the poverty line; they are people who had to work hard to survive in their home countries and now are doing the same in the United States. Many work long shift hours to pay their monthly bills, and many take two or more jobs to meet their needs. Many have suffered unspeakable hardships in their home countries; some have fled wars and terror, while others came to the United States to escape endemic poverty.

They are in search of better opportunities, which are not always considered in terms of monetary outcomes but, rather, in educational gains for their children. In their home countries, many parents in the community had few opportunities for education themselves or for their children. Although life in their new country is not always easy, the main difference now is that, here, education is for all, and it is free. As a group, the families in this community envision their young ones as educated adults who can have better chances to live in this country with fewer struggles than in their home country.

The 8 parents in this study proportionally reflect the diversity of the larger community. Two parents immigrated to the United States from El Salvador and the others came to the United States from Colombia, Guatemala, Honduras, Mexico, Sierra Leone, and Somalia. Their literacy and education levels in their native language varied widely: One parent had never attended school, and the others had been enrolled for 2, 3, 4, 6, 9, 12, and 13 years ($\mu = 6.1$ years). The 2 parents with the most years of schooling had earned high school diplomas, and 1 had begun university studies. Seven were mothers (although one was an aunt who worked most directly with her niece and nephews because her own children were in secondary school and older) and the other participant was a father.

The 8 families had a total of 17 children of preschool and elementary school age living with them. (Three of the families also had children who were still living in their home countries.) Five of the children were enrolled in pre-K or were younger, 7 were in kindergarten or first grade, and 5 were in second to sixth grades.

As immigrants, one of their greatest challenges has been to learn English to move forward in their lives and to build strategies for supporting their children's learning in schools with unfamiliar expectations of parents' roles. These common needs reflect a unity of purpose among our diverse participants. Learning a new language as an adult is difficult and takes many hours of practice, which parents struggle to find because their working hours are long. They need English to be able to work and feed their families but also to effectively communicate with teachers and administrators in their children's schools. Spoken English is needed during parent-teacher conferences, but reading and writing are much-needed skills as well. Parents often receive written notifications from teachers (and society in general), and if they don't understand and can't reply, then they won't be able to help their children.

The Intergenerational Literacy Project (ILP) that the participants attend offers English literacy classes to immigrant parents so that they can improve their own opportunities and support their children's education in U.S. schools, while maintaining their existing rich literacy and language practices within the family. Adults are (a) provided instruction in reading and responding to literacy materials of adult interest; (b) supplied a selection of children's books, strategies, and ideas for use with their children; and (c) encouraged to share their children's stories and drawings and to discuss literacy events and their importance in their lives and the lives of their children. Emphasis is placed on family contexts for literacy with specific emphasis on family storybook reading. Parents attend classes four days per week for two hours per day; classes meet in a space provided within the school system's Early Learning Center. Although the family literacy classes are independent of the classroom instruction of the school-aged children, the family literacy teachers come to know the children through various events and activities sponsored by the ILP.

Learning English literacy in this program is a community effort as learners support each other. During much of the instructional time, participants work in small groups, a practice that allows learners with different language abilities to work together and to help each other. Participants feel comfortable in the classroom because the atmosphere is one of acceptance and support. Everyone in the room understands each other as most have been through similar experiences of being circumstantially forced to learn a new language when arriving in the United States.

For some of the participants, the literacy project has been their first contact with a literate world as they could not read or write even in their native tongue. For others, who previously did read and write, the program has been an introduction to a different culture, one in which print literacy is essential to economic progress, often in contrast to its role in their home countries.

How We Learned About Writing in Immigrant Families

To understand the ways parents and children wrote in the home setting, we collected three types of data. First, the teachers in the ILP explained to parents that we were interested in learning more about the purposes and types of writing that they and their children used at home. The teachers provided each parent with large manila envelopes and asked them to collect household writing samples, place them in the envelopes, and return the envelopes to class. We stressed our interest in collecting as many samples as possible from all family members. We called these data collection periods "writing sweeps," and we conducted three sweeps, each over a four-day period. Envelopes were distributed on Thursday and returned on the following Monday. The samples were collected from late February through mid-April 2004.

Second, we anticipated that parents and children might be unable or unwilling to include all writing samples. So that such items would be represented in our analysis, we provided a form on which we asked parents to describe samples that were not submitted in the envelope.

Third, after we collected all writing samples, we chose 8 of the participants to study in depth (the 8 that were previously discussed). The 8 participants were chosen because they had turned in at least three envelopes with samples, had children under age 18 living at home, and were willing to dedicate more time to the study. We then conducted research conversations with each of these 8 participants to learn about the context in which each writing sample was composed. No time constraints were imposed on these conversations, and the learners had the choice of expressing themselves in English or in their first language. In addition to discussing each writing sample and each entry on a Reported Writing Form, parents were also asked to talk in general about writing at home and their (and their children's) purposes, frequency, language choices, and catalysts. We had these conversations audiotaped and later transcribed.

We treated each participant as an individual case study, analyzing and recording the purpose, language, genre, participants, catalyst, and audience of each submitted writing sample and reported writing event. We also analyzed and coded interview data with attention to writing purposes, forms, language choices, participants, and frequency. We examined patterns in the data within the individual cases and then across the 8 cases.

What We Learned About Family Writing

To organize our "lessons" about family writing, we have divided the evidence into two sections. The first describes what we learned about parents' writing; the second describes what we learned about children's writing.

Parents' Writing

Evidence related to parents' writing fits into five categories: frequency, purposes and genres, language choice, influence of parents' education, and influence of parents' participation in the ILP.

Writing Frequency. All the parents in the study wrote frequently, regardless of their English proficiency and literacy proficiency in their first language or English. Three of the 8 participants reported writing at least weekly, and the remaining 5 reported daily writing. Those who wrote daily reported established writing routines and described systematic times and places for writing, while those who wrote less frequently described a more spontaneous and incidental occurrence of writing.

Most participants (6 of 8) reported substantial differences in the types and frequency of writing in the United States as compared to writing in their own countries. For learners with little formal education (between 0 and 4 years), this was a straightforward consequence of lack of educational opportunity and, consequently, writing knowledge—they had not learned to write in their first languages. For learners with more formal education (6 years or more), it is difficult to know whether the reported increase in types and frequency of writing is an outcome of participation in the ILP, where reading and writing at home are explicitly and routinely emphasized and discussed or, rather, the influence of American society in general and the value placed on reading and writing.

Writing Purposes and Genres. Like the parents described by Heath (1983) and Taylor and Dorsey-Gaines (1988), the parents we studied wrote for a variety of purposes and used a variety of writing genres. They wrote to learn, to manage daily tasks, to communicate, and to express their feelings and ideas. Across parents, writing to learn was found to be the most common writing purpose, with 6 of the 8 participants reporting or demonstrating that they wrote specifically to practice the English language. As a group and as individuals, they used different genres to fulfill this goal, sometimes composing clearly school-like tasks, such as the vocabulary and spelling practices illustrated in Figures 6.1 and 6.2, while, at other times, using writing with the deliberate intention of both practicing oral and written English and also mediating a routine task, as in the shopping list displayed in Figure 6.3.

Figure 6.1 A Parent's Writing Showing Vocabulary Practice

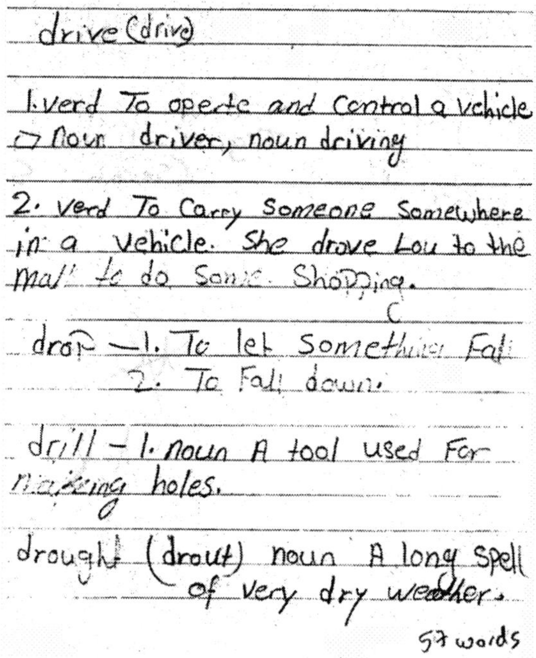
drive (drive)

1. verd To opecte and control a vehicle
→ noun driver, noun driving

2. verd To Carry Someone Somewhere in a vehicle. She drove Lou to the mall to do Some Shopping.

drop — 1. To let Something Fall
2. To Fall down.

drill — 1. noun A tool used For making holes.

drought (drout) noun A long spell of very dry weather.

57 words

Figure 6.2   A Parent's Writing Showing Spelling Practice

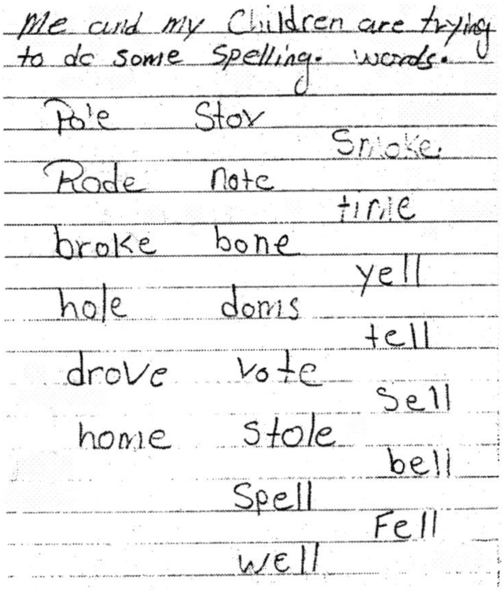

Me and my Children are trying
to do some Spelling. words.

Po'e	Stor	
		Smoke.
Rode	note	
		time
broke	bone	
		yell
hole	doms	
		tell
drove	vote	
		Sell
home	stole	
		bell
	Spell	
		Fell
	well	

Figure 6.3   A Parent's Shopping List

Beyond the evidence provided by examination of writing samples, parents were explicit during interviews in articulating the language-learning goals they attached to writing. Marina's explanation of one of her writing samples provides one example:

Marina: Yes, these are the numbers in English. I took them from a book from this library.

Researcher: From the library here?

Marina: Yes, and I can count up to 12! [laughs]

Researcher: Great! So you learned the numbers by writing them in this paper?

Marina: Right, because here I wrote them the way they were written in the book.

Interviewer: A good practice.

Marina: Because I want to improve...I would like to learn both things.

Researcher: Spanish and English?

Marina: I would like to learn English because...here you have to find your way around with English. It's more important.

(Marina, Interview 1, March 2004)

Of the 6 parents who wrote to support their own learning, 3 also used writing to support their children's English-language and literacy learning. These participants varied in their educational levels, each having completed 4, 6, or 9 years of formal education. As her daughter read a story aloud, Eliana recorded words she wanted her daughter to practice and learn (Figure 6.4). She underlined words that were the subject of pronunciation practice immediately after the child finished reading.

Four of the 8 participants in the study reported that writing was integral to managing routine tasks, a category that combines the categories Heath (1983) and Taylor and Dorsey-Gaines (1988) identified as "memory-aids writing" and "financial writing." For the parents in our study, writing to accomplish routine tasks included bill paying, preparing for grocery shopping, and searching for a job. This mother's explanation was typical of others:

> I write it because of my mind is not good, sometime when I, I can want something that I want to buy at the store, but...soon as I get to the store I forgot what I supposed to buy and want buy something else. So, my daughter told me "Mommy, the best thing that you have to do [laughs], you have to do a list that everything that you wants," so I said, "That is a good idea." So we try to make the list of what we are going to go shopping. So, we check in the refrigerator anything that we need, and write it, so the [unintelligible] shopping and we keep on looking at the paper. (Sanaa, Interview 1, March 2004)

Parents also engaged in what Heath (1983) and Taylor and Dorsey-Gaines (1988) called "social-interactional" writing. Five of 8 parents provided samples (e.g., notes, messages, letters) and talked about writing specifically as a way to maintain family and social ties with family members and friends living apart from them. Susana's example is representative of others:

> I write to my family...in El Salvador, to my mother, my father, my girlfriends left behind...and to my sister in Texas...and, well, my brother who is.... I don't know if I should say this but he is detained, okay, then I write to him...twice a month or every other week. I write to him, he writes to me to learn how, how the

Figure 6.4   Eliana's List of Words for Her Daughter to Practice

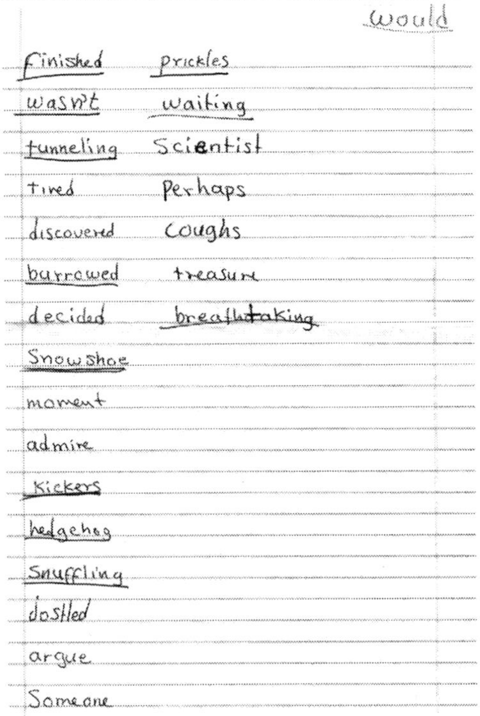

would

Finished   prickles
wasn't   waiting
tunneling   Scientist
tired   Perhaps
discovered   coughs
burrowed   treasure
decided   breathtaking
Snowshoe
moment
admire
kickers
hedgehog
Snuffling
Jostled
argue
Someone

problem and everything are going because I cannot go...on visiting days. Then we visit him by letter. (Susana, Interview 1, March 2004)

Finally, for at least half of the parents, writing also provided a way to reflect on events in their daily lives or to express personal feelings. The following examples illustrate the unique explanations with which they shared these experiences with the written word:

I think it helps us...to feel more relaxed, write what one...sometimes what one feels. Parts of things one feels.... And there are things one writes, sometimes one has a lot a stress,...we write like taking the bad out of our body to feel better [laughs], that's why we write. (Susana, Interview 1, March 2004)

I write about everything, about my...daily things, about at home, with my childrens...yes, sometimes I write about my life [laughs]. I like to write because I think when I write about my life my heart is relax. (Eliana, Interview 1, March 2004)

As in writing to support their children's learning, we found no patterns in the incidences of this type of writing and parents' years of education. For these parents, the range of education was from three to nine years. The specific reasons and the forms of writing also varied among the 4 participants: One was primarily motivated by her desire to provide a legacy for her children, one wrote a diary in the form of letters, one wrote her worries and concerns, and one expressed feeling liberated by writing. In addition to this, the need to reflect was not always related to personal feelings or experiences but also to religious practices or beliefs. In the words of one parent, "And the passages from the Bible [reads] that I need to reflect on. I write them and then hang them in a visible place, so I can read them during the day, so I then remember that it's important" (Eliana, Interview 2, April 2004).

Language Choice. Across these different writing purposes and genres, we observed that language choice was influenced by three factors: the nature of the task, the explicit intention of practicing English, and parents' desire to involve their children in writing.

Most participants chose to write in their first language when their purpose was to express feelings or to reflect. However, the relationship between first language and self-expression did not always hold true. One parent, Eliana, explained her deliberate attempt to represent "complex thoughts and ideas" in English rather than in her native Spanish. (See the poem displayed in Figure 6.5.) In her words, "I can write this in Spanish in only five minutes. But I need to free my mind, my thoughts, and the ability of my hands to write in English, and to think in English" (Eliana, Interview 2, April 2004).

When writing to accomplish routine tasks (e.g., shopping lists, money orders, checks), parents typically wrote in English. In some instances, this decision was related to the demands of the tasks, for example, writing a check to an American company. In others, the decision was governed by parents' desire to practice English while managing a certain task (for example, writing a shopping list in English). At yet other times, the involvement of children dictated the language choice. Seven of the 8 parents reported choosing English when writing for or with their children for different purposes. Ana explained one such instance:

> Sometimes my daughter asks me, "What are we going to buy?" And as she only writes in English, I tell her, "We are going to buy this." And I write that. And so for her to understand what I'm doing, I write it in English. (Ana, Interview 1, March 2004)

Figure 6.5   Example of a Parent Writing in English to Express Her Feelings

How much pain are in my heart.
How much Sadness to drag my life.
I living my life on wail.
The guilty is your love.

Never imagine the pain.
That your love bring,
at my heart.

My heart Speak but.
Your heart not reply.
Even it a one idea
to be Cling.

Conquer your love.
Was our purpose.
But as never obtain answer.
He feeling Sad and walk,
on the Sadness.

Since then he roam.
on the world as punishment.
For the pain that your,
Love bring it.

Related writing samples were mostly composed for or with young children (ranging from 2 to 12 years with a mean age of 6.6 years); all but 2 of these children had received school instruction in English only. We found it interesting that in most cases parents' written language choice reflected their children's language preference rather than their language knowledge. That is, 7 of the 8 participants reported that their children preferred to speak English at home, although parents most often spoke to them in their first language. In the single instance where a mother recorded her hopes and dreams for her children in her first language (Spanish), the children were older (ages 9 and 12) and had been schooled in Spanish in their home country (Honduras) before coming to the United States.

Relationship Between Writing Purposes and Language Choice. Parents' writing purposes and language choice were found to relate to their level of education. Those with more years of education (μ = 10 years) commonly reported using English while composing for varied purposes and in varied genres. Moreover, they were deliberate in using writing for the dual purposes of managing daily responsibilities and advancing their English-language learning. For example, one parent reported that she routinely composed her food shopping list in English, explaining that making a list helped her to spend her money more wisely and also gave her an opportunity to practice and use the English language.

This was not the case for participants with fewer years of formal schooling (μ = 2.25 years) and more limited literacy in their first language. These parents were engaged in both primary literacy development (in English and/or their first language) and English-language learning simultaneously. Although they wrote for as many purposes overall as did the more highly educated parents, they tended to separate their writing tasks to focus on a single purpose at a time. When writing for purposes unrelated to learning (e.g., social communication, task management), they wrote in their first language. When writing to support language and literacy learning, they wrote in English. An exception was Marina, who was learning to write in both English and Spanish, and therefore, in her case, both languages related to the purpose of learning.

Relationship Between Family Writing and Participation in the Literacy Program. We also found writing at home to be related to the participants' experiences in the ILP. Six of the 8 parents reported being influenced by the program when writing to improve their own or their children's English. Two of the participants in particular adopted one of the program's writing assignments—writing about daily events and experiences—as a home writing-practice routine. The writing sample displayed in Figure 6.6 prompted the following conversation between Ana and the researcher:

Researcher: This, I'm curious. Did you write it?

Ana: Yes, we go to the movies frequently. This movie that my husband wanted to see because of the dancing.

Researcher: So why did you write this?

Ana: Well, to tell the teacher that we had gone to...the activities. Sometimes we go to the park, or to the store, but mainly to the parks.

Researcher: And your teacher asked you to do this? To write about the things you had done?

Figure 6.6   A Parent's Home Writing Practice

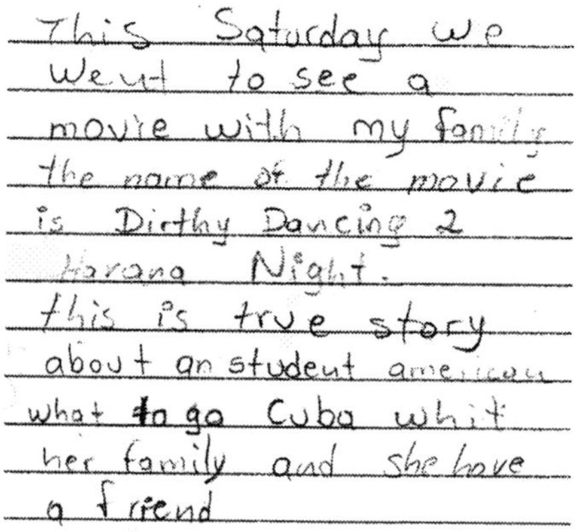

> This Saturday we
> went to see a
> movie with my family
> the name of the movie
> is Dirthy Dancing 2
> Havana Night.
> this is true story
> about an student americou
> what to go Cuba whit
> her family and she love
> a friend

Ana: Let's say they ask us to narrate the activities we've done. So when
                I'm home I start writing: This day I did—this is becoming a routine.
                Sometimes there are things you don't want to forget and so you
                write it, and then you say: Oh, that day we went to this and that
                place, and all.

Researcher: So the teacher always asks you what you did...and 'cause you don't
                want to forget, you write it?

Ana: Yes, because sometimes I can't come to school.

Researcher: Oh, so if you don't come you write this down anyway.

Ana: I always, we sit together with the kids.

                (Ana, Interview 1, March 2004)

Marina, the parent with the most limited literacy proficiency, wrote at home in
an attempt to build on what she did in her class. Interestingly though, although
she wrote sentences in class, at home she only copied words. Like many Central
American learners with little formal education, she believed in the value of
copying words and phrases she read, even though that was not a technique that
was taught or modeled in class.

Children's Writing

We organized the findings from our analysis of children's writing into three
categories: frequency, purposes and genres, and writing as a family event.

Writing Frequency. Like their parents, children in these families wrote frequently.
In 7 of the 8 families, at least 1 child wrote daily. However, 4 of the school-age
children wrote exclusively to complete tasks assigned by teachers or parents. The 8
children who self-initiated writing—all girls—chose to write in a variety of genres
and on a daily basis. For these children, writing served as entertainment and as an
expression of affection; they frequently gave what they wrote to family members or

friends, their classroom teacher, or the teachers in the ILP. Parents described their children's self-initiated writing in these ways:

> It is like a little poem that she writes, those are like poems. She writes a lot or...like, she also writes like riddles, like riddles, poems, everything that is.... It's like that, she does.... (Juana, Interview 1, March 2004)

> For example, on Saturdays or Sundays, when she's at home all day. Sometimes I think she gets bored of playing and she comes to me, "Mom, do you give me permission to write?" "Oh, yes," I say. And she starts writing while I'm doing other things around the house. (Eliana, Interview 2, April 2004)

Writing Purposes and Genres. With few exceptions, children wrote for three purposes: learning, recreation, and social interaction. Writing genres were diverse and varied according to age groups. Children in pre-K and younger (5 children) composed mostly drawings and, in a few cases, scribblings. Children in kindergarten to first grade (7 children) composed mostly drawings, many of them labeled or captioned narrations of daily events, and letters to family, friends, or teachers. Children in grades 2 to 6 (5 children) wrote letters, shopping lists, poems, songs, and stories and also completed many school-assigned worksheets. (Samples that are typical of the writing we collected are displayed in Figures 6.7, 6.8, and 6.9.)

Types of school-assigned writing varied widely by teacher. In some cases, assignments consistently required only one-word or short-answer responses. In other cases, assigned tasks required extended writing. Parents were involved in their children's school-related writing in two ways. First, they actively monitored their children's completion of homework assignments, providing paper and a pencil, designating homework space and time, and, in some cases, sitting side by

Figure 6.7   Child's Letter to the Tooth Fairy

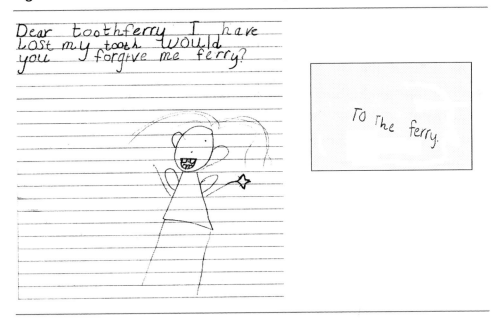

Figure 6.8   Child's Poetry Writing in English and in Spanish

Figure 6.9   Child's Signed Drawing

side to provide help or attention, actions that were encouraged and often discussed during ILP classes. Sanaa's comment is typical:

> They bring from school mathematics, English, science every Friday. Every Monday they give them like four piece of papers that they bring home, everything is homework here, so on Fridays they return it back to the teacher. So when she is doing the homework that she is doing, she need like a little bit of help, more of homework that she can do by herself, so that I mean she knew someone like sitting by [unintelligible] so she cannot make mess. (Sanaa, Interview 1, March 2004)

In addition, 4 parents frequently extended school learning by assigning school-like writing activities after the children had completed their homework. One mother described these writing activities this way: "We finish the homework...we give you the paper, we write in the practice for me" (Aicha, Interview 1, March 2004). Or, as Julio explained,

Julio: So at home I say [to] my son, "Jefrrey, you take the piece of paper and the pencil. And you writing." I say, "You write." And I say, "My name is Jefrrey."

Researcher: So you dictate words to him?

Julio: Yes, because for him is good, because he practice.... I spell this part and he write.
                     (Julio, Interview 1, March 2004)

Another parent motivated and encouraged her preschool- and kindergarten-age children to write by creating blank books for them:

Ana: Oh, I make books for them. And I tell them, "Let's make a book for each of you." But I make it like this [folds the page to make it look like a book] and staple them. And I write...I make the cover, or just write their names, so they can do the drawings.

Researcher: So the rest are blank pages for them to use.

Ana: For them to use in whatever they want to do, to write, to draw. For David sometimes I put pages so he can...here is the staple.
                     (Ana, Interview 1, March 2004)

Language Choice. Children's language choice varied by age group. In the kindergarten and first-grade age group, all the samples collected were in English; in the second- to sixth-grade age group, the samples were primarily, but not exclusively, in English. We believe that this finding relates to children's educational experiences. The younger children had attended school only in the United States, in English-only classrooms, whereas the 2 children in the second- to sixth-grade age group who composed samples in their first language were first schooled in their home country. Both were enrolled in transitional bilingual education classrooms when they first entered U.S. schools, where they were encouraged to write in both their first language and in English.

Writing as a Family Event. In 5 of the 8 families, writing in the home usually took place in a context in which members of the family sat together with the explicit purpose of writing. Four of the parents were deliberate in modeling writing and providing materials for their children to participate; in the fifth case, family writing was less structured and more spontaneous. The following excerpts illustrate these sessions:

Sanaa: Like, we have like 25 minutes every night, OK, that we spend our time writing, me and my kids, because they need more reading and more writing. So every 20 minutes after we read, they can have their dinner and go to bed, OK. So every day except like Fridays, we do like 10 minutes because the following day is a weekend so they can have a rest.

Researcher: So it is 20 minutes a night.

Sanaa: At night we try to read books. Try to take books from the library so we can read.

Researcher: And also, it is also related to writing.

Sanaa: Yeah, because we can read it, but at the same time we try to make a word so with my children, like when we see something that is fun, we try to make it in writing. Like if I see something that is interesting on the reading, I try to tell my children, "Can you write something about this?" Like the animals, or the colors, something like that, OK, everybody writes. Everybody, even my 2-year-old: "Mommy, can I have a pen? A pen?" [laughs] (Sanaa, Interview 1, March 2004)

Juana: My daughters do it in the living room, or we make a circle, when we are doing some work we make a circle and start writing in the living room, together...when we write something.

Researcher: When you write what, for example?

Juana: When my daughter is writing.... Because sometimes.... Each one of us writes his/her own work, they write what they want to write, what they think, and so do I.

Researcher: But then, every time you do it, you do it together, or not?

Juana: Sometimes together, sometimes each one separately. My daughter, the one who writes songs, is almost always writing. And she writes and sends, and writes the songs, listens to them on the CD, and she starts to write them. She writes and then sends them, a lot of pages for copying. She copies everything she writes, she send the music to the copier.... Yes, she sends to copy the music for storing them later on. Yes, or to give them to her school classmates. I don't know now. Oh yeah, yeah, yeah, to share them, to share them with her classmates. (Juana, Interview 1, March 2004)

This kind of family writing also appeared to create a context that motivated younger children to write. In 3 of the families we studied, older siblings served as a catalyst for writing. Parents reported that when younger children saw their older siblings write, either for homework or for pleasure, they asked for paper and tried to duplicate their siblings' work. In most cases, they scribbled or engaged in invented spelling, often with the older sibling helping in this task. As Sanaa explained,

Yeah, they sit, they sit together. When Melina sees Karima is doing something, she tries to come closer to Karima and know what Karima is doing. "Can I look this so I can write mine?" Try to look the letters and write...and writes. (Sanaa, Interview 1, March 2004)

Applying the Evidence to Classroom Practice

As we reviewed our findings, we were pleased to confirm that many of these parents and their children were interested in writing at home and were eager to use writing in both their daily lives and as a means of supporting their English-language and literacy development. At the same time, we were dismayed to note how many opportunities we had missed to incorporate family writing into our instruction. Although we were confident that our classroom routines were supporting parents in reading on their own and with their children, we had provided few cues for families to engage in shared writing. We wanted to find ways to extend class writing into the home that would allow all learners, even those just beginning to learn to read the alphabet, to continue learning at home and to embed writing into their families' daily lives.

We composed the following instructional guidelines to help us to act on the findings:

1. Parents of all levels of oral and written language proficiency are capable of writing at home and of engaging their children in family writing activities.

2. Writing occurs most frequently in families where there are established writing routines. Explicit explanation of such routines may be helpful to parents who are developing as writers.

3. Involving their children in writing is a powerful motivator for parents. Writing tasks that require parent–child collaboration have the potential to increase writing frequency for both adults and children in the household.

4. In some families, homework provides the context for family writing. Homework assignments that engage parents and children in writing tasks that are both extended and require critical thinking have the potential to increase the frequency and quality of home writing.

5. Girls seem more likely than boys to self-initiate writing. Family writing tasks that are framed with attention to content and context that will engage young and adolescent boys as well as girls have the potential to mediate this finding.

We then planned three strategies to help us respond to these guidelines. The first was implemented on the first day of the next ILP academic term. We began by asking parents to introduce themselves to us and to each other. We told the parents that we wanted to get to know all of the members of their families and asked them what kinds of information they or their children might want to share with us. Responses included children's names, ages, grades in school, interests, parents' jobs, home countries, and hobbies. We provided each parent with a kit that included a piece of poster board; several sheets of loose-leaf paper, first-grade lined paper, and blank copying paper; a pencil; and a small box of crayons. We asked them to work at home with all of their family members to create a poster or series of letters that introduced their family members to the class. To account for our learners' range of English-language and literacy proficiency and their children's ages and literacy development, we proposed several ways they could approach the task: We reminded them that they could choose to write in English or in their first language; we suggested cutting out pictures from magazines and writing words that provided captions, having each member of the family write a paragraph about himself or herself or another family member, drawing captioned pictures, and responding to open-ended sentences, such as "When I have free time, I like to...." We were explicit in encouraging parents and children to work together and to support each other in describing themselves.

To provide models and to build the classroom sense of community, teachers and tutors in the ILP class engaged in the same activity with their own families and brought them in to share with the class. Over the next week, learners flooded the classroom with posters; some consisted mostly of captioned pictures, while others were covered by pages of loose-leaf paper with parents' and children's elaborate introductions (Figure 6.10). The teachers and tutors also introduced their families, modeling a pictorial-and-written format and strengthening the sense of community. In addition to letting all of us know a little more about the families with whom we collaborate, these posters served as the backdrop for instruction throughout the cycle. When we discussed and read about ways to prevent teenage drinking, for example, we looked to the posters to give us more information about the interests and goals of our learners' teenagers as we brainstormed approaches for building on their children's interests and keeping them away from dangerous activities.

While the posters were successful, we also realized that using the classroom to support embedded writing in the home required a more sustained effort. The second strategy related to the dialogue journals that had long been a staple of the ILP classroom. Parents write in their journals once a week, and their writing partners (a teacher or tutor) respond to the learners' thoughts, extending the dialogue by sharing their own related experiences and asking learners to clarify or expand what they've written. Parents write in their dialogue journals in class, and prior to our study of out-of-school writing, we had seldom asked them to engage in extended writing at home. Our review of the findings made it clear to us that our learners were most commonly using writing at home to extend their English literacy, but that we were not taking advantage of their interest in linking learning in the classroom to writing at home.

We decided to expand the dialogue journal routine to include a second at-home component that would build on parents' interest in more systematic and routine opportunities to write at home; strategies for involving their children in their writing; and tasks that linked what they had read, written about, and discussed in class with writing at home. We purchased composition books for in-home dialogue journals to allow ample space for both parents and children to write.

We first introduced the concept of the journals near the end of an ILP class day in which parents had read an article about parent–child activities in our local community. After learners had discussed the article in small groups, we gave them the composition books and wrote on the chalkboard, "What activities would you like to share with your family?" Then we asked them to head the first page of their books with the question and to write their own suggestions for family-friendly activities that weren't mentioned in the article. We then reunited as a whole class for parents to share their suggestions, and we asked parents to take the books home and ask their children to add to their parents' list. We encouraged parents to work with their children in brainstorming activities that they might like to do, in addition to excursions they had already shared. We also emphasized involving all members of the family and suggested that parents invite young children to draw pictures, which parents could annotate; older children could write lists of words, sentences, or descriptive paragraphs. We were careful to mention explicitly that, while this opportunity provided parents with an opportunity to practice writing in English, they (and their children) should write in the language of their choosing. To make sure that the learners with the most limited literacy felt comfortable with the task, we also suggested that parents might want to take home the day's reading to help them come up with words to use and reminded the class that their responses could be lists of words, sentences, or paragraphs. The next day, parents eagerly shared their families' comments with teachers, tutors, and each other. Teachers asked the

Figure 6.10 Examples of Families' Written Self-Introductions

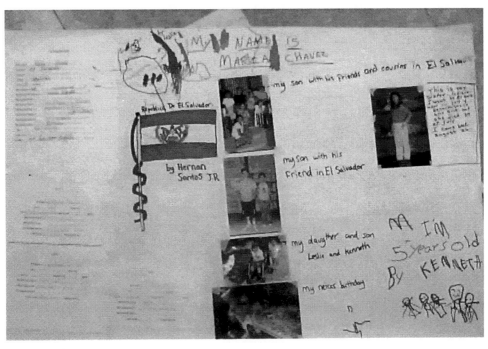

learners to share orally new suggestions that they had brainstormed with their families and wrote them on the board, thereby providing a model of "correct" writing and spelling without directly pointing out learners' errors.

Although nearly all of our learners responded enthusiastically to their first at-home journal writing opportunity, we realized that the task could become burdensome if parents felt obligated to add a writing assignment to their and their children's long days. Further, some of the topics we read and discussed in class were not as clearly relevant to family writing. At the same time, we were also aware that several learners were already engaging in writing to support their own learning at home and to reflect on their lives. We decided to provide parents with a question at the end of each class day, which we wrote on the board. We then asked learners to take their journals home to share the writing prompt with their families, but we were careful to let parents know that this was a suggestion, not a requirement. We also spent five minutes each morning reviewing the previous night's question and noting their responses on the board. This review allowed us to both reinforce the previous day's lesson and incorporate the voices of all family members into our adult literacy classroom.

The third strategy was planned to respond to our evidence that the highest incidence of writing was found in families where there were established routines and to the evidence that in all of our families, girls were more likely than boys to self-initiate writing. We decided to focus a series of four instructional days on writing in our daily lives and to target strategies for encouraging reluctant writers to see the importance of writing as a means of accomplishing tasks.

Based on what we had learned from our family writing study, we were aware that shopping lists were used by many of our learners. Because all family members have a stake in what is bought at the supermarket, the shopping list seemed a perfect first lesson. We began by asking our learners what considerations they used in shopping. Did they plan a new list each time they shopped based on a weekly menu, or were they more likely to make slight modifications to a preset list? Who was involved in writing the shopping list? Did they write it just before they went to the store, or did they post a running list that was added to over time? In the store itself, did they select items based on price, sale items in a flier, brand name, or family members' preferences? Did they use coupons? We graphed some of our findings on the board and discussed commonalities. We then read a short article on tips for saving time and money in the supermarket. After discussing the reading in small groups and as a whole class, we asked the parents how they could involve their families in writing a shopping list. We requested that they think especially of ways to include children who could not yet write or who chose not to write. After brainstorming in small groups, the learners reconvened with a range of suggestions for both early and reluctant writers. For their youngest children, they suggested keeping a set of index cards with the names of different foods that children could copy onto the list, keeping old packages and labels that children could copy, and leaving space for children to draw pictures. To involve their children who didn't want to help with the family shopping list, one parent suggested dividing up the shopping list task into different sections (e.g., dairy, produce, frozen foods) and having each member of the family come up with items for a section of their choice. Another mother proposed having children look through the kitchen cabinets to come up with what was in limited supply and adding those items to the list. Parents also suggested writing the list as a family, with different members taking turns writing down others' suggestions, or offering children an opportunity to add a treat of their choosing to the list if they had come up with a sufficient number of items the family actually needed. As with other discussion topics, we sent parents home with their journals to encourage family members to offer their thoughts on how to construct a shopping list.

Subsequent lessons—focused on note writing and message writing, constructing chore or task schedules, and budget writing—followed the same format of encouraging parents to generate strategies for incorporating all members of the family in routine writing activities.

Final Thoughts

As we began this work, our purpose was to document the writing routines that commonly occur in families in which adults and children are both acquiring English as a second language and in which adults have relatively few years of formal education. As has happened so often in our work with families in this particular community, we end this phase of our work gratified by the opportunities for learning afforded to us by our association with these men, women, and children.

Our study of their writing lives taught us several important lessons: that parents of all levels of oral and written language proficiency are capable of writing at home and of engaging their children in family writing activities; that established writing routines seem to increase the incidences of family writing; that involving children in writing is a powerful motivator for parents to initiate writing at home; and that for young family members, writing may be gender-related—girls in our study were more likely than boys to self-initiate writing. But perhaps more important than any of these lessons was one that seemed to override all others—in families where parents and children wrote most, they perceived and used writing as a way to mediate social interaction and social–emotional events in their lives.

Our analysis reminded us once again that, at its base, writing is a social act—and that if we are to succeed at engaging learners of all ages and abilities in daily and sustained writing, we must position writing both in and out of the school as an activity that has the potential to mediate events that are important and purposeful in our students' lives. In closing, we return to the words of Eliana—words that we believe capture the importance of helping our students experience the many ways writing can make a difference in their lives: "When I write about my life my heart is relax[ed]."

REFERENCES

Ada, A.F. (1988). The Pajaro Valley experience: Working with Spanish-speaking parents to develop children's reading and writing skills in the home through use of children's literature. In T. Skutnabb-Kangas & J. Cummins (Eds.), *Minority education: From shame to struggle* (pp. 223–238). Philadelphia: Multilingual Matters.

Akroyd, S. (1995). Forming a parent reading-writing class: Connecting cultures, one pen at a time. *The Reading Teacher, 48,* 580–584.

Baghban, M. (1984). *Our daughter learns to read and write: A case study from birth to three.* Newark, DE: International Reading Association.

Bissex, G.L. (1980). *Gyns at wrk: A child learns to read and write.* Cambridge, MA: Harvard University Press.

Cazden, C.B. (2001). *Classroom discourse: The language of teaching and learning* (2nd ed.). Portsmouth, NH: Heinemann.

Compton-Lilly, C. (2003). *Reading families: The literate lives of urban children.* New York: Teachers College Press.

De Temple, J.M., & Tabors, P.O. (1995). Styles of interaction during a book reading task: Implications for literacy intervention with low-income families. In C. Kinzer, D. Leu, & K.

Hinchman (Eds.), *Perspectives in literacy research and practice* (pp. 265-271). Chicago: National Reading Conference.

Edwards, P.A. (1991). Fostering early literacy through parent coaching. In E.H. Hiebert (Ed.), *Literacy for a diverse society: Perspectives, practices, and policies* (pp. 199-213). New York: Teachers College Press.

Ferreiro, E., & Teberosky, A. (1982). *Literacy before schooling*. Exeter, NH: Heinemann.

Gadsden, V.L. (2000). Intergenerational literacy within families. In M.L. Kamil, P.B. Mosenthal, P.D. Pearson, & R. Barr (Eds.), *Handbook of reading research* (Vol. 3, pp. 871-888). Mahwah, NJ: Erlbaum.

Goldenberg, C.N. (1989). Making success a more common occurrence for children at risk for failure: Lessons from Hispanic first graders learning to read. In J.B. Allen & J.M. Mason (Eds.), *Risk makers, risk takers, risk breakers: Reducing the risks for young literacy learners* (pp. 48-82). Portsmouth, NH: Heinemann.

Heath, S.B. (1983). *Ways with words: Language, life, and work in communities and classrooms.* Cambridge, UK: Cambridge University Press.

McCarthey, S.J. (1997). Connecting home and school literacy practices in classrooms with diverse populations. *Journal of Literacy Research, 29*(2), 145-182.

Palmer, B.C., Alexander, M.M., & Olson-Dinges, C. (1999). Journal writing: An effective, heuristic method for literacy acquisition. *Adult Basic Education, 9*(2), 71-89.

Paratore, J.R. (1993). Influence of an intergenerational approach to literacy on the practice of literacy of parents and their children. In C. Kinzer & D. Leu (Eds.), *Examining central issues in literacy, research, theory, and practice: 42nd yearbook of the National Reading Conference* (pp. 83-91). Chicago: National Reading Conference.

Paratore, J.R., Homza, A., Krol-Sinclair, B., Lewis-Barrow, T., Melzi, G., Stergis, R., et al. (1995). Shifting boundaries in home and school responsibilities: Involving immigrant parents in the construction of literacy portfolios. *Research in the Teaching of English, 29,* 367-389.

Paratore, J.R., Melzi, G., & Krol-Sinclair, B. (2003). Learning about the literate lives of Latino parents. In D.M. Barone & L.M. Morrow (Eds.), *Research-based practice in early literacy* (pp. 101-120). New York: Guilford.

Purcell-Gates, V. (1995). *Other people's words: The cycle of low literacy.* Cambridge, MA: Harvard University Press.

Quintero, E., & Huerta-Macîas, A. (1990). All in the family: Bilingualism and biliteracy. *The Reading Teacher, 44,* 306-312.

Reutzel, D.R., & Fawson, P.C. (1990). Traveling tales: Connecting parents and children through writing. *The Reading Teacher, 44,* 222-227.

Rhoder, C.A., & French, J.N. (1995). Participant-generated text: A vehicle for workplace literacy. *Journal of Adolescent & Adult Literacy, 39,* 110-118.

Rogers, R. (2004). Storied selves: A Critical Discourse Analysis of adult learners' literate lives. *Reading Research Quarterly, 39,* 272-305.

Schickedanz, J.A. (1990). *Adam's righting revolutions: One child's literacy development from infancy through grade one.* Portsmouth, NH: Heinemann.

Straub, S. (2003). Read to me: A family literacy program for young mothers and their babies. In A. DeBruin-Parecki & B. Krol-Sinclair (Eds.), *Family literacy: From theory to practice* (pp. 184-201). Newark, DE: International Reading Association.

Taylor, D. (1983). *Family literacy: Young children learning to read and write.* Exeter, NH: Heinemann.

Taylor, D., & Dorsey-Gaines, C. (1988). *Growing up literate: Learning from inner-city families.* Portsmouth, NH: Heinemann.

Taylor, M.C., & Blunt, A. (2001). A situated cognitive perspective on literacy discourses: Seeing more clearly through a new lens. *Canadian Journal for the Study of Adult Education, 15*(2), 79-103.

Teale, W.H. (1986). Home background and young children's literacy development. In W.H. Teale & E. Sulzby (Eds.), *Emergent literacy: Writing and reading* (pp. 173-206). Norwood, NJ: Ablex.

Volk, D., & de Acosta, M. (2003). Reinventing texts and contexts: Syncretic literacy events in young Puerto Rican children's homes. *Research in the Teaching of English, 38*(1), 8-48.

Yaden, D., & Paratore, J.R. (2002). Family literacy at the turn of the millennium: The costly future of maintaining the status quo. In J.E. Flood, D. Lapp, J.R. Squire, & J.M. Jensen (Eds.), *Handbook of research on teaching English language arts* (2nd ed., pp. 546-565). Mahwah, NJ: Erlbaum.

Zakaluk, B.L., & Wynes, B.J. (1995). Book bridges: A family literacy program for immigrant women. In L.M. Morrow, S.B. Neuman, J.R. Paratore, & C. Harrison (Eds.), *Parents and literacy* (pp. 84-89). Newark, DE: International Reading Association.

SECTION TWO

Writing in the Middle and Secondary Years

Chapter 7

Middle School Writing: 9 Essential Components Model

James Flood, Diane Lapp, and Wendy L. Ranck-Buhr

arly adolescence is a period of rapid development and significant change in every person's life (Blasingame & Bushman, 2005; Glatthorn & Shuse, 2003; Jackson & Davis, 2000). The human organism develops in all spheres of its existence during early adolescence, including physical, emotional, cognitive, and linguistic growth. In the area of language growth, early adolescents begin dealing with three distinct language registers in their oral and written language encounters: a social register that they use in their homes with family members, an ever-expanding academic register that they use to communicate and learn in school, and an increasingly more difficult (and specific) peer register that they use in social settings with their friends (Chamot & O'Malley, 1994; Larson & McKinley, 1995). All three registers have their own vocabulary and contexts in which they are used (Adger, 1998).

Although middle schoolers' social and peer registers can be different in grammatical form from their academic registers, their social and peer registers include all the functions of language (e.g., requests, commands, questions, greetings, declarations), and they require great attention to maintain inclusion in each of these important groups. Early adolescents interact in social settings as they make sense of their world by processing their life experiences; familiar social settings enable them to acquire new and expanded lexicons that they need for learning new academic concepts. It is through their existing vocabularies that they make connections between verbal and written forms of communication. It must be noted that their social registers are not superficial or unimportant to their academic growth as many media illustrations (television shows, magazines, and even novels) purport. In school, children encounter academic language that frequently differs from their home registers; their social registers, then, often serve as their bridges to academic learning. Especially during the middle school years, students experience dissonance between topic and language because they constantly encounter interactions with impersonal topics within the various disciplines (force, density, eminent domain, allegory) that require more formal uses of English in writing, reading, speaking, and listening than they were using before this time.

The conflicting demands on the adolescent from the home, their peers, and their teachers can be daunting. For many early adolescents, this is the most challenging (maybe even terrifying) time in their lives; their language patterns are largely inadequate for dealing with all of the new information that they are expected to learn (Jackson & Davis, 2000). Most early adolescents find the transition to learning new and complex concepts difficult even when their language background matches the language of the curriculum. For children whose first language is not English, for many African American Vernacular English (AAVE) speakers, for children who have not succeeded in academic tasks, and for children who have not been exposed to the requirements of academic language, the journey through early adolescence is particularly foreboding.

Frameworks for Writing Instruction in the Middle School

Any discussion of writing instruction and the middle schooler must begin with an acknowledgment of the complexity of what writing encompasses in the middle schooler's life as well as the complexity of the middle schooler's swirling psyche. On the one hand, we rightfully should ask questions such as "What kind of writing?" (e.g., personal, expository) and "For whom and for what purpose?" On the other, we should wonder about "Which middle schooler, on which day, and in what context?" We knew that the task of designing a writing program for middle schoolers would be daunting, so three years ago, we invited a group of middle school teachers to join us in a conversation about best practices.

We decided to begin with a full-blown gripe session with teachers about how middle schoolers disappointed them as writers over the years. What hadn't happened? The initially reticent group worked themselves into a frenzy before the session was over.

> They write about nothing. I never have to watch television because all of their "creative" pieces are rehashes of sitcoms, action shows, and made-for-TV maudlin melodramas.

> They never revise. Oh, they pretend to; they recopy the same misspelled words, alter "zero" sentences, and even recopy whole paragraphs twice.

> They summarize through lexical paraphrasing. How kind we're being; they sometimes change a word. They shift focus in a piece as frequently and blithely and randomly as a toddler struts through an airport.

> When you ask them not to answer "I don't know" to your question "Who's your audience?" they stare their vacant stare.

> "Eats, shoots, and leaves" *seems* as plausible to them as "eats shoots and leaves." They've never met a comma they didn't invite for dinner.

> Sometimes their sentences contain an "and" or "but"; on the whole they religiously follow NVO [noun–verb–object] patterns and never even think about combining two thoughts.

Professional Development

In order to design a program that would help middle school students write well, we knew that we had to begin with teachers' professional development. Lee Shulman

(1987) suggests that professional growth requires the development of knowledge and expertise in three areas:

1. content knowledge—specific subject-area knowledge of the depth generally expected of advanced study in the subject area;
2. pedagogical knowledge—general knowledge regarding how to teach; and
3. pedagogical-content knowledge—content-specific knowledge regarding best practices in the subject area.

A great deal of research has been conducted that illustrates the ways in which teachers can grow professionally in their knowledge of and ability to teach writing skills to middle schoolers (Blasingame & Bushman, 2005; Killion, 1999). Joellen Killion states,

> to face the complexities of educating middle-level students, teachers must engage in staff development that increases their knowledge and skills, challenges their beliefs and assumptions about education, provides support and coaching to develop comfort with new practices and engages them as active participants in the study and reform of the school culture. (p. 6)

In Douglas Reeves's (2000) "90/90/90" studies (schools where 90% of the children represented minority populations, received free or reduced-price lunch, and achieved the standard benchmarks for success), he examined how schools were organized for instruction. Reeves found that conversations among teachers about writing instruction were a universal characteristic of schools that excel. Although his intention had not been to focus on writing instruction per se, his observations led him to conclude that teachers who talked with one another in professional groups not only expanded their overall pedagogical knowledge but they also expanded their knowledge about writing instruction.

Andy Hargreaves (2003) maintains that in order to prepare students to function in a knowledge society and a knowledge economy, teachers must pursue deep and continuous professional learning that includes regular discussions with colleagues. Not surprisingly, Hargreaves notes that this type of debate and discussion among colleagues is rarely seen in professional development structures at low-performing schools.

Consensus Scoring as a Context for Professional Conversations

Recently, we have been involved with a professional development activity that expands upon Reeves's fortuitous finding that teachers who talk together about writing instruction create achieving schools. The context for our work is two large, urban middle schools: Johnson Middle School in Albuquerque, New Mexico, and Monroe Clarke Middle School in the San Diego City Heights Educational Program, California. The professional development program, titled Consensus Scoring, has shown remarkable promise during the past three years (Fisher, Lapp, & Flood, 2005). It is based in part on the British notion that multiple measures are needed to fully understand children's writing efforts (Silvernail, 1996). We began our program with middle school teachers in Albuquerque and San Diego because they were becoming increasingly concerned about the depressed writing scores of their middle school students. By synthesizing and integrating teachers' key ideas with ours, we have found that combining the best research-based ideas for writing instruction in middle schools and then implementing a schoolwide process results in significant changes in student achievement.

Consensus Scoring Components

Fisher et al. (2005) have found through consensus scoring that teachers (a) gain an increased understanding of the content and performance standards that guide their instruction, (b) work together to assess student work, (c) provide quality instruction, and (d) reteach writing skills and content as necessary to ensure student achievement. The process of consensus scoring is implemented in a series of five steps.

Step 1: Unpacking the standards. In consensus scoring, teachers examine the content and performance standards for their grade and subject. While most teachers know the key standards for writing at the middle school, discussions about what the standards can look like in action are often not held. As Wiggins and McTighe (1998) suggest, the careful analysis of standards, including the development of pacing guides and materials lists, is critical in teaching writing.

Step 2: Developing common assessments that are standards-aligned. The second step in consensus scoring is to develop standards-aligned assessments, which can be given at the end of major units of study or as groups of standards are completed. In the two schools in which we implemented this approach, teachers met approximately every six weeks to plan common assessments. We based this practice on evidence that such assessments provide teachers, administrators, parents, and students with regular feedback and opportunities for midcourse corrections (Guthrie, 2002; Langer, 2001). The difference between our consensus scoring model and common practice is that all of the teachers who teach the same grade or content were required to give the same assessment in addition to any other assessments they were using.

Step 3: Providing quality curriculum and instruction in writing. We believe that the key to meeting increased accountability demands lies in providing quality curriculum and instruction. During consensus scoring meetings, teachers discussed the types of instructional texts that are particularly useful in helping students to achieve the identified standards. In addition, teachers discussed the instructional strategies that were especially effective in helping students to achieve shared benchmarks.

Step 4: Collecting assessment information. By creating pacing guides and common assessment tools before writing instruction, teachers commit to collecting specific assessment information at designated times. The main purpose of this collection is to ensure that every teacher has chosen student work to discuss during the consensus scoring meetings. Collecting assessment data during a common window in time ensures that all of the writing standards will be addressed, and the year will not end with students who have not mastered appropriate middle school writing skills.

Step 5: Discussing results, implications, improved practice, and next steps. This final step is the heart of consensus scoring. It is the time we use to evaluate the entire assessment to instruction to student growth process while looking forward to the next steps needed to ensure continued progress. In this discussion, teachers score the common assessments, look for patterns in the data, and discuss the instructional implications. Through these conversations, gaps in students' knowledge and process needs are identified and beneficial instructional strategies are identified. As part of these conversations, representative papers are analyzed in depth. At Johnson Middle School, the papers presented in Figures 7.1–7.4 were written as persuasive letters by the students to their principal about the school's dress code. The papers were scored during conversations by teachers as 1, 2, 3, and 4, respectively.

During discussion about each piece, the teachers concluded that the paper rated as 1 was weak in several areas, including format, coherence of argument, organization, sentence and paragraph structure, and mechanics. The paper rated as 2 included more attention to the norms of format for a persuasive letter but was lacking in coherence, sentence structure, and clear point of view. The paper rated as 3, which is decidedly longer than the lower-ranked papers, included a coherent argument and well-organized paragraphs but lacked sentence control. The paper rated as 4 showed sophistication with all elements from coherence to cogency and careful attention to mechanics.

These conversations typically not only focus on students' writing and the criteria for judging students' work but also provide individual teachers with an opportunity to reflect on their teaching content (the standards) and their instructional repertoires.

Figure 7.1 Sample of Middle School Student's Letter to the Principal: Rating of 1

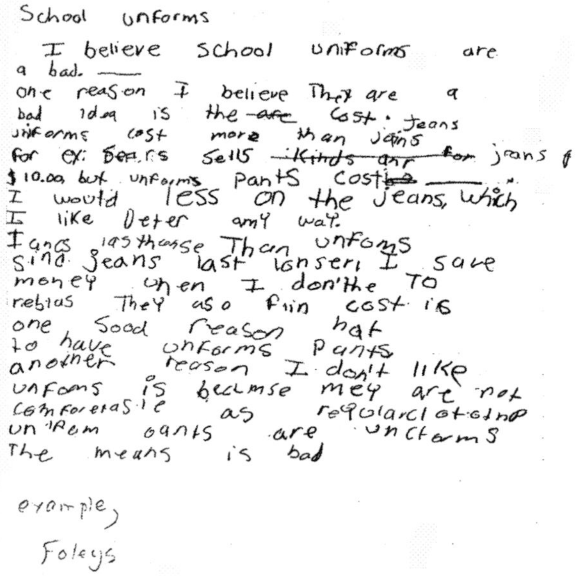
School unforms

I believe School uniforms are a bad.

one reason I believe They are a bad idea is the ~~are~~ cost. uniforms cost more than jeans
for ex: Sears sells ~~kinds an for~~ jeans $10.00, but unforms pants cost ___.
I would less on the jeans, which I like beter any way.
Jeans lasthasse Than unfoms sind jeans last longer, I save money when I don'the TO rebias They aso fiin cost is one good reason hat to have unforms pants.
another reason I don't like unfoms is becamse mey are not comforetasle as regolarclotghing unifom oants are unfforms The means is bad

example,

Foleys

Figure 7.2   Sample of Middle School Student's Letter to the Principal: Rating of 2

Dear Mr. Agustin,

The students at John Adams Middle really Don't like Dress Code we Don't like Dress Code because we dont want to wear these Clothes Even though they are nice. I think we should be able to wear Jeans With a Striped or whatever colored Polo Shirts. I think if the Dress Code was Jeans and a Striped or Whatever colored Polo Shirt untucke. Students Would follow the Dress Code alot more Better than we do now. So if you Considered this we would appreciate it alot

Figure 7.3   Sample of Middle School Student's Letter to the Principal: Rating of 3

Dear Mr Agustin,

I am concerned about the JAMS school dress code. As I have seen teachers everyday check school uniforms very strictly, student are sent to the office beccause of pants and etc. I was thinking that if students are constantly being sent out of class, that they are loosing lots of valuable time. In which they can be getting an education. If student don't get the knowledge that is provided, the school is not reaching its goal in giving students their education. All of that hazard just because some students are out of dress code. How students dress should not have nothing to do with their education, but now it is getting to that point.

Uniforms now in days are very expensive. Many people can not afford them. Some just say, Why not just wear the casual pants, but that are the same color. Stretch pants and jeans are still pants. They cover the same area on the body, why not wear them to school. That is another reason students are getting in trouble.

In my way of thinking an I am sure many others think the same way, is that uniforms are not such a good idea after all. Thank you for your patience.

Figure 7.4   Sample of Middle School Student's Letter to the Principal: Rating of 4

> Dear, Mr. Agustin
>
>   The situation about the dress code here at John Adams, is that we have to wear certain shirts and pants. The shirts have to be pollo style and certain colors. The pants have to be dress pants and certain color. There are no gang related clothing.
>
>   I think that the dress code is reasonible, Although I would not chose to dress like this everyday, at school I think that's fair. I know that you would like us to look nice, instead of looking like hooligans and I understand that and respect you guy's for that.
>
>   I don't think you should change the dress code I think It is fine allready. Frankly the only reason that I don't mind the dress code is because I just don't care. I don't care about how you want us to dress at school As long as its only at school and I still have my freedom of dress off campus.

Transporting the Program Between Schools

Based on our experience in Albuquerque, we were interested in testing the consensus scoring model with a middle school in San Diego, California, that provides an education to 1,460 students in grades 6–8; 99% of the students qualify for free lunch. More than 30 languages are spoken at this school, and 76% of the students are English-language learners. Public schools in California are evaluated according to the Academic Performance Index (API), a ranking for accountability. Each school receives an annual API score based on students' performance on standardized and standards-based tests. When we began our project, the school's API score was one of the lowest in the city. In 2003, the API score increased by 167 points, the highest change among all middle schools in the district. The writing sample scores also improved dramatically; prior to our project, 78% of the children received scores of 2 on the state rubric (the range was 2–8 with two raters scoring each paper 1–4). In 2003, only 18% of the students in this school received scores of 2.

What changed at this school that allowed it to post among the highest gains in achievement in the county? While we have acknowledged the significant changes in professional development provided to the teachers at this school in previous papers (e.g., Fisher, Frey, Lapp, & Flood, 2004), we also know that a focus on consensus scoring has had a significant impact on student achievement.

The teachers at this school regularly meet in grade-level teams and engage in the process of consensus scoring. They have spent significant amounts of time reviewing writing standards and creating pacing guides to ensure that students have access to a standards-aligned writing curriculum. The discussions that teachers have during the Consensus Scoring sessions have resulted in the creation of an after-school reading and writing intervention program for over 600 students two days per week; individualized tutoring for over 200 students; significant changes in the ways in which spelling, vocabulary, and writing are taught at all grade levels; and significant increases in student achievement, including that which is measured by state accountability systems.

Even with all of their success, the teachers realized that they had a good model for attending to standards, but they did not yet have the instructional model that tied together all of the pieces of the middle school writing puzzle. They hoped for an instructional framework that was comprehensive, manageable, and effective.

Identifying an Appropriate Instructional Framework

In searching for an appropriate framework that would be comprehensive and flexible enough to be responsive to all of the demands of an effective middle school writing program, we analyzed frameworks that were based on a genre approach to writing instruction, a disciplinary approach, and a rhetorical approach. None seemed broad enough to meet the demands of the middle school literacy teacher who needed to teach his or her children to write stories, poems, and information texts; to construct logical arguments; to take notes that would actually help them in the future; to paraphrase and summarize; to respond to literary texts; to respond to propaganda; to persuade others to their point of view; and to write with a personal voice all their own. None of the existing frameworks captured the robustness necessary to engage early adolescents.

Most of the frameworks could be divided into the traditional curricular categories defined by Edmund Farrell (1991), which are mastery, with its overemphasis on mechanics; transmission, with its overemphasis on specific cultural knowledge; and process, with its overemphasis on time-consuming reflections. None of the frameworks had the flexibility that we knew middle schoolers and their teachers need.

As the teachers talked through their concerns about the papers they were scoring, they began to realize that the components of writing could be divided into distinguishable patterns that could be coded. They noted that errors seemed to be occurring around sense of audience, coherence of ideas, organization of information, construction of sentences and paragraphs, and use of spelling and mechanics. As they discussed their observations, we told them about the work of Ruth Culham (2003) with primary traits. She identified the following primary traits of written language: Ideas, the core of the message; Organization, the pattern or internal design or structure of the lesson; Voice, the author's way of communicating thoughts, ideas, feelings, and convictions; Word Choice, the language choices that convey the author's message; Sentence Fluency, the flow and connectedness of the text; Conventions, the use of grammar and mechanics; and Presentation, the form, layout, and delivery.

In researching the ways in which Culham's (2003) framework has been implemented, we noticed in the literature that the word *scoring* was continually attached to the words *primary traits* ("primary trait scoring"). In this chapter we argue that the primary traits model is insufficient for developing the writing skills of middle schoolers. Although we found Culham's list very attractive, we were disappointed not to find Audience, Paragraph Writing, and Presentation among the primary traits. In our work with middle school teachers, we developed our own 9 Essential Components Model as a framework for teaching writing.

Teaching Middle School Writing Through the 9 Essential Components Model

Our model has three major interactive components: a writer, a text, and a context. We acknowledge that middle school writers come to the task of writing with individual skills, strengths, and needs that have an impact upon the texts that they produce. We also acknowledge that writing occurs in specific contexts that vary with each student; these contexts include the teacher, the classroom, the home, and the community. In recommending our 9 Essential Components Model, we also acknowledge the work of Culham (2003) and other writing researchers and educators who have preceded us.

Audience

As students progress toward middle school, they generally become less and less interested in writing exclusively for a teacher audience. However, the struggle to fill a page with thoughts almost vanishes when middle school students have an authentic audience to address in their writing.

Publication Celebration. Popularized by Nancie Atwell (1998), publication celebrations are an excellent method to encourage students to consider their audience while writing. In some middle school classrooms where we work, a publication celebration is held at the end of every unit of study. Invitations are sent to parents, teachers, administrators, and community members. Students post their writing, and the invited guests are encouraged to respond to the students' writing on a response sheet posted next to each piece of student writing.

RAFT. The acronym RAFT (Santa & Havens, 1995) signifies the choices students are expected to consider prior to drafting their work. *R* stands for the role that the student author will take when writing the text. *A* stands for the audience that the student will address. *F* indicates the format of the writing. *T* stands for topic. Initially, the teacher assists students by guiding their choices (in the beginning, perhaps, even assigning each component), but eventually teachers should encourage students to create their own RAFT.

The RAFT technique is particularly useful because it links together more than one of the nine essential components of writing that we have identified in our work with middle school students. Figure 7.5 displays how the RAFT technique was used to help students analyze the writing components evident in the novel *Nothing But the Truth* by Avi (1991). In this novel, the story of a high school track star, Phillip Malloy, is told through a series of different text types, such as telephone calls, journal

Figure 7.5　Implementing the RAFT (Role, Audience, Format, Topic) Technique

Role	Audience	Format	Topic
• Phillip Malloy • Principal • Mrs. Malloy • Mr. Malloy • Journalist • Phillip's English teacher • Community member	• Journal entry • Memo • Letter to the editor • School newspaper column • Conversation • Speech • National newspaper article	• Lies that have gone out of control • School policies • Freedom of speech • Students' rights	• Self • Staff at the school • Community members • Other students

Adapted from Santa, C., & Havens, L. (1995). *Creating Independence through Student-owned Strategies: Project CRISS*. Dubuque, IA: Kendall-Hunt.

entries, news articles, and so forth. It is an excellent novel for introducing students to a variety of text formats. In addition, the content of this novel rarely fails to evoke rich discussions about fairness, justice, and lies that get out of control.

Ideas

Middle school teachers, as we noted earlier in this chapter, are often inundated with writing that reads like a replay of the hottest television sitcoms or the diary entry of melodramatic pop star. However, our work demonstrated that with the right support and encouragement, students are able to produce writing that is both creative and thought provoking (Fisher et al., 2005).

Rich Classroom Library Collection. In order to generate ideas for writing, students need to have access to a wide range of texts and resources. Providing students with exposure to a wide range of texts allows them to explore possibilities in their own writing. A well-stocked middle school classroom library collection should include a range of texts and text types. Students who are struggling with ideas for their writing can browse the classroom collection as a means to jumpstart their own ideas. As students browse the collection to generate ideas, the teachers should encourage them to keep a list of possible writing topics that would serve as an ongoing collection. Some of the classroom library resources that we have found useful are listed in Figure 7.6.

Talk Time. Prior to any writing activity, students should be provided with time to talk with partners or in small groups about their ideas for writing. In order to facilitate the discussion, the teacher may provide question prompts that are appropriate for the type of writing that students will be doing. For example, if students are writing an information article, question prompts might include the following:

Figure 7.6   Useful Classroom Library Resources

Books	Magazines	Newspapers	Audiotapes
• Short fiction • Short-story collections • Nonfiction • Biographies • Poetry collections • Student-produced books	• *Time for Kids* • *Newsweek* • *Teen Ink* (a student-produced magazine that includes a range of text types)	• Local newspaper • School newspaper • Classroom newspaper	• Books on tape • Young adult authors talking about their work and how they get their ideas • Class-produced tapes

Adapted from Santa, C., & Havens, L. (1995). *Creating Independence through Student-owned Strategies: Project CRISS.* Dubuque, IA: Kendall-Hunt.

Why did you pick this topic?

How is it important to you personally?

Why should other people care about this topic?

How might this information be useful?

Organization

Assisting students in the organization of their writing can be challenging for teachers. However, it is a critical step in the process that helps writers clarify their thinking, select the most important ideas, and eliminate extraneous details. It is not enough to tell students how to organize their writing. Developing writers need to be shown a variety of techniques for organizing their writing. Perhaps most important, the writer must struggle through the organization of the text in order to communicate ideas clearly.

Graphic organizers are an excellent tool to help students organize their ideas for writing (Lapp, Flood, & Hoffman, 1996). For schools with access to software such as Inspiration, a variety of graphic organizers can be created from a single brainstorming session. Inspiration is also an excellent tool to use to generate ideas as a whole class and then organize the ideas into a logical sequence; the program's simple interface allows you to move between a cluster diagram and an outline format with the click of the mouse.

Voice

When we first mention voice to our middle school students, we find that they are often not familiar with the term as it refers to writing. A helpful first step to developing an understanding of voice is to identify and distinguish other writers' voices. One of the best techniques for doing this is using model texts.

Model Texts. This technique requires selecting and reading aloud texts in which the author's voice is especially apparent. Picture books, excerpts from longer texts,

Figure 7.7   **Texts That Model the Concept of Voice in Writing**

Title and Author	Ideas for Teaching
Voices in the Park by Anthony Browne	This picture book is an excellent resource to introduce students to the idea of voice in writing. In the story, Browne has four different characters go to a park, but each character has a different experience there based on his or her unique point of view. Text features such as different fonts for each character's story and clear distinction between each of the characters' voices provide supports for students in the early stage of identification of voice.
The True Story of the 3 Little Pigs *Squids Will Be Squids* *Stinky Cheese Man* by Jon Scieszka	These picture books are always popular with students at all levels. Scieszka's distinctive voice appeals to middle school students.
Joey Pigza Swallowed the Key *Joey Pigza Loses Control* by Jack Gantos	The humorous and distinctive voice of Jack Gantos appeals to middle school students. Excerpts from these novels engage middle school students and provide excellent examples of Gantos's voice as an author.
Maniac Magee *Who Put That Hair in My Toothbrush?* by Jerry Spinelli	Jerry Spinelli has excellent insight into the minds and hearts of middle school students, and his unique voice appeals to them.
Dogzilla *Captain Underpants* series by Dav Pilkey	Dav Pilkey's style and humor appeal to middle school students. Many middle school students have selected Pilkey's work on their own for independent reading. Because of his unique voice, Pilkey is good a choice when teachers are in the early stages of working with students on voice.

and news articles are all good choices. Once students begin to recognize the voice of a few authors, try reading a text to the students without telling them the author; ask them to name the author, and provide examples from the text that illustrate the author's voice. Figure 7.7 provides examples of some titles that are useful as model texts.

Word Choice

Helping middle school students expand their vocabularies is a never-ending task for the middle school teacher. Frequent and wide reading is a critical factor in this effort, as well as regular word work in the classroom.

Word Walls. Although some practitioners may associate word walls with elementary classrooms, they are also useful for word study in middle-level classrooms. Word walls provide the opportunity to post new and interesting words in a public place in the classroom where students are likely to have easy access and multiple encounters with them, an essential element of successful word study. Word games that support the development of "word consciousness" (Scott, 2004) are especially useful in helping students to make new vocabulary part of their writing and speaking vocabularies.

Show, Don't Tell. Use student work to demonstrate revisions that focus on word choice. Encourage the students to show the reader what is happening rather than tell the reader what is happening. We have found a two-column chart like the one shown in Figure 7.8 to be a useful tool to track changes from tell to show. We keep this chart on display in the classroom following the initial lesson on word choice as a reminder to students to revise for word choice.

Sentence Fluency

Sentence fluency relates to the flow and connectedness of the text. In order for sentences to flow and connect, students need to work on developing more complex sentences. We have found that working with the whole class or a small group of students using a common text works well to help middle school writers develop their skills in this area.

Sentence Combining. Use either a student-generated text or a teacher-generated text to demonstrate to students a variety of techniques for combining sentences.

Sentence-Level Edits. In this activity, students are given a sentence and directed to work in pairs or groups to express the same idea in a variety of different ways. We explain to students that it is like a thesaurus for sentences. (See Figure 7.9 for an example of the sentences generated by one group of students.)

Paragraph Structure and Organization

Many of the middle school teachers with whom we work tell us that they spend a great deal of time teaching students how to structure paragraphs. To address this need, we suggest the use of paragraph frames, best described as a graphic organizer for paragraph structure. Paragraph frames provide the skeletal structure for student-created paragraphs, and they assist students in internalizing the basic paragraph structures as part of their writing repertoire. (See Figure 7.10 for two sample paragraph frame structures.)

Language Conventions

Grammar and punctuation lessons never seem to be much fun. However, with some creativity even writing conventions can be fun. We emphasize game-like activities that focus students' attention on the importance of careful editing. For example, to call students' attention to the importance of appropriate use of commas, we ask them to read sentences like these and to describe what is happening:

- Marcel eats, shoots, and leaves.
- Marcel eats shoots and leaves.

Figure 7.8   Show, Don't Tell Chart

Don't Tell	Show
It was hot while we played basketball.	The sweat poured off my face as the sun beat down on the hard asphalt court.
I was afraid.	I could feel my knees shake and I started to get goose bumps on my neck.

Figure 7.9   A Thesaurus of Sentences

Teacher-Provided Sentence
I felt so sad when my best friend moved away.

Student-Generated Rewrites
My heart was broken when my best friend left our small town.

I could feel a lump forming in my throat whenever I thought about my best friend moving away.

I was very depressed when my best friend moved away.

I was lonely and depressed when my best friend moved away.

Figure 7.10   Sample Paragraph Frames

Sequential
A champion wrestler does many things to prepare for a match.

First, _____

Next, _____

Then,   _____

Finally, _____

Main Idea
There are many sources of water pollution.

First, _____

Second, _____

Third,   _____

Finally, _____

So, _____

Presentation

The form, layout, and delivery of a written text must be considered in context with the audience and the purpose for the text. Too often middle school students spend the bulk of their writing time producing written text only on white lined paper. However, with ever-increasing access to computers and other forms of technology, teachers need to consider the variety of ways that students can present their written texts. PowerPoint slide shows have been a presentation method for written research in content area classrooms for over a decade. More and more middle school students are posting their writing to websites and participating in informal writing via chat rooms and e-mail exchanges. An emerging genre that is gaining popularity is known as hyperfiction. Hyperfiction is not merely fiction that is online; it is fiction that uses electronic media to communicate narrative text. It is basically any type of online writing that presents fiction in a new, exciting, different manner. Some hyperfiction sites that are currently available are ongoing stories created by visitors to the site. In Figure 7.11, we present a list of websites that teachers and students have found useful in exploring different ways to present their texts through electronic media.

Figure 7.11   Presentation Websites

Name of Website	URL	Site Summary
Kids Bookshelf	www.kidsbookshelf.com	This site will publish selected student work. Guidelines for submission are included on the site.
Scholastic: Writing With Writers	www.teacher.scholastic.com	Go to the online component of this site and then to Writing With Writers. This is an outstanding website that gives students the opportunity to work with the authors that they have read about in class.
Teen Ink	www.teenink.com	This website has a variety of resources for both teachers and students. This site publishes student work on the site as well as in their print magazine.
White Barn Press	www.whitebarnpress.com	This is another website that publishes student writing. Publishing guidelines are included as well as suggestions for teachers who want to set up their own website for the purpose of publishing student work.

Concluding Thoughts

Working with middle school writers as they develop the writing skills they will need for high school and beyond is challenging. We have found that by working within the framework of the 9 Essential Components Model of writing, teachers are able to plan and develop writing lessons that are focused on the specific needs of students, and, in turn, students are able to develop their skills as writers.

REFERENCES

Adger, C.T. (1998). Register shifting with dialect resources in instructional discourse. In S.M. Hoyle & C.T. Adger (Eds.), *Kids talk: Strategic language use in later childhood* (pp. 151-169). New York: Oxford University Press.

Atwell, N. (1998). *In the middle: New understandings about writing, reading, and learning* (2nd ed.). Portsmouth, NH: Boynton/Cook.

Blasingame, J., & Bushman, J.H. (2005). *Teaching writing in middle and secondary schools.* Upper Saddle River, NJ: Pearson/Merrill Prentice Hall.

Chamot, A.U., & O'Malley, J.M. (1994). *The CALLA handbook: Implementing the cognitive academic language learning approach.* Reading, MA: Addison-Wesley.

Culham, R. (2003). *6 + 1 Traits of writing: The complete guide grades 3 and up.* New York: Scholastic.

Diederich, P.B. (1974). *Measuring growth in English.* Urbana, IL: National Council of Teachers of English.

Farrell, E. (1991). Instructional models for English. In J. Flood, D. Lapp, J. Squire, & J. Jensen (Eds.), *Handbook of research on teaching the English language arts* (pp. 63-84). New York: Macmillan.

Fisher, D., Frey, N., Lapp, D., & Flood, J. (2004). Improving literacy achievement and professional development through a K-12 urban partnership. In D. Lapp, C.C. Block, E.J. Cooper, J. Flood, N. Roser, & J.V. Tinajero (Eds.), *Teaching all the children: Strategies for developing literacy in an urban setting* (pp. 137-152). New York: Guilford.

Fisher, D., Lapp, D., & Flood, J. (2005). Consensus scoring and peer planning: Meeting literacy accountability demands one school at a time. *The Reading Teacher, 58*, 656-666.

Glatthorn, A., & Shuse, D. (2003). Secondary English classroom environments. In J. Flood, D. Lapp, J. Squire, & J. Jensen (Eds.), *Handbook of research on teaching the English language arts* (2nd ed., pp. 512-531). Mahwah, NJ: Erlbaum.

Guthrie, J.T. (2002). Preparing students for high-stakes test taking in reading. In A.E. Farstrup & S.J. Samuels (Eds.), *What research has to say about reading instruction* (3rd ed., pp. 370-391). Newark, DE: International Reading Association.

Hargreaves, A. (2003). *Teaching in the knowledge society: Education in the age of insecurity.* New York: Teachers College Press.

Inspiration 7.0 [Computer software]. (2000). Portland, OR: Inspiration Software.

Jackson, A.W., & Davis, G.A. (2000). *Turning points 2000: Educating adolescents in the 21st century.* New York: Teachers College Press.

Killion, J. (1999). *What works in the middle: Results-based staff development.* Oxford, OH: National Staff Development Council.

Langer, J.A. (2001). Beating the odds: Teaching middle and high school students to read and write well. *American Educational Research Journal, 38*(4), 837-880.

Lapp, D., Flood, J., & Hoffman, R. (1996). Using concept mapping as an effective strategy in content area instruction. In D. Lapp, J. Flood, & N. Farnan (Eds.), *Content area reading and learning: Instructional strategies* (2nd ed., pp. 291-306). Boston: Allyn & Bacon.

Larson, V.L., & McKinley, N.L. (1995). *Language disorders in older students: Preadolescents and adolescents.* Eau Claire, WI: Thinking Publications.

Reeves, D.B. (2000). *Accountability in action: A blueprint for learning organizations.* Denver, CO: Advanced Learning Press.

Santa, C., & Havens, L. (1995). *Creating Independence through Student-owned Strategies: Project CRISS.* Dubuque, IA: Kendall-Hunt.

Scott, J. (2004). Scaffolding vocabulary learning: Ideas for equity in urban settings. In D. Lapp, C.C. Block, E.J. Cooper, J. Flood, N. Roser, & J.V. Tinajero (Eds.), *Teaching all the children: Strategies for developing literacy in an urban setting* (pp. 275-293). New York: Guilford.

Shulman, L.S. (1987). Knowledge and teaching: Foundations of the new reform. *Harvard Educational Review, 57*(1), 1-22.

Silvernail, D.L. (1996). The impact of England's national curriculum and assessment system on classroom practice: Potential lessons for

American reformers. *Educational Policy, 10*(1), 46-62.

Wiggins, G., & McTighe, J. (1998). *Understanding by design*. Alexandria, VA: Association for Supervision and Curriculum Development.

LITERATURE CITED

Avi. (1991). *Nothing but the truth: A documentary novel*. New York: Orchard Books.

Browne, A. (1998). *Voices in the park*. New York: DK Publishing.

Gantos, J. (1998). *Joey Pigza swallowed the key*. New York: Farrar, Straus, and Giroux.

Gantos, J. (2000). *Joey Pigza loses control* New York: Farrar, Straus, and Giroux.

Pilkey, D. (1993). *Dogzilla*. New York: Harcourt.

Pilkey, D. (2002). Captain Underpants series. New York: Scholastic.

Scieszka, J. (1993). *The Stinky Cheese Man and other fairly stupid tales*. New York: Viking.

Scieszka, J. (1996). *The true story of the 3 Little Pigs*. New York: Viking.

Scieszka, J., & Smith, L. (1998). *Squids will be squids: Fresh morals, beastly fables*. New York: Viking.

Spinelli, J. (1984). *Who put that hair in my toothbrush?* Boston: Little Brown.

Spinelli, J. (1999). *Maniac Magee*. Boston: Little Brown.

Chapter 8

Creating Independent Writers and Thinkers in Secondary Schools

Douglas Fisher, Nancy Frey, and Rita ElWardi

econdary schools have a critical responsibility as the capstone institution for preparing youth for their lives beyond school. This responsibility is especially complex in terms of creating independent writers and thinkers who can participate in higher education, engage in the workplace, and meet their civic responsibilities. Teachers in secondary schools must build on the writing instruction provided in elementary and middle schools in order to extend students' abilities to write and think independently and to fill in the gaps in students' learning. In addition, in many classrooms, teachers are challenged to respond to students who are newcomers to the United States, having not participated in schooling or instruction in the English language. Whatever students' backgrounds, secondary school teachers are charged with the responsibility to ensure that all students develop a lifelong love of reading, writing, speaking, listening, and viewing.

In 1999, the International Reading Association published a position statement on adolescent literacy, which reads, in part:

> The expanding literacy demands placed upon adolescent learners includes more reading and writing tasks than at any other time in human history. They will need reading to cope with the escalating flood of information and to fuel their imaginations as they help create the world of the future. The Association's recommendations for focusing on the literacy needs of adolescent learners include providing them with
>
> • access to a wide variety of reading material that appeals to their interests;
>
> • instruction that builds the skill and desire to read increasingly complex materials;
>
> • assessment that shows their strengths as well as their needs;
>
> • expert teachers who model and provide explicit instruction across the curriculum;
>
> • reading specialists who assist students having difficulty learning how to read;
>
> • teachers who understand the complexities of individual adolescent readers; and

---

Learning to Write, Writing to Learn: Theory and Research in Practice edited by Roselmina Indrisano and Jeanne R. Paratore.
Copyright © 2005 by the International Reading Association.

- homes, communities, and a nation that supports the needs of adolescent learners. (Moore, Bean, Birdyshaw, & Rycik, 1999)

Although many of these statements specifically address reading, we believe the opening lines indicate that the position statement also applies to writing, writing instruction, and writing assessment.

Fortunately, there are schools across the country in which the responsibilities of educating students well are being met (e.g., Fisher, Frey, & Williams, 2002; Langer, 2001). An examination of the ways in which successful schools meet the needs of their students allows us to identify practices and structures that can be used in other schools. Studies of secondary schools in which students experience success indicate a fair amount of consistency, at least in terms of writing instruction and development. This chapter will explore several of these effective practices and structures, including developmental writing instruction in English classrooms, instruction in writing genres, peer feedback, writing to learn in content area classrooms, the importance of wide reading, and consensus scoring of common writing prompts. In doing so, we act on advice from Brozo and Hargis (2003) that student voices and experiences must be represented in any serious discussion of adolescents' achievement.

Each of our recommendations for writing in the secondary school is grounded in the experiences of our students, some of whom you will meet in this chapter. The three of us teach at Hoover High School in San Diego, California. Hoover educates just over 2,300 students in grades 9–12. Of these students, 100% qualify for free or reduced-price lunch and 76% speak a language in addition to English at home. Hoover is an urban, inner-city school that has posted significant gains in student achievement over the past several years (e.g., Fisher, 2001). As one example, the percentage of students who have passed the High School Exit Exam, which includes a writing task, on their first attempt has increased from 18% to 55%.

"I Didn't Know I Could Write"—Developmental Writing Instruction in English Classrooms

The first of several students you'll meet in this chapter is Edgar Castro, a ninth-grade student at Hoover High School. Edgar speaks both Spanish and English. During his ninth-grade year, Edgar began to express himself in writing (in addition to expressing himself with his clothing and hairstyle choices). He learned to do so as his teacher implemented a developmental writing curriculum. At the beginning of the school year, Edgar's reading was assessed on the Gates–MacGinitie Reading Test (MacGinitie, MacGinitie, Maria, & Dreyer, 2000). He scored at the 3.8 grade level in vocabulary and 4.2 grade level in comprehension. When asked to respond to a five-minute timed writing, he averaged 17 words per minute with 3.2 errors per sentence.

Gradual Release of Responsibility Model

Edgar's English teacher used a developmental approach that was based on a gradual release of responsibility model (Pearson & Gallagher, 1983). The gradual release of responsibility model stipulates that the teacher moves from assuming "all the responsibility for performing a task...to a situation in which the students assume all of the responsibility" (Duke & Pearson, 2004, pp. 200–211). This gradual release may occur over a day, a week, or a term. We will review each of the instructional strategies that were used to ensure that Edgar's writing improved (adapted from Fisher & Frey, 2003). Although we will profile a student who would be considered "struggling" or "at risk," the gradual release of responsibility model of writing instruction is not limited to such students (e.g., Ruddell, 2005). Different teachers start at different points in the model, depending on the needs of the students in the class.

Language Experience Approach (LEA)

This approach dates back 40 years (Ashton-Warner, 1959; Dixon & Nessel, 1983). Adolescents without strong independent writing skills are typically unwilling to participate in activities that highlight their skills or lack thereof. In a typical LEA lesson, the students have a discussion and then agree upon a sentence or two. The teacher then scribes the sentence on the board while students observe. For example, early in the term, Edgar's class had a visit from a World War II veteran. Following the visit, the class had a discussion and reached a consensus on a few sentences that the teacher recorded on chart paper, including "Mr. Hernandez lied about his age to get into the Army. He was sent to fight in World War II. He used a 50 caliber machine gun to down two German fighters."

The language experience approach is an important first step in writing instruction for two reasons. First, it helps students develop an understanding of speech-to-print connections. In other words, it is useful when students do not know how to record their thoughts or spoken conversations. Second, it can be used to develop a trusting environment when students are unwilling to write in front of their peers. Too many adolescents have had years of experience telling them that they were not strong writers, and they are often unwilling to demonstrate that in front of the whole class. The writing done via the language experience approach is accomplished with substantial teacher support. The teacher scribes almost everything and looks for opportunities to teach aspects of language structures and conventions that are relevant to the learners. In other words, while the students come to a consensus on a message, the teacher can discuss some aspect of language or writing (mechanics, spelling, grammar, vocabulary, and so forth).

Interactive Writing

Interactive writing has historically been used with emergent young writers (Callella & Jordano, 2002; McCarrier, Pinnell, & Fountas, 2000). Given the success of this instructional strategy, it seemed reasonable to suggest that it might work with struggling adolescent writers who, like their younger peers, are also in the emergent stages of writing (Fisher & Frey, 2002). Interactive writing is used in large- and small-group settings to engage students in meaningful conversations that include the purposes and conventions of writing. Similar to the language experience approach, interactive writing follows "from ideas, to spoken words, to printed messages" (Clay, 2001, p. 27). The difference is that the students write the message on the dry-erase board as it is repeated by the whole class. Because students now scribe each word on the board, the teacher can focus on teaching elements of written language from conventions of print to clarity of message. Thus, language lessons are based on students' thinking and speech. In addition, the instructional value of interactive writing lies in the opportunities for oral language development as students collaborate to plan the message as well as in the repeated oral readings that occur as the message is composed. Among the challenges of interactive writing instruction is the adaptability demanded of the teacher. The process requires immediate recognition of students' confusions and their insights that are on display as students attempt to use written language to represent their thoughts. Such incidents are widely viewed as "teachable moments"—opportunities that effective teachers seize in order to teach new understandings or to reinforce insights that are on their way to being internalized.

Because students take control of the pen, interactive writing can test the level of trust in the classroom. Any threat of embarrassment in front of peers can undermine a lesson, so it is essential that students view their mistakes as an opportunity for everyone to learn. The teacher is responsible for building this atmosphere of collaboration. Deep knowledge of the students' control of words and vocabulary, and especially their understanding of structural analysis, is vital to an interactive writing lesson. For example, following a discussion about a photograph of a statue in a park covered in snow, the class agreed on a sentence that read, "As the snow falls, the rider wonders why he was left alone." The teacher calls on individual students to write a word on the board. As each student walks away from the board, the whole class repeats what is written on the board as well as what has yet to be written. Edgar is invited to the board to write the word *rider*. He writes *riter* and steps away. The teacher says, "there's a small error in the way that word was written. The root is *ride*, like he's riding a horse." Edgar listens and changes the *t* to a *d*, and the teacher begins reading aloud the sentence (including the part that is written and the remainder from memory) with the students.

Writing Models

Using existing writing as a model for new writing is another way to engage these young writers. To develop an understanding of various writing text genres, students are asked to begin by reading published writing. These writing models provide a pattern or scaffold that students may follow when they begin to compose original writing. Consistent with a gradual release model, writing models increase the amount of student control but provide them with a framework that supports their individual creations. One common example of a writing model is the popular "I Am" poem in which students complete sentence starters (Figure 8.1) that all focus on one main idea (Fisher & Drake, 1999; Moretti, 1996).

At one point, Edgar's teacher shared the poem "If I Were in Charge of the World" by Judith Viorst (1981). Students were provided the opportunity to use the poem as a model and write their own poems using the sentence frames that Viorst originally wrote. Some of Edgar's lines included the following:

> If I were in charge of the concert
> I'd cancel bouncers, bras, beer and also posers
> If I were in charge of the concert
> There'd be free food, loud music, and a mosh pit.

Figure 8.1   Stanzas for an "I Am" Poem

1. I am (special characteristics or nouns about you)
2. I wonder (something you are curious about)
3. I hear (an imaginary sound)
4. I want (an actual desire of yours)
5. I am (repeat first line of poem)
6. I pretend (something you pretend to do)
7. I feel (an imaginary feeling)
8. I touch (an imaginary touch)
9. I worry (something that truly bothers you)
10. I cry (something that makes you very sad)
11. I am (repeat the first line of the poem)
12. I understand (something you know is true)
13. I say (something that you believe in)
14. I dream (something you dream about)
15. I try (something you make an effort about)
16. I hope (something you actually hope for)
17. I am (repeat the first line of the poem)

At other times, the teacher wrote paragraph frames on the dry-erase board and asked students to complete them, such as "I was walking through the halls when.... I turned to see.... To my surprise.... Thankfully,...." At each ellipsis, students insert their own writing to create a paragraph that makes sense.

Writing models release additional responsibility to students as they have increased control over the content of their writing, but their choices are constrained by the grammar structures of the sentences as well as the overall topic.

Generative Sentences

Edgar's teacher noticed that Edgar, along with many of his peers, often made mistakes at the sentence level. To help students to focus on the accuracy of individual sentences, generative sentences were introduced. These are quick activities that last a few minutes per day. Fearn and Farnan (2001) call this practice a "given word sentence" (p. 87).

For example, one day, the teacher asked Edgar and his classmates to write the letter *v* on their paper. Then the teacher asked them to write a word with the letter *v* in the third position. The teacher recorded the list of these student-generated words on the dry-erase board. The teacher asked students to examine the list and notice the variation of words that share this characteristic—*love, have, give, dove, advice*, and so on. Following this, the teacher asked students to use their word in a sentence. Over time, the task becomes more complicated. For example, the teacher asked students to complete the following generative sentences (Edgar's responses are in the right column):

1st position	HAVE	Have you seen my hair?
2nd position	THEY'RE	If they're late, they will have to stay after school.
4th position	THEIR	I don't believe their story.
Last position	THERE	I don't even want to go there.

Power Writing

Power writing is a fluency activity that requires students to write as many words as they can on a topic as fast as they can. In addition to increasing writing fluency, power writing provides students with self-created material to revise. As Fearn and Farnan (2001) suggest, power writing is "a structured free-write where the objective is quantity alone" (p. 501). The instruction for power writing is very simple. The teacher provides students with a topic or choice of topics based on class activities. Students are given one minute to write everything that they can on the topic. At the end of the minute, students count the number of words they have written on the topic. This sequence is repeated two more times, and students record their best score on a personal chart. Besides building fluency and providing students with material to revise, power writing requires that students get to writing right away. This daily procedure is in stark contrast to the often-observed adolescent writing strategy of procrastinating.

In many classes, students are assigned to power writing groups. These groups are heterogeneous—a mix of stronger and emerging writers. Each day, one randomly selected group can be assigned to take their power writing home and return the following day with an edited form. Then the members of the group review these edited versions, revise them as needed, and submit them to the teacher. This procedure is useful for a variety of reasons. First, most teachers cannot read 24 to 36 papers per class per day. However, reading five papers per day per class is manageable. In addition, students are more likely to take the power writing activity seriously if they never know which day they will be asked to provide an edited version to the teacher.

In terms of Edgar's development, he started the term averaging 17 words per minute. By the end of the term, he could consistently write more than 40 words per minute. His personal best was 61 words in a minute. Toward the end of the term, he wrote the following:

> Memorial Day is more than a day off school. It is a day for me to think about war and to remember the poeple I miss the moust. I wonder what other poeple think about on the day we shud remember. I hope they [timer rings]

Although there are still errors in his writing, Edgar now has his thoughts down on paper and he has something to edit.

Independent Writing

Independent writing is the goal of all writing instruction. However, we must remember that students who require significant amounts of scaffolding are likely to revert to old writing habits when they are given open-ended prompts. As Carol Jago (2002) notes, "teachers must strike a balance between giving students too much and too little choice in writing prompts" (p. 15). Teaching students how to analyze the prompt in advance of responding is an important step in a gradual release model.

In the final weeks of the class, Edgar was asked to write a reflection on his semester. This independent writing prompt required that he review his writer's notebook, consider the progress he made over the term, and identify what he needed to do to further improve his writing. He titled his piece "I Didn't Know I Could Write" and commented on how he "had ideas but didn't know how to write them all." He also indicated that he "couldn't write fast enough to get my idea before it was gone." By the end of the term, it was clear that Edgar was on his way to becoming a writer and thinker. Although he will require instructional interventions to continue to improve and extend his writing, his English teachers are ready to provide him that support.

"What Does It Mean, Persuade?"—Genre Instruction

In addition to a focus on writing development, students need instruction in specific genres of writing (Dickson, DeGraff, & Foard, 2002; Fearn & Farnan, 2001). Although this is most often accomplished in English classrooms, more and more schools are taking a schoolwide approach to writing and requiring teachers in specific content areas to focus on specific genres of writing. For example, the science department may take responsibility for teaching "reports of information," while the social studies department may assume the task of teaching "persuasive writing."

We learned a lot about the importance of genre instruction from Raquel Ramirez-Gomez, a 10th grader who speaks both English and Spanish at home. She lives with her sister, who is a single mother of two infants. Her parents, who have yet to gain permission to enter the United States, live in a remote village in Mexico and do not have access to telephones or other modes of communication.

In addition to the developmental writing instruction described in Edgar's case, Raquel's teachers also focused on specific genres in which she needed to learn to write. They used samples of text, both informational and fictional, to scaffold their students' understanding of the various genres and text structures.

Raquel's teachers noted that students needed two additional components of instruction to ensure that they understood the requirements of writing in different genres. First, they required daily practice expanding sentences from simple to complex within specific genres (Cudd & Roberts, 1993/1994; Sedgwick, 1989). For example, students needed to expand their use of descriptive words when writing in response to literature. Similarly, students needed to embed facts into their informational reports. Teachers scaffolded the daily practice by modeling (within the context of whole-class lessons) how to identify and incorporate elements of the focal genre and by providing small-group guided practice and then individual homework.

Second, the teachers provided beginning-of-year paragraph practice. Although students know that there is no hard-and-fast rule about the size or length of a paragraph, they are introduced to the basic idea that paragraphs have topic sentences and supporting details (Baines, Baines, Kunkel, & Stanley, 1999; Morris, 1993; Speer, 1995). The teachers start the year by composing paragraphs, in specific genres, with the whole class. They introduce and reinforce the idea that a paragraph has an opening sentence, a number of sentences with details, and then a closing sentence. Over time, the teacher provides instruction on the composition of cohesive and coherent paragraphs in small groups. As groups complete their assigned genre-based paragraphs, the writing sample is provided to another group, which then analyzes the paragraph to determine the main idea and the supporting details. Students practice writing paragraphs within particular genres by focusing on topics that are relevant to them: a persuasive essay about the dress code, a descriptive piece about an ideal living area, a letter to the principal about an important issue such as school lunch or the tardy policy, and a response to a short story.

Over time, students internalize variations of paragraphs as they translate their ideas into writing. At one point, Raquel was asked to write a persuasive letter about the U.S. immigration policy; later in this unit, Raquel wrote a personal narrative about her experience with immigration; she then examined her narrative and created a found poem. A found poem requires that a writer use existing text to create a free-verse poem. Raquel's poem read,

Time has to pass
and
I had to say good-bye.
I felt careless about leaving
everything
I was decisive, no impediments
The decision was made
I knew I was going to come back
I wish I said "I love you, dad"
Mom, please don't cry
She knew that I wasn't coming back.

"She Knows How to Tell Me"—The Power of Peer Feedback

Deasia Maye is an African American 10th grader who embodies what we have learned from Jay Simmons (2003), namely, that students must be taught how to respond to one another's papers. We know that peer feedback on writing is an important component of the writing workshop (e.g., Calkins, 1994). We also know, as Simmons does, that students are more likely to use global praise and not provide helpful feedback unless they are taught to do so. In Figure 8.2, we present Simmons's suggestions for teaching students to respond to the writing of their peers.

You'll note that Simmons provides specific instructions for the teacher and the students in developing the ability to provide peer feedback. As we used these techniques with the students in our classrooms, Deasia made clear why peer response succeeds: Peers listen to one another. In the following excerpt from a teacher–student discussion, notice how Deasia responds to a peer's offer to help her revise:

Teacher: Have you all read you partners' papers?

Students: Yeah.

Teacher: So, what do you think about the characters in *Always Running* [LA Vida Loca, Gang Days in L.A. (Rodriguez, 1993)]. What did your partners think about your papers?

Figure 8.2   Techniques to Teach Peer Responses

Technique	What the Teacher Does	What Students Do
Share your writing	Share a piece of writing and ask for responses	Offer comments on the teacher's writing
Clarify evaluation versus response	Show that evaluation is a product, while response is to the writer	Understand that response is personable and helpful
Model specific praise	Show how you tell a writer what you like as a reader	Learn that "cheerleading" is too general to be helpful
Model understanding	Restate the meaning of the piece	Learn that reflecting back the piece to the writer is helpful
Model questions	Create questions about what you don't understand	Learn that questions help the writer clarify his or her purpose
Model suggestions	Clarify writing techniques	Appreciate that a responder leaves a writer knowing what to do next
Comment review	Read the comments of peers to writers	Get teacher feedback on comments

Adapted from Simmons, J. (2003). Responders are taught, not born. *Journal of Adolescent & Adult Literacy, 46,* 684–693.

Shannell: My paper's good. I described them all right.

Deasia: Yeah, I got it. These were some bad folk. They be all in your face.

Teacher: Did you write that in your paper? I mean did you describe how really bad it was?

Deasia: Yeah.

Teacher: I see that you started your paper talking about the gangs here in San Diego. Did you think about maybe an opening paragraph about the impact of gangs?

Deasia: That could work.

Shannell: Ya know, I think she means that you could talk about some gang stuff they do and how they try to get you to jump in and when you do, you get in trouble for doin' in initiation.

Deasia: Ohh, yeah, like the thing with Anthony. Yeah.

Teacher: And how about the end?

Shannell: Deasia's paper don't really end yet. I can help her at our table.

Deasia: Yeah, she knows how to tell me.

Deasia understands that she writes for different audiences and for different purposes. But what she taught us was that she also knows that peer feedback works because students understand one another. A trusted peer who has been taught to respond can provide feedback in ways that are understood and useful. In addition, peer feedback ensures that the teacher can serve as a guide and facilitator and have the time to meet with each individual and small group as they write.

"Writing Is Everywhere"—Writing to Learn in Content Area Classrooms

Although Edgar, Raquel, and Deasia learned a good deal from the various instructional strategies we introduced, their successes would have been limited if they were not provided with opportunities to write to learn. (For a full discussion of the connections between writing and learning, see Armbruster, McCarthey, & Cummins in this volume.) Despite the evidence that writing supports students' acquisition of content knowledge, in some secondary school classrooms, many students go days without being asked to write. Although our data are only anecdotal, we have spent extensive amounts of time moving in and out of secondary school classrooms, and our observations bring to mind Nell Duke's (2000) study of nonfiction reading. Duke reported that first-grade students spend less than 3.6 minutes per day reading nonfiction texts. We suspect that systematic examination would find that many secondary school students spend just as little time writing. For some students, the absence of such opportunities may be the difference between academic success and failure. We were determined to make secondary school classes at Hoover different from what we believe to be the norm. Let's meet another student and examine the opportunities he has to write in his classes.

Abdurashid Ali, a senior at Hoover High School, noted that "writing is everywhere. All of my teachers have me write, almost every day." Abdurashid and some of his family fled Ethiopia when he was 8 years old. He lived in a Kenyan refugee camp with no formal schooling for four years before being granted permission to immigrate into the United States. He arrived at Hoover speaking four languages—Oromo, Amharic, Swahili, and Somali. Following him during a typical day reveals the number of opportunities he has to write and to receive feedback on his writing each day. Hoover High School operates on a block schedule, meaning that students attend four 90-minute classes per day. These classes each last a term, September to January or February to June.

Abdurashid, a student who was not in school for four years and who did not speak any English upon his arrival during the ninth grade, begins his day as a senior in Advanced Placement (AP) Physics. Upon entering the room, he notices a prompt on the board, which reads, "There are two mechanisms by which sunlight is scattered by clouds. Explain the difference between Rayleigh and Mie scattering." Because this is a daily occurrence in his classroom, Abdurashid begins to respond to the writing prompt in his journal. After approximately four minutes, the physics teacher invites the class to discuss their responses to the daily "bellwork" writing prompt from the board. Following the class discussion, the teacher begins a lecture. Abdurashid automatically turns the page in his journal, ready to take notes. He creates a Cornell note page (Figure 8.3) and begins taking notes. The class also watches a short video and Abdurashid takes notes during this activity as well. As the class ends, students are presented with another writing

Figure 8.3   **Sample Cornell Note Page**

Name:_____ Subject: _____ Date: _____

Key Points | Notes

Summary

prompt, this one an exit slip, which reads, "Indicate which of the two forms of sunlight scattering is responsible for the blue skies we often see in San Diego." Abdurashid responds to this prompt in his physics journal before leaving class.

During second period, Abdurashid has an AP English class. As might be expected, there is a significant amount of writing in this class. Students regularly complete a number of responses to literature prompts in which they analyze characters, plots, themes, and settings. They explore, through writing, their thinking about literature and prepare for the AP exam. On the particular day in question, Abdurashid enters the classroom to find a number of essay questions on the board based on the class novel, Voltaire's *Candide* (1759/1930). Each member of the class selects one prompt to respond to. As they finish, students meet with a peer to discuss their responses, be challenged on their thinking, and revise their papers.

Third period at Hoover is 20 minutes longer than all of the other classes. The first 20 minutes are used for silent sustained reading (SSR), as will be discussed in the section that follows. Following the 20-minute independent reading session, Abdurashid's Government and Economics teacher begins discussing an upcoming assignment. She asks students to briefly describe, in writing, how they spend their time. Abdurashid writes for about three minutes about going to school, studying, sleeping, playing sports, and eating. As they finish writing, the teacher distributes a short article from *Newsweek* about the ways in which teens spend their time. They read the article and discuss it in groups of four using reciprocal teaching (Oczkus, 2003; Palincsar, 1987), taking turns summarizing, questioning, clarifying, and predicting. As they finish the article, the teacher introduces the assignment, which involves keeping a minute-by-minute log for seven days and then writing an analysis of how time was spent. The opening two paragraphs of Abdurashid's paper can be found in Figure 8.4.

Abdurashid's fourth and final class of the day is Algebra II. As he enters the room, following lunch, he sees a "do now" on the overhead projector. A "do now" in math (a specific type of bellwork) requires that students solve a familiar math problem and write out in words how the problem is solved. After about five minutes, the teacher asks for volunteers to solve the problem and to discuss how the solution was obtained. He then introduces new material while students take notes. Again, Abdurashid uses a Cornell note-taking system to record the information being presented. Approximately 25 minutes later, the class is provided with a number of problems to solve while the teacher walks around speaking with individual students. Students are encouraged to work in groups and to discuss their solutions and approaches to solving the problems. The class ends with a homework assignment of 25 problems.

Based on this typical day of 360 minutes of class time (not including the 20 minutes of silent reading), Abdurashid spent 53 minutes (15%) of the day actively writing by responding to prompts, 76 minutes (21%) actively writing by taking notes, and another 20 minutes (5%) writing by completing math problems. In all,

Figure 8.4   Opening Paragraphs of Abdurashid's "Time Budget" Paper in Economics

Over seven days, I maintained a record of how I spent my time. This was a very important project for me as I was moving out of my father's house at the time and into my own apartment. It was good for me to have to analyze how I spent time, especially since I would have a lot less structure to my time when I lived in my own apartment. The assignment was given at the perfect time for me to think about budgeting my time to get my work done. If I were writing a newspaper article about this project, I would title it, "Teen Spends Too Much Time on Homework!"

However, this is not a newspaper article, it is a report of information and a reaction to the data and some additional readings. I will first discuss my reaction to the data I collected then I will comment on three things that I noticed when I first saw the data presented in a pie chart. I will conclude this paper by reacting to the additional readings provided in the information packet.

41% of Abdurashid's day involved him holding a writing instrument and writing for a variety of reasons and audiences. It's no wonder he says, "Writing is everywhere!" (And perhaps it is no wonder, then, given what we know about the connections between writing and learning, that Abdurashid will attend the University of California at San Diego and major in premedicine.)

We know that writing across the curriculum is an important component of the success at Hoover High School, and the evidence from highly successful schools bears this out (Reeves, 2000). As such, we have collected some of the writing to learn prompts that we have observed to be particularly effective across content area subjects (Frey & Fisher, in press). They include the following prompts:

- Bellwork—One of the most basic forms of writing-to-learn prompts is bellwork. These are writing prompts posted on the board each day in anticipation of the arrival of students who are instructed to begin writing as soon as they are settled into their seats.

- Entry and Exit Slips—An entry slip is a writing-to-learn prompt that must be completed before the next class, whereas an exit slip is a writing-to-learn prompt that must be completed before leaving the class. These prompts typically require students to use material from the lesson in responding.

- Crystal Ball—This prompt allows students to make predictions by writing what might come next. The crystal ball prompt is useful in developing comprehension because students must use the information already provided to make their predictions.

- Yesterday's News—This prompt requires that students summarize what has already happened. Like the crystal ball prompt, it is useful in developing comprehension because students must synthesize what they know and present it in writing.

- Found Poems—The found poem writing prompt usually follows a reading activity. Working in groups or individually, students select key words and phrases from their readings to create a free verse poem that provides readers with information about the larger reading. These words and phrases can be rearranged to maintain a poetic flow, but only those that appear in the text may be used.

- Golden Lines—This writing-to-learn prompt provides students with an opportunity to explore their thinking in response to a specific line from a text. In some cases, the teacher selects the line and asks all of the students to respond to the same line. In other cases, students each select their own lines and explore their understandings and confusions.

- RAFT—A creative means for assessing students' literal and inferential understanding is through the use of a writing-to-learn prompt called RAFT (Santa & Havens, 1995). These letters form a mnemonic to shape a student's written response to text:

  Role—the role of the writer

  Audience—to whom are you writing?

  Format—the form of writing (letter, poem, telegram, essay, etc.)

  Topic—the subject of the piece

For example, students in a world history class may be asked to respond to the following:

R—a sailor in Hawaii, December 7, 1941
A—people on the mainland
F—e-mail
T—we've been attacked!

(For additional discussion of RAFT, see Flood, Lapp, & Ranck-Buhr in this volume, who discuss its use in middle school classrooms.)

Naturally, there are many more writing-to-learn prompts that teachers can use (e.g., Hand & Prain, 2002; McIntosh & Draper, 2001). Regardless of the prompt, students must write across the curriculum and receive feedback from all of their teachers about their writing (Aulls, 2003; Fisher & Frey, 2004).

"I Remember Reading This Book"—The Importance of Wide Reading

Although we know that providing students with time to read materials of their choice during the school day is considered by some to lack an empirically strong research base (e.g., Shanahan, 2004), we have learned from our students that this reading time provides them with fodder for their writing. We agree with Ivey and Broaddus (2001) that "just plain reading" matters.

Although we have many examples of students' use of ideas and rhetorical structures from literature (e.g., Frey & Fisher, 2004; Johnson, 2002), a recent example struck us as especially significant. Khoi Le is an outstanding student who was salutatorian of his class and will attend San Diego State University as a business major. He based his commencement address (Figure 8.5) on a book he read during SSR at Hoover High. Khoi's family immigrated from Vietnam when he was 3 years old. He reads, writes, and speaks English and Vietnamese. When asked, he said that he spent a lot of time thinking about what to say to his friends who were graduating with him that day. As he was discussing his speech with a teacher, she asked him if there was a book that he really connected with. Khoi thought for a moment and said, "Yeah, I remember reading this book during 3R [the SSR period] in freshman year." At that point, he knew exactly what he wanted to say and sat down to write his speech. A book that he picked up during his freshman year for silent reading, *The Giver* (Lowry, 1993), had such an impact on him that he chose to relate the idea from this book to his peers.

It is clear that Khoi would have written and given a fine commencement speech regardless of his opportunity to read this particular book during school hours; nonetheless, the positive consequence of a period of the school day devoted to students' self-selected reading cannot be denied. Khoi and his peers have taught us that providing time to read during the school day is an important factor in their writing. As with any other school-day routines, there are both effective and ineffective ways to implement SSR. Figure 8.6 provides an overview of the factors that Janice Pilgreen (2000) identified as critical in the success of SSR initiatives.

Figure 8.5   Graduation Speech

Khoi Le, Hoover Class of 2004

Welcome, family, friends, faculty, administrators, and honored guests, on behalf of the class of 2004, I thank you for joining us on this special day as we depart from our childhood and enter into adulthood. At this time, I want to compare our journey with the experiences of Jonas from a piece of valued literature titled *The Giver*, by Lois Lowry.

Some of us are familiar with *The Giver* because we've read it during middle school or high school. But for those of you, who are not familiar with this book, I would like to take a brief moment in explaining the key concepts and lessons that unfold in *The Giver*.

The Giver is about a society with no color; meaning everyone is black and white. The citizens of this society live in a sheltered world where everything is plain and simple. They have no choices; therefore they cannot take risks. However, there are consequences to this sameness.

This book illustrates one person, Jonas, whose triumph was to search for change and self-refinement. He finds the courage through memories passed onto him by a man known as "The Giver."

As the class of 2004 embarks into the future, we leave behind our pains and our fears. With the fond "memories" of our high school experiences, we will be granted opportunities to change for the better. As we move from our childhood and proceed on this bright path to adulthood we will find our contribution and place in society.

Referring back to *The Giver*, I found it intriguing how a society which lives behind walls can find protection and bliss. In many aspects, Hoover is like the society described in *The Giver*. Behind the walls of Hoover, we are protected by our friends and our teachers. In contrast to that, Hoover has one thing that the society in *The Giver* does not. That is the concept of love. Behind these walls, we have learned to love one another. We have learned to love our teachers, and most importantly, we have learned to love ourselves.

Behind these walls, we have watched one another grow. We've helped one another plant the seeds of wisdom in ourselves, and in the souls of others. The time for change has arrived. It is time to breach these walls of love, and protection just as Jonas did in order to seek out the true colors of life. For better or for worse change is inevitable; let us use the knowledge that we have acquired at Hoover to guide us towards an ever changing future.

These past four years have been an emotional rollercoaster with many twists and turns. Nevertheless, through all the fiery loops and corkscrews, we prevailed. The long epic ride has granted us memories behind every turn, and every twist. There are some memories that are more pleasant than others. However, all these memories contributed to our unforgettable experience. We are all receivers and givers of memories. Just like Jonas, we are absorbing the memories that shape our character. One day, we will be able to turn into the givers and pass down our memories to the next generation. There's no distinction between giving and receiving memories because if we lack the ability to receive, we cannot give. When I look at these bright faces today, I see a world filled with memorable memories, and a world filled with hope.

Let hope guide our way to seek for our place and contribution in society. Most importantly, let hope allow us to find personal freedom. In *The Giver*, Jonas' sense of hope lies in the life of Baby Gabriel; Gabriel portrays the purity of life. So let me ask you the Class of 2004, what is your hope? How do we find our place in society? Is it by obtaining a rank or living by a reputation or status? No. Finding our place simply means finding our

(continued)

Figure 8.5   Graduation Speech (continued)

state of happiness. Once we have achieved happiness, then and only then will we find personal freedom. As quoted from the book, "There is an elsewhere where we came and an elsewhere to where we are going." It is our choice to determine what that "elsewhere" means to us. Thank You.

Before I leave the podium, I would like to congratulate the class of 2004 for all your hard work and achievements. I would like to thank everybody in the audience again. Thank you parents, teachers, mentors, administrators, and counselors. Without you, we wouldn't be sitting here today. Thank you for sharing with us this defining moment in our lives.

Figure 8.6   Factors for a Successful Silent Sustained Reading (SSR) Program

1. **Access**. This principle deals with getting reading materials into the hands of students, which Pilgreen sees as the responsibility of the teachers and the schools. This involves more than simply telling students they must bring something to read.

2. **Appeal**. This factor deals with student interests, the variety and range of materials we offer to our students, and yes, even making sure that the materials offered are "classroom appropriate."

3. **Environment**. This has to do with physical comfort, alternatives to the traditional classroom setting, and the possibilities of reading as a social interactive activity for those students for whom reading in silence is not conducive to the freedom associated with SSR.

4. **Encouragement**. This includes modeling, discussions, and postreading opportunities for sharing, and enlisting parent support and involvement.

5. **Staff training**. Providing training in SSR, answering organizational and how-to questions, and encouraging all teachers to provide a specific set daily time for SSR are discussed.

6. **Nonaccountability**. While students are not required to complete the usual types of formal assessment, such as book reports or tests of content knowledge, SSR practices do provide for informal accountability through opportunities for sharing in discussion, writing, or other formats.

7. **Follow-up activities**. SSR, Pilgreen says, needs to provide ways for students to "sustain their excitement about the books they have read" (2000, p. 16). Activities and shared experiences are very effective in encouraging further voluntary reading.

8. **Distributed time to read**. Habits—including the habit of reading—are formed through sustained efforts over time. Occasional lengthy periods of time set aside for free reading are not as powerful as shorter periods of 15 to 20 minutes at least twice a week.

From Miller, H.M. (2002). [Review of the book *The SSR handbook: How to organize and manage a sustained silent reading program* by Janice Pilgreen]. *Journal of Adolescent & Adult Literacy, 45,* 434–435.

Consensus Scoring of Common Writing Prompts

In addition to all of the instructional approaches and systems we know must be in place for adolescents to become skilled writers and thinkers, there should be a schoolwide procedure in place to ensure that teachers regularly calibrate or fine-tune their writing instruction. In chapter 7 of this book, James Flood, Diane Lapp, and Wendy Ranck-Buhr describe their work with middle school teachers using the process of consensus scoring and the 9 Essential Components Model (see also Fisher, Lapp, & Flood, 2005). We expand on that discussion here, this time within the context of secondary school teachers. Consensus scoring is described elsewhere as collaborative analysis of student work (e.g., Langer, Colton, & Goff, 2003).

At Hoover High, the process begins with teachers meeting in course-alike groups (e.g., English I, Chemistry, World History). Within these groups, they identify key standards and develop a pacing guide. As part of the pacing guide, they outline the materials they need. In addition, they develop a common assessment. This assessment is given to all students enrolled in a course regardless of the teacher. In other words, all students who are enrolled in a biology class take the same common assessment. This can be in addition to any assessments that the teacher uses for planning instruction or grading. In this case, we are focused on writing. A common writing prompt is identified and given to students; later, teachers meet in groups to analyze the results. The first step they take during the consensus scoring meeting is to rate each writing sample using the rubric developed in advance. They then examine each item on the rubric and complete an item analysis. They ask themselves, "On which items or components are our students doing well and where do they need to grow?" In course-alike groups, they analyze the results and discuss implications. They then select a sample paper for each grade on the rubric using a 4-point scale similar to the one provided by the California Department of Education. Thus, we select four sample papers to represent the range of learning performances among students. The course-alike group studies the sample papers and discusses each in turn. They ask themselves, "What instruction does this student need to advance to the next level?"

It is this conversation, focused on future instruction, that we find most helpful. Teachers share ideas with one another and discuss their favorite approaches to improving the outcomes for students. As teachers notice commonalities among groups of students, they discuss the need to reteach specific components, the need to revise the pacing guide, or the need to revise the assessment.

Conclusion

It takes the whole school to ensure that adolescents become independent writers and thinkers. As teachers in a secondary school, we perceive our first role to be to ensure that our students develop the writing and thinking skills they need. However, our work does not end there. We must also help our colleagues see that writing across the curriculum is not only a powerful way to ensure that students increase their knowledge of writing but also a way for them to refine their thinking skills and deepen their content knowledge. Further, we must ensure that the students in our schools have the opportunity to read widely, both at school and at home. This may mean that we must advocate for time during the school day in which students can "just read." It may also mean that we have to provide students access to books and other reading materials that they can take home to read. Finally, we must ensure that we meet regularly with our colleagues to review student writing samples. The conversations we have with our colleagues about students and their writing and thinking are powerful ways of ensuring that students are being taught to write. Although the ultimate goal is to create independent readers and writers, we have learned that an interdependent process of writing instruction and assessment across grade levels and content areas is required to achieve this objective.

REFERENCES

Aulls, M.W. (2003). The influence of a reading and writing curriculum on transfer learning across subjects and grades. *Reading Psychology, 24*(2), 177-215.

Baines, L., Baines, C., Kunkel, A., & Stanley, G.K. (1999). Losing the product in the process. *English Journal, 88*(5) 67-72.

Brozo, W.G., & Hargis, C.H. (2003). Taking seriously the idea of reform: One high school's efforts to make reading more responsive to all students. *Journal of Adolescent & Adult Literacy, 47*, 14-23.

Calkins, L.M. (1994). *The art of teaching writing* (New ed.). Portsmouth, NH: Heinemann.

Callella, T., & Jordano, K. (2002). *Interactive writing: Students and teachers 'sharing the pen' to create meaningful text*. Huntington Beach, CA: Creative Teaching Press.

Clay, M.M. (2001). *Change over time in children's literacy development*. Portsmouth, NH: Heinemann.

Cudd, E.T., & Roberts, L.L. (1993/1994). A scaffolding technique to develop sentence sense and vocabulary. *The Reading Teacher, 47*, 346-349.

Dickson, R., DeGraff, J., & Foard, M. (2002). Learning about self and others through multigenre research projects. *English Journal, 92*(2), 82-90.

Dixon, C.N., & Nessel, D. (1983). *Language experience approach to reading (and writing): Language-experience reading for second language learners*. Hayward, CA: Alemany.

Duke, N.K. (2000). 3.6 minutes per day: The scarcity of informational texts in first grade. *Reading Research Quarterly, 35*, 202-224.

Duke, N.K., & Pearson, P.D. (2004). Effective practices for developing reading comprehension. In A.E. Farstrup & S.J. Samuels (Eds.), *What research has to say about reading instruction* (3rd ed., pp. 205-242). Newark, DE: International Reading Association.

Fearn, L., & Farnan, N. (2001). *Interactions: Teaching writing and the language arts*. New York: Houghton Mifflin.

Fisher, D. (2001). "We're moving on up": Creating a schoolwide literacy effort in an urban high school. *Journal of Adolescent & Adult Literacy, 45*(2), 92-101.

Fisher, D., & Drake, L. (1999). Connecting geometry to students' experiences. In S. Totten, C. Johnson, L.R. Morrow, & T. Sills-Briegel (Eds.), *Practicing what we preach: Preparing middle level educators* (pp. 128-131). New York: Falmer.

Fisher, D., & Frey, N. (2002). Accelerating achievement for adolescent English language learners: Interactive writing grows up. *California English, 7*(4), 24-25.

Fisher, D., & Frey, N. (2003). Writing instruction for struggling adolescent readers: A gradual release model. *Journal of Adolescent & Adult Literacy, 46*, 396-405.

Fisher, D., & Frey, N. (2004). *Improving adolescent literacy: Strategies at work*. Upper Saddle River, NJ: Merrill Prentice Hall.

Fisher, D., Frey, N., & Williams, D. (2002). Seven literacy strategies that work. *Educational Leadership, 60*(3), 70-73.

Fisher, D., Lapp, D., & Flood, J. (2005). Consensus scoring and peer planning: Meeting literacy accountability demands one school at a time. *The Reading Teacher, 58*, 656-666.

Frey, N., & Fisher, D. (2004). Using graphic novels, anime, and the Internet in an urban high school. *English Journal, 93*(3), 19-25.

Frey, N., & Fisher, D. (in press). Prompting understanding: Ten things every teacher should know about writing to learn. In V. Miholic (Ed.), *Strategies for writers and teachers of writing*.

Hand, B., & Prain, V. (2002). Teachers implementing writing-to-learn strategies in junior secondary science: A case study. *Science Education, 86*(6), 737-755.

Ivey, G., & Broaddus, K. (2001). "Just plain reading": A survey of what makes students want to read in middle school classrooms. *Reading Research Quarterly, 36*, 350-377.

Jago, C. (2002). *Cohesive writing: Why concept is not enough.* Portsmouth, NH: Heinemann.

Johnson, V. (2002). Urban adolescents jump into young adult literature. *Michigan Reading Journal, 35*(1), 12-16.

Langer, G.M., Colton, A.B., & Goff, L.S. (2003). *Collaborative analysis of student work: Improving teaching and learning.* Alexandria, VA: Association for Supervision and Curriculum Development.

Langer, J.A. (2001). Beating the odds: Teaching middle and high school students to read and write well. *American Educational Research Journal, 38*(4), 837-880.

MacGinitie, W.H., MacGinitie, R.K., Maria, K., & Dreyer, L.G. (2000). *Gates-MacGinitie reading tests* (4th ed.). Itasca, IL: Riverside.

McCarrier, A., Pinnell, G.S., & Fountas, I.C. (2000). *Interactive writing: How language and literacy come together, K-2.* Portsmouth, NH: Heinemann.

McIntosh, M.E., & Draper, R.J. (2001). Using learning logs in mathematics: Writing to learn. *Mathematics Teacher, 94*(7), 554-557.

Miller, H.M. (2002). Book review: The SSR handbook. *Journal of Adolescent & Adult Literacy, 45,* 434-435.

Moore, D.W., Bean, T.W., Birdyshaw, D., & Rycik, J.A. (1999). *Adolescent literacy: A position statement.* Newark, DE: International Reading Association. Retrieved August 10, 2004, from http://www.reading.org/resources/issues/positions_adolescent.html

Moretti, C. (1996). *Literary creativity with art: A resource teacher project.* La Mesa, CA: Grossmont Union High School District.

Morris, R. (1993). Sentence strips. *Writing Notebook: Visions for Learning, 11*(1), 35-38.

Oczkus, L.D. (2003). *Reciprocal teaching at work: Strategies for improving reading comprehension.* Newark, DE: International Reading Association.

Palincsar, A.S. (1987). Reciprocal teaching: Can student discussion boost comprehension? *Instructor, 96*(5), 56-58, 60.

Pearson, P.D., & Gallagher, M.C. (1983). The instruction of reading comprehension. *Contemporary Educational Psychology, 8*(3), 317-344.

Pilgreen, J. (2000). *The SSR handbook: How to organize and manage a sustained silent reading program.* Portsmouth, NH: Boynton/Cook.

Reeves, D.B. (2000). *Accountability in action: A blueprint for learning organizations.* Denver, CO: Advanced Learning Press.

Ruddell, M.R. (2005). *Teaching content reading and writing* (4th ed.). Hoboken, NJ: Wiley.

Santa, C., & Havens, L. (1995). *Creating Independence through Student-owned Strategies: Project CRISS.* Dubuque, IA: Kendall-Hunt.

Sedgwick, E. (1989). Alternatives to teaching formal, analytical grammar. *Journal of Developmental Education, 12*(3), 8-10, 12, 14, 20.

Shanahan, T. (2004). Improving reading achievement in secondary schools: Structures and reforms. In D.S. Strickland & D.E. Alvermann (Eds.), *Bridging the literacy achievement gap grades 4-12* (pp. 43-55). New York: Teachers College Press.

Simmons, J. (2003). Responders are taught, not born. *Journal of Adolescent & Adult Literacy, 46,* 684-693.

Speer, T. (1995). Re-conceiving the five-paragraph essay in an era of uncertainty. *Teaching English in the Two-Year College, 22*(1), 21-29.

LITERATURE CITED

Ashton-Warner, S. (1959). *Spinster, a novel.* New York: Simon & Schuster.

Lowry, L. (1993). *The giver.* New York: Bantam Doubleday Dell Books for Young Readers.

Rodriguez, L.J. (1993). *Always running: LA Vida Loca, Gang Days in L.A.* East Haven, CT: Curbstone Press.

Viorst, J. (1981). *If I were in charge of the world and other worries: Poems for children and their parents.* New York: Aladdin.

Voltaire. (1930). *Candide.* New York: Three Sirens Press. (Original work published 1759)

Chapter 9

Writing and Response in the Secondary School

Richard Beach, Tom Friedrich, and David J. Williams

> Response to writing is often difficult and tense. For the teacher, it is the
> schizophrenia of roles—now the helpful facilitator, hovering next to the writers
> to lend guidance and support, and now the authority, passing critical judgment
> on the writer's work; at one moment the intellectual peer, giving "reader-based"
> feedback...and at the next, the imposer of criteria, the gatekeeper of textual
> standards. —Christopher Anson (1989, p. 2)

Response, author and scholar Christopher Anson (1989) reminds us, is
multiple: It is given by teachers as an invitation to students to participate
more fully in their education, refining the work they do not only as
writers but also as readers—of their own texts and literary ones. This chapter
focuses on two different meanings for response—using writing to foster literary
response and using a response-based pedagogy to help students learn to respond
to their own and others' writing. By helping students learn to use writing to
respond in specific, critical ways to literary texts, teachers are also helping them
learn to reflect on their own and others' texts in a writing classroom.

In this chapter, we argue that instruction in ways of responding to literature
transfers over to how students respond to their own and their peers' writing,
thereby integrating reading and writing instruction. We will illustrate this
integration of response pedagogy in reading and writing with examples from the
high school literature classes of David Williams, a coauthor of this chapter and a
veteran English teacher at Hopkins High School of the Hopkins, Minnesota, School
District. As we will illustrate in this chapter, David strongly believes in the value of
combining reading and writing instruction, and he believes that in learning ways of
responding to texts, students also learn to respond to their own texts.

Reader-Response Theories: How Readers Construct Text Meaning

Reader-response theory emerged in the 1960s and 1970s as a reaction to the New
Critics who advocated a narrow focus on the text to the exclusion of the reader's

experience of that text (Rosenblatt, 1995; Tompkins, 1980). Since that period, a range of different theories of response to literature have been put forth, theories that now go beyond the original focus on the transaction between the reader and the text that prevailed in the 1970s and 1980s (Beach, 1993; Galda & Beach, 2001; Sumara, 2002). Those who support these theories assert that meanings do not reside "in" a text but are constructed by readers according to the particular stances, perspectives, agendas, or purposes they adopt as members of a community of literary learners. For example, Jeffrey Wilhelm (1996) defines three dimensions of response: the "evocative dimension," in which readers first construct the story world by relating to characters, showing interest in their actions; the "connective dimension," in which readers connect the story world with their own lives; and the "reflective dimension," in which readers consider the text's significance and then evaluate the author and self as reader.

Calling for the need to reexamine notions of experience employed in reader-response theory, Mark Faust (2000) notes that teachers who adhere to reader-response approaches often experience a double bind. On the one hand, they promote the value of students' own autobiographical experiences, while on the other, they require students to justify their responses by citing textual authority. The familiar teacher statement—"Students can respond in any way they wish as long as they back up their point of view with evidence from the text"—illustrates this bind. This stance assumes that a valid interpretation is based on meaning "in" the text as an autonomous entity distinct from the experience with the text.

To resolve this split, Faust (2000) turned to John Dewey's (1934) notion of an aesthetic experience, an idea that influenced Louise Rosenblatt's (1995) theory of response. Text and reader interpenetrate with the "transformation of evocations (initial ideas and impressions) into responses (more comprehensive, coherent, and satisfying formations)" (Faust, p. 15); response, then, is a "socially-mediated composing process" (p. 22) in an "experiential space" in which students develop evidence as "the tangible trace of past and present experience, which is the focal point of perception and as such constitutes the content of whatever sense of continuity a person is able to achieve in a particular situation" (p. 25). This sociocultural theory of response goes beyond a focus on subjective transaction between reader and text to highlight how both readers and texts are constituted by larger cultural and institutional forces. Teachers can therefore use students' literary experiences to foster reflection about their responses and stances as shaped by these larger forces, leading to adopting a critical stance on texts and the world.

Using Writing to Foster Literary Response

Writing can be used as one tool for fostering students' development of their responses and their reflection on those responses. Unfortunately, a lot of writing about literature occurs solely as highly prescribed worksheets, book reports, and five-paragraph essays, tasks that do not invite students to extend their thinking through exploration of alternative perspectives leading to adopting a critical stance.

Informal Writing About Literature

In contrast to prescribed formal writing, informal writing is exploratory, tentative, subjective, even contradictory (Burke, 2002; Elbow, 1998). Responding to literature through notes, lists, freewriting, journal entries, maps, or diagrams, students create records of their thoughts, tentative hypotheses, or ideas. Students can review informal writing material to inductively extract certain patterns in their responses for use in creating interpretive arguments. For example, students may use a journal or a reading log in which they react to texts (Anson & Beach, 1995). Using a dual-entry approach, students can write their reactions on one side of a page and then reflect on their reactions on the other side; students may move back and forth between sides, triggering further reactions. Students may also use a dialogue-journal exchange of entries to react to each others' responses, pose questions, or challenge positions, creating dialogic tensions between their own and others' interpretations (Atwell, 1998). When they engage in dialogic writing, they begin to anticipate others' reactions to what they have to say, reflecting Mikhail Bakhtin's (1981) notion of "answerability"—that all utterances anticipate some potential reaction from others. This anticipation invites them to further extend their responses or to formulate counterargument in response to their partners' perspectives.

Teachers can also respond to students' entries by posing questions that model certain heuristics or interpretive strategies or critical approaches (Atwell, 1998). Questions as simple as "I wondered why the character did that?" or as complex as "How were the characters trapped within their own western European ideologies?" can foster students' internalization and application of these ideas, supporting more elaborated interpretations.

Formal Writing About Literature

In contrast to their informal writing, students also write formal essays about literature. In more formal essay writing, students pull together material developed from informal writing to formulate a sustained, systematic analysis or interpretation. In devising formal writing assignments about literature, teachers must not only specify response tasks, but they also need to define specific expectations for their students' responses, including criteria for what constitutes successful response to a text. Students may misread teachers' expectations simply because they do not understand what those expectations are (Sperling & Freedman, 1987). For students to concur with a teacher's evaluative response to their writing and actually make use of that response, they need to understand the teacher's expectations and assessment criteria (Kim, 2004). The clearer the teacher's construction of the purpose, audience, and context, along with criteria for what constitutes successful writing in that context, the less difficulty students are likely to have in interpreting the rhetorical context (Clare, Valdes, Pascal, & Steinberg, 2001). Further, effective teachers apprentice students to a range of roles and stances. For example, in a study of a first-grade teacher, Larson and Maier (2000) found that as the teacher modeled the roles of teacher, author, coauthor, and "overhearer," her students adopted similar roles; in this "participation framework," the social practices of "read to three then me" rule and an Author's Tea led students to sharing their writing with peers. In this context, students began to value themselves as contributing members of an authoring community.

The social context of the classroom can also be used to create tensions and challenges that serve to foster students' exploration of alternative responses to texts. Based on how they are addressed and responded to, students construct themselves as certain kinds of people in the classroom through adopting different, multiple voices. This involves much more than making simple textual changes. Nancy Welch (1998) identifies revision as a performative space where students entertain voices that may differ from certain, more familiar voices. To realize this, Welch advises against "foreshadowing" textual possibilities—that is, shutting down exploration of alternative voices with such comments as "What I hear you saying..." and "What you might consider now...." She recommends instead that students and teachers "sideshadow," a practice she describes as engaging in a "marginal conversation with their writing...[that] disrupts the pattern of student composes-and-teacher-comments...draw[ing]...students into considering the competing discourses, cultural norms, conflicting intentions, and textual ideals that shape and unshape a draft" (p. 382). In a move that also supports the entertainment of multiple voices, Tim Lensmire (2000) proposes that teachers foster students' reflection on their writing by capitalizing on certain "opposing moments" in the classroom. He has students consider why events do not always turn out positively by taking a realistic perspective on social forces shaping characters' and students' lives. Students then explore a range of different, competing voices that reflect the tensions portrayed in a text.

An important aspect of formal writing assignments is the extent to which students have a clear understanding of the criteria used to assess their writing. Rather than importing generic criteria, criteria should be designed with a specific context in mind (Broad, 2003). Some of the following criteria could be used in evaluating students' responses to literature:

Ability to Adopt a "Point-Driven" Stance. One key criterion is the student's ability to adopt a point-driven stance (Hunt & Vipond, 1992), to read a text for its larger symbolic or thematic meanings. This means more than recalling textual information (an information-driven stance) or describing engagement (a story-driven stance). It means that students can recognize that characters' actions or an author's description have certain symbolic meanings (for example, the meaning of the appearance of ghosts in *Hamlet*).

Ability to Develop and Elaborate on Hypotheses or Positions. Another important criterion has to do with the students' ability to develop and elaborate on their hypotheses or positions. Students need to be able to use not only specific material from a text but also other related ideas, theories, texts, and experiences.

Organizational or Genre-Based Criteria. Teachers also evaluate the student's organization and development of a text. Students need to be able to formulate an organizing principle or framework and then signal to the reader their uses of that principle or framework (Flash, 2002).

A Teacher's Support of Written Responses to Literature

In giving assignments to his high school students at Hopkins High School, David Williams provides his students with criteria to use in assessing their writing about Shakespeare's plays. For example, in assignments involving literary analysis of text passages in the plays, he organized criteria according to three areas: content summary, thematic context, and extrapolation and transfer. These three areas refer to what he asked students to do in these essay assignments: summarize the content of the passage; then explain the context of the passage relative to a thematic thread of the play; and then extrapolate an aspect of the human condition and explore and explain a parallel from literature or life. These criteria provided clear expectations for completing this assignment.

Content Summary of Passage

Establish the immediate circumstances of the situation, including the setting, the character who is speaking, and the character(s) to whom the passage is spoken.

Focus only on the content of the passage.

Restate or rephrase the content of the passage using parallel or synonymous vocabulary.

Be specific: line by line, idea by idea, sentence by sentence; cover the entire passage.

Explain metaphors.

Thematic Context

Introduce and briefly explain a theme that ties this passage to other relevant passages or events in the text.

Present at least four thematically relative passages or events from the entire text that logically lead to and follow from this passage and which track the theme throughout the text.

Be specific regarding the passages and events to which you refer; use textual references (act, scene, line) and short quotations.

Interpret how each passage or event is relevant.

Clearly tie passages and events mentioned to the articulated theme.

Extrapolation and Transfer

Choose and name a specific aspect of the human condition distilled from the passage.

Describe, explain, and explore in detail a specific parallel situation from personal experience, current events, historic events, or another text (not from Shakespeare) in which this same aspect of the human condition can be found.

Tie the parallel example back to the passage from the text; clearly show the connections of your parallel situation to the Shakespearian passage.

Specifying these tasks and articulating related criteria provided students with a sense of the ground rules for successfully completing this assignment, ground rules that served as the basis for David's feedback to their writing.

Responding to Students' Writing

We now turn to a discussion of how teachers may draw on theories of response to literature to inform their responses to students' writing. A primary purpose for responding to students' writing is to help them improve the quality of their work through fostering revision. This departs from the traditional formalist assumption that held sway in the 1950s and 1960s that "correcting" students' errors on final drafts supports students' writing growth. Built around the "outline, draft, edit" model (Fitzgerald, 1992), student revisions in this period involved making surface changes and editing (Emig, 1971; Sommers, 1982). With form-based, vague comments such as "wordy," "awkward," or "choppy" prevalent, students' revisions often consisted of editing or tidying up drafts, as opposed to reworking ideas or organization. These findings led to increased attention to teacher feedback that fosters self-assessment and revision (Beach, 1989). In one such study, Mlynarczyk (1996) found that a shift away from comments related to surface matters to open-ended comments about content invited substantive revision.

Despite such findings, research shows a continued focus even today on form instead of content. A meta-analysis of the data-based instructional research on writing (Hillocks, 1986) shows the "outline, draft, edit" model still in place, with an attendant lack of focus on prewriting or revision. Hillocks found that teachers reinforce these practices, concentrating on organization to the exclusion of the ideas addressed in student work.

Other evidence suggests that changing the approach, by itself, may not necessarily lead to improved student writing. For example, Yagelski's (1995) study of a 12th-grade advanced composition class indicated that despite an emphasis on revising multiple drafts and receiving peer feedback, 81.7% of revisions involved surface and stylistic changes, while only 18.3% of revisions involved more substantive structural and content changes. Moreover, Yagelski reported that if students only receive feedback on final drafts, they will not engage in revision of rough drafts. Van Gelderen's (1997) study of fifth- and sixth-grade students' revisions yielded similar findings: Simply making revisions did not improve the quality of their writing.

In yet another study of the importance of the type of feedback teachers provide to students, Patthey-Chavez, Matsumura, and Valdes (2004) examined the influence of 11 teachers' feedback to 64 middle school students' revision of drafts. Most of the teacher feedback focused on editing matters. Analysis indicated that 58% of the students' revisions were surface-level or editing revisions, while 34% were content revisions involving deleting, organizing, adding information, or responding to teacher questions. However, when the quality of the early drafts was held constant, whether the students received content or editing feedback did not predict improvement in the quality of their drafts because many of the revisions simply amounted to adding information requested by the teacher. The few students who made substantive revisions that improved quality received specific guidance as to how to improve their draft (suggestions, for example, to include evidence to support claims or to formulate a summary conclusion).

Findings from these studies point to the need for teachers to provide content-based feedback and to show or direct students on how to use that feedback to improve the quality of their drafts. In some cases, particularly with older students, teachers need to go beyond simply providing "reader-based" feedback and also interrogate or challenge students' taken-for-granted assumptions, a process Amy Lee (2000) contends leads to students "re-envisioning" their beliefs and attitudes.

Providing Helpful Written Feedback

Written feedback, as marginal or final comments, is often perceived by students as less helpful than oral comments in conferences because these written comments often consist of pro forma statements, do not address key issues, focus on editing, are highly inconsistent, and are not clearly understood or are misinterpreted by students (Freedman, 1987; Sommers, 1982; Straub, 1997). Nonetheless, most teachers rely at least some of the time on guiding students' writing through written feedback, so it is important to understand the types of written feedback that contribute to students' ability to improve their writing. Students report that they prefer specific comments that give them advice, provide explanations for feedback, employ open-ended questions, and clarify the meaning of symbols; in addition, it is important to note that students prefer that these written comments be supported by backup conferences during which teachers elaborate on comments (Bardine, Bardine, & Deegan, 2000).

Teachers must also give praise where it is due (Crone-Blevins, 2002), as negative comments may limit students' motivation to improve. But praise must be specific and point to the elements of students' writing that contributed to engaging and comprehensible text (Straub, 1997), as overly general feedback is not useful (Beach, 1989; Burkland & Grimm, 1986). This suggests the value of specific reader-based feedback that describes how teachers processed and engaged with texts (Elbow, 1998; Johnston, 1983). For example, teachers might identify the parts of the text that engaged, entranced, moved, involved, disturbed, intrigued, or puzzled them.

However, some evidence suggests that positive but indirect feedback may not be useful for some students (Hyland & Hyland, 2001). One study of Chinese- and Spanish-speaking students' perceptions of peers' responses indicated that these students actually preferred specific, negative comments that identified problems in their drafts (Nelson & Carson, 1998). In another study, Sweeney (1999) found that college students who received more direct feedback made more improvements than those who received more indirect feedback.

Teachers also need to provide students with explanations that specify why certain sections of an essay succeed or fail. In a study of 172 first-year college students, Straub (1997) found that students wanted explanations about the quality of their writing, particularly comments that reflected a careful reading and provided more specific or elaborated details rather than global or vague comments, such as "just generalize" or "tighten up" the writing.

In formulating their responses, effective teachers take into account a student's zone of proximal development (ZPD) (Vygotsky, 1934/1978) by not overwhelming students with overly sophisticated responses and, at the same time, challenging them in ways that lead to seminal changes. A student's ZPD relative to his or her abilities, experience, and knowledge can be ascertained by examining a student's past writing, yet teachers must recognize the variability of students' writing across different assignments.

Teachers should also attempt to prioritize their comments, selecting those aspects of the text that are especially weak, for example, a consistent lack of supporting evidence for claims (Ferris, 2003). Finally, comments should be targeted to the student's phase or stage of development, providing feedback that focuses on the formulation of ideas during prewriting, on the development and organization of ideas during drafting, and on editing during the editing phase.

Responding to students' journal entries, which are typically more informal pieces of writing, requires a different type of written feedback. In responding to journal entries, teachers may continually encourage students to employ an informal exploratory writing style that entertains alternative perspectives and contradictions, interrogates assumptions, and asks questions of readers to invite their response (Anson & Beach, 1995). Taking the form of dialogic correspondence, teachers' written comments ought to have the feel of a conversation, involving informal yet specific insights and reactions about a particular student's work (Atwell, 1998; Todd, Mills, Palard, & Khamcharoen, 2001). Nancie Atwell (1998), for example, writes letters to her students in which she poses "one good, thoughtful question" in order to foster a dialogue between herself and the students (p. 178). In doing so, she models question-asking strategies for students, with the expectation that students will internalize the question-asking strategy and, over time, will pose questions about their writing on their own, leading to elaboration of their writing.

Mary Kooy and Jan Wells (1996) recommend that teachers comment on students' response journal entries using criteria that rate students' responses on a continuum: lower-level responses simply summarize the text, make improbable predictions, fail to pose questions, cite stereotyped responses, or confuse the text; higher-level responses explore different levels of meaning, formulate interpretations and predictions based on textual analysis, explore character motivation, draw connections to other texts, recognize reasons for writers' choices, and examine the relationships between students' own beliefs and those expressed in the text.

In responding to journals, teachers also can provide feedback by audiotaping comments on cassette or digital tapes (Anson, 1997; Mellen & Sommers, 2003). This medium enables teachers to communicate more information with greater ease than is possible with written responses.

More recently, many teachers have chosen to employ online feedback through e-mail or message boards that allow more time to reflect on and develop comments, while synchronous online interactions allow for discussions about writing that are similar to those that occur in face-to-face conferences (Honeycutt, 2001). In another example of ways to take advantage of new technology, teachers use speech-feedback and word-prediction software with learning-disabled students' journal writing, resulting in production of longer, high-quality entries (Williams, 2002). (To explore in greater depth the ways that technology may support the development of writing and writers, see Bruce & Comstock in this volume.)

Factors That Influence Students' Use of Teacher's Feedback

Certain kinds of feedback work better in certain situations than other kinds. Comments that request specific changes, ask for information, or address grammar and mechanics may be easier for students to act on than questions that challenge students' ideas or arguments (Conrad & Goldstein, 1999; Ferris, 2001). Consequently, written comments that ask students to add details or examples, improve coherence, or edit may well facilitate revisions, but when matters concerning students' ideas or arguments are at hand, it may be more useful to use a face-to-face conference to engage students in discussions about those ideas or arguments (Ferris, 2003).

Students' use of written comments also can be supported by teachers' use of checklists with specific criteria that reflect the rhetorical demands of a specific assignment—as opposed to generic features—and by engaging students in reflective self-assessments that are evaluated as part of the students' grades (O'Neill, 1998).

Peer- and Teacher-Written Feedback in David's Classroom

We now turn to some examples of peer- and teacher-written feedback employed in David's senior-year, intermediate-level short story literature class. Most of the 28 students in his literature class plan to attend postsecondary institutions. In this nine-week course, which meets every day for 90 minutes, students read short stories and discuss the use of story-writing techniques in the stories. Students also select stories on their own, read them, and respond to the stories based on a template in which they write plot summaries and record analyses of the character relationships, thematic meanings, and the use of story-writing techniques. They also engage in a discussion of the relationship between the story and their own lives, other texts, or current or historic events. As was the case with his Shakespeare assignment, by using a template, David provides students with specific criteria linked to specific tasks. By tracking the primary topics on which he provides feedback to students, David notes specific areas in which students experienced difficulties and focuses his instruction on those areas.

In addition to engaging in response to the literature they read, David's students also write a short story. This, too, is based on a template assignment, and students are guided by specific criteria linked to the template. To help initiate their stories, David has students write some initial first sentences, and then, using a computer projector, the students explore ways to develop their stories. They also participate in character development activities, and they share oral narratives that address plot development. As they develop ideas for their stories, they create notes as evidence that can be shown to and reviewed, first by classmates, then by an adult outside of the class, and finally by David.

The students then write drafts of their stories and provide each other with written feedback; they also rate their peers' drafts based on the specified criteria: unity of protagonist, antagonist, conflict, and climax; use of characterization; development of characters; a plot with an introduction, development, and resolution; a discernable theme; a consistent narrative voice; originality; title that is relative to the story; use of varied text types, such as narrative, descriptive, expository, and dialogue; purposeful use of language and word choice; and a holistic image of the story from the reader's perspective.

David's use of peer feedback reflects a practice of training peers to provide feedback in pairs, small groups, chat rooms, or "read-arounds" in which students place papers on their desks and other students write comments on response sheets (Christian, 2000). The success of peer conferences or classroom workshop feedback depends on the degree to which students are trained on effective methods of feedback (Barnard, 2002). Trained writers are better able to provide feedback that leads to substantive revisions that, in turn, lead to higher quality writing (Berg, 1999; Simmons, 2003; Straub, 1997). Without effective training, students can exclude certain peers, adopt highly judgmental or negative modes of feedback, or, out of concern for their social relationships, provide only praise (Henkin, 1995).

To train students to engage in peer editing, David models uses of descriptive, reader-based feedback and then has his students practice feedback by responding to the same draft in a large group. Different groups of students function as specialists on one of the story-writing criteria. Each of the students' stories is read by four other "criteria specialist" readers and by the writer, discussed briefly, and scored based on the grading criteria. Other narrative comments can be written on the drafts, and the writer also takes notes on verbal feedback to help direct the revision process. This assignment creates legitimate interactions between writer and readers throughout the process without requiring David to be the sole responder to the students' writing.

Analysis of Three Students' Writing and Feedback

To illustrate the peer-feedback process, we focus on the responses of three students—Rebecca, Clayton, and Greg (pseudonyms)—to peers' drafts and each student's subsequent revisions. Rebecca is a white female who is self-motivated. She is conscientious about her coursework; she sees a writing assignment as just that—a writing assignment—and she gets it done, usually well. Her story is situated in the peer and work worlds in which she participates; it culminates in the car crash and death of the main character and her boyfriend as a result of irresponsible drinking at a party. The twist she begins to develop from the beginning is that the main character is present at her own funeral, a ghost watching the proceedings.

Clayton is a black male who is an able and willing student—participating actively in class discussions and informed on current events. He also plays on the school's varsity basketball team. In his story, Clayton describes a suburban high school basketball star's team's surprise state championship success over a perennial urban power—a team for which the main character had previously played, with a coach who had failed to honor his talent.

Greg is a white male who is very sharp and often works with the school's Tech-Ed teachers. In the short story class, Greg acts out the script of the typical, suburban, male student: He knows how to do school very well. Greg's story portrays the demise of two suburban boys' friendship as they vie for a girl's affection. Replete with a final drag-race scene, it is a class-based narrative of the working class main character's moral decline. Turning to reselling pot bought from an inner-city dealer to his suburban peers to gain access to a sports car, he works to outmatch his middle class challenger's easy access to material goods—and loses.

To encourage these and other students to make suggestions that will help their peers improve their writing, David asked them to provide comments about why "this story [is] good" and also comments about how the story could "be improved." The students focused their comments on the need for character development, lack or strength of dialogue, evidence of a story theme, development of the plot, and the strength of the conclusions—comments that went beyond simply referring to the rating criteria. Rebecca, for example, commented on Clayton's plot development in the story of the basketball team's championship bid:

"I like how the story builds and builds up until the final sentences of the story," reflecting her use of the story development criteria.

Many of the students' responses draw directly on the terminology included in the assessment form David developed for them. For example, commenting on the lack of dialogue in Rebecca's draft, Clayton pointed out the need for her to use a greater variety of text types: "You should try to use all the text types in your story; you're missing dialogue." Rebecca responded by adding more dialogue to her story. Clayton's comment reflects two important elements of David's instruction: his emphasis on modeling effective ways to provide feedback and the identification of specific criteria for judging writing.

In general, students provided more elaborated suggestions for revision when they commented on how their peers could improve their writing than they did when commenting on what made the writing "good." For example, although most of his comments are brief, Greg's suggestions for how Clayton's piece could be improved were facilitative: "Needs a title. Work on developing stronger theme"; in contrast, his comments about the strengths in the piece were largely evaluative, but might not help the student reproduce the "good" practice: "Good details." The same pattern was evidence in Rebecca's response to Greg's drag-race story. She praises specific details: "I like the relation to cars. I like the theme of the story." By contrast, addressing how Greg's piece could "be improved," she writes: "Maybe develop Ricky [the middle class rival] & Tony [the working class main character] more. I kind of get a picture of what Ricky looks like being a football player, but not Tony."

Students' praise is often reader based while their criticism is criterion based. In their comments, criterion-based language features prominently when the students address how pieces under review could be improved, while reader-based feedback focuses on readers' interest in and ability to identify with what is said, a stance that led at times to uncritical assessments. For example, the sense of familiarity limits Greg's possible challenge to Rebecca to deal more explicitly with class differences in her character descriptions: "great looking couple with Eric's 6' stature, and blonde hair, and dazzling green eyes and my 5'4" stature, sandy blonde hair, and hazel eyes. We were the envy of our friends. Everyone knew we were going to be the couple to last forever." Although class distinctions figure prominently in Greg's own story, he makes no effort to challenge Rebecca's claims or encourage her to develop more complex characters. Instead, he writes, "Easy to relate to story, characters are just average kids."

Students also drew on David's evaluation criteria by combining them to address particular issues of story development. Explaining her rating of Greg's "Use of characterization; development of characters," Rebecca noted Greg's need to clarify his theme: "You could develop Ricky more. Tony is obviously jealous. Is Ricky very built? How is Tony jealous?" The matter of what Tony loses by the end of the story—and of what he continues to have—is left unexplained in this draft, a matter Rebecca addresses in her feedback; by doing so as she requests development of Tony, she shows understanding of the rhetorical context, and she points to the possibility of substantive revision.

Although these students' suggestions often did not lead to substantive revision, their comments demonstrated engagement with assignment criteria. When there were revisions that went beyond making surface-level changes, they involved further development of stories through additional character description or elaboration on final, climactic scenes that helped resolve conflicts or clarify themes. For example, in Rebecca's draft, she quickly deals with a climactic car crash, failing to adequately explain how the narrator is still able to watch the scene and failing to address the complexity of what had just happened. She wrote, "I can't remember the impact of the truck because I had died instantly. But I remember standing on the sidewalk looking at the car seeing the two of us laying there motionless and wondering how I could have been so irresponsible. If only I had listened to what others had told me maybe I would be alive to at least say I'm sorry." A peer responded to the ending by commenting, "The end is a little weird because you can't tell the narrator is dead at the beginning." In her revision of the ending, Rebecca clarified the fact that the narrator is still dead but is appearing as a ghost, reflecting on the fact that she has been irresponsible to herself, her boyfriend, and her family.

Though students sometimes made few revisions in response to each other's comments, it would be unfair to say that they did not respond to their group members' perspectives. A sense of "answerability" (Bakhtin, 1981) guided how they composed their drafts, which is to say that they anticipated peer responses and drew on the assignment criteria as they crafted their initial drafts; they chose topics of common interest, and they worked to interpret and enact the rhetorical values of the assignment through considering rubric criteria as they drafted.

In his own written feedback, David used a response form similar to that used by the students, and he also recorded marginal and end comments. Although, at times, he takes up themes similar to those commented on by the students, he also takes up alternative ones. For example, David joins Greg in asking Clayton to make clearer the role of the player–coach conflict in the story's movement toward the championship game. Greg asks Clayton to "Work on developing [a] stronger theme," and David notes that Clayton needs a more "discernable theme." But David takes it further, suggesting that Clayton improve the "use of characterization; development of characters." David wrote: "What is the point? Could this be stronger?" and "How could you enhance Tyus [the player] and Harris [the coach]?" In revision, Clayton added an illustrative flashback that explained the coach–player conflict. In general, David notes that he concentrates less on surface matters than his students do, and he focuses more on issues of story organization and development.

These peer- and teacher-written comments provide helpful, respectful feedback that serve to foster revisions in the students' stories. The reader-based comments provide writers with an understanding of their readers' subjective experiences in reading the stories—feedback that serves to verify their sense of their stories' abilities to engage their readers. The "needs improvement" comments that draw largely from the criteria that David explicates provide specific suggestions for elaborating on characterization or plot in ways that reflect larger notions of effective narrative development. As previously noted, central to the quality of the written peer comments is David's modeling ways of providing effective feedback.

Feedback Through Teacher and Peer Conferences

While written comments can foster revision, one of the advantages of providing feedback in conferences is that teachers can provide students with more elaborate explanations for their feedback and can query students about their perspectives on their drafts (Anderson, 2000; Black, 1998; Frank, 2001; Kaufman, 2000). Students can voice their purposes, practice self-assessing, and formulate alternative revisions (Beach, 1989). If students are having difficulty self-assessing, teachers can model the self-assessing process (McIver & Wolf, 1999). Conferences with English as a foreign language (EFL) and English as a second language (ESL) students are particularly valuable for EFL/ESL students given their need to address language translation issues by verbalizing their thoughts to a teacher (Ferris, 2003).

Teachers may focus conference feedback on the specific issues facing a student. In prewriting conferences, they may employ heuristic strategies for exploring ideas or construction of the rhetorical context. In drafting conferences, they may focus on issues of organization and development of ideas. This focus involves inquiry directed at a paper as a whole—at students' audiences, their larger purposes—and at specific sections of a draft. Questions such as "What do you want your audience to do or think?" and "What are some things you could do to improve this?" address the former category, while questions such as "What are you trying to say or show here?" or "What are the different parts or chunks of material, and how could you name them?" address specific sections of a draft. In editing conferences, teachers may focus on aspects of readability and clarity; having students read aloud their drafts may lead to self-editing, although such oral approaches may only benefit more proficient readers (Moran, 1997).

Teachers also adopt different styles of conferencing depending on differences in students' ability to self-assess (Patthey-Chavez & Ferris, 1997). For students who are capable of extensive self-assessing, a teacher may adopt a highly facilitative, open-ended style—simply asking students "what works" and "what needs work" (Glasswell, 2001). For students who need more direction, a teacher may assume a more directive style that addresses specific problems in students' writing, modeling ways of reflecting on problems and potential revisions. In working with students for whom writing is a challenge, teachers may simply focus on having students talk out their ideas, which the teacher transcribes into writing, or have the student then write down those ideas (Schneider, 2003). Finally, it is helpful to conclude conferences by negotiating a mutually agreed-upon plan or contract for subsequent revisions, particularly if students assume that there is no need for further revision. When students considered their stories complete, a teacher's conference feedback aimed at supporting their revisions had little effect (Nickel, 2001).

Teachers also have used technology to provide written comments in online chat sites or as "comments" on text files (Blair, 2003). One advantage of online feedback is that students can save copies of feedback to refer to at a later point when revising their drafts (Hewett, 2000). One study found that online feedback results in a larger number of comments and subsequent revisions than was the case with traditional feedback (Liu & Sadler, 2003). There are a number of commercial online programs—Dadaelus, CommonSpace, Redline, Textra—that can be used for structuring and organizing online peer response (for a comparative review, see Wolfe, 2002). For example, in CommonSpace, students put their draft writing in a left column; peers then highlight sections of the draft and write comments on the adjacent right column—comments that are permanently linked to the original draft (Tannacito & Tuzi, 2003). Free, noncommercial chat room sites (such as www.tappedin.org, www.moodle.org, or www.nicenet.org) create and send e-mail transcripts of online feedback to students and provide them with a record of comments that they can then use for working on their revisions (Yuan, 2003).

Asynchronous feedback through e-mail or message boards allows for more time to reflect on and develop comments, while more synchronous online interactions allow for more discussions about writing issues similar to that which occurs in a conference (Crank, 2002; Honeycutt, 2001). If a teacher shares online comments with other students, all students may benefit from reviewing those comments (Monroe, 2002). On the other hand, asynchronous feedback can be problematic when students do not respond to comments or simply do not participate in online interaction (Blair, 2003). With synchronous feedback, students can coach each other or discuss issues and potential revisions in real-time chat.

ESL teachers can also employ online feedback to readily correct grammatical errors (Jones, Iannacone, Melby-Mauer, & Tanner, 2003). Teachers used speech-feedback and word-prediction software to provide feedback to learning-disabled students' journal writing, resulting in production of longer, higher quality entries (Williams, 2002).

David's Conferencing Practices

David's conferences are face-to-face, individual sessions, conducted after he has reviewed the student's draft. The conferences are based on the students' particular needs, phase of development, and degree to which they have successfully addressed the assignment criteria. Each conference involves the following steps:

1. A preliminary, informal discussion, not focused on the paper.
2. A generally supportive statement about the piece and a review of David's main points.
3. A discussion of the difference between proofreading and revision, in which David draws the distinction between surface-level fixes and substantive changes in order to support both, but also to focus the conference on the student's ideas and content and to encourage the student to make substantive revisions later.
4. A brief focus on surface-level fixes.
5. An extended, dialogic exchange about possible ways of developing ideas, which David begins with questions to students about their purposes and intentions concerning theme, plot, character development, and so forth.
6. Formation and revision of developing theories through student response, continued questioning by David, and often several suggestions made by David to support substantive revision while "sideshadowing" (Welch, 1998) alternatives.
7. A review of what was discussed.
8. A proposal of an informal contract to revise, when David asks the student if he or she is willing to revise the draft based on what they have discussed in the conference.
9. The student's acceptance of the contract.

Though David sets the agenda for these conferences, he adopts a nondirective stance, suggesting different ways students can develop their stories, asking students whether he has understood their intentions and purposes, and reminding them that they need not take his suggestions. David thereby maintains space for multiple voices by occupying a range of roles and stances in these sessions (Larson & Maier, 2000). He does not always play the part of teacher but rather, at times, adopts a peer or pop-culture-critic stance. In these alternative roles, he uses humor to distance the writer from writing, making his criticism of underdeveloped or unclear aspects of the draft a bit less threatening, thus encouraging the writer to be more open to revision.

In a conference with Rebecca, David addresses how the lack of character development in her story influences the rhetorical effect of the story:

David: Your description is sort of police line-up info. You give us height, hair color. Without being so clinical, so "police," how could you bring these characters to the reader? What kinds of things could you tell about the characters to describe them to the reader other than sounds like the FBI's most wanted list?

Rebecca: [laughs]

David: What could you tell me about a person?

Rebecca: Um.

David: I mean imagine in your mind this girl. What else could you tell me about a person? I mean, imagine in your mind this girl. What might you tell me about her other than "she's 5'4"..."?

Rebecca: Well, more of her interests and stuff. Do it based on stereotypes and that.

David: OK. So, you could look at interests. Here's what I wrote. "Can you find other ways to give readers a visual image?" Is she athletic? Does she look like a movie star? Is she the girl next door? You could play on some of those stereotypes. Because when we get to know her better, we get deeper into the story. You know, the better you know the character, the more you feel about what they're doing. So that might be something important, a way to bring the reader into the description.

David draws from his written comments to focus on the evaluation criterion of character development. At the same time, he actively "sideshadows" (Welch, 1998)—using humor in his stance of pop-culture critic, working to create distance between the writer and her text, clearing space for her "stereotypes" comment by suggesting a range of alternative descriptions she could use.

David works similarly with Clayton to support substantive revision in his basketball story related to portraying conflict between the player, Tyus, and the former Coach Harris. David notes that the ending of the story draft shows Tyus's new team's victory over his former team, but that it fails to show directly Tyus personally confronting Coach Harris. After Clayton confirms that what matters most to Tyus is beating Coach Harris, David clears space for consideration of alternative perspectives on how the narrative might end.

David: How can a player show up another coach? What would be a way that you could sort of embarrass or that you could show this other coach that he's just not as good? In a basketball game, how does a coach look bad? How can you make a coach look bad? You've seen enough basketball.

Clayton: Well, if someone is making gestures, saying things that don't have anything to do with basketball.... Those sorts of things can be done.

David: OK. So, sort of personal things could come into the game.

Clayton: Yeah.

David: What else makes a coach look really bad in a game?

Clayton: Certain situational things where a coach thinks you're going to do one thing, and you do something else, and he doesn't know what to do.

David: Can I throw out some possibilities?

Clayton: Sure.

David: Might there have been something that this coach taught Tyus that he could use against this guy in that final game? That might be a way to embarrass him. And, I'll tell you one of the things that I think is most embarrassing for coaches is when you do something as a coach and as a result somebody goes to the free throw line all by himself.

Clayton: Oh, they get a technical?

As their conference continues, Clayton decides to go with David's technical foul idea, but it is the work they do to move beyond the preliminary draft's regulation-time, game-winning buzzer shot conclusion that makes this alternative possible. How the game's ending can be "personal" is a matter they work through by entertaining multiple voices. Clayton revises the preliminary draft's final sentence—"[Tyus] Sanders sinks the shot at the buzzer to beat his former team and win the state title"—to read, "Sanders sinks the shot at the buzzer to send the game into overtime." As Clayton extends the conclusion, the personal conflict builds and is resolved: The coach runs out onto the court, screaming; Tyus misses his first shot; he looks over at the coach, "seated on the bench with his head in his hands"; he sinks the shot. The player–coach conflict theme is clear, in the end, through conference dialogue, through substantive revision.

In contrast to his written comments, in these conferences David is able to explain his feedback in more detail; he is also able to model self-assessing processes within the student's ZPD. The students are able to formulate possible revisions that address these needs, exploring the efficacy of those revisions with David. Conferences therefore serve as an arena in which students practice self-assessing in a supportive context, practice that transfers to writing on their own.

Students' Construction of Identities

In responding to students' writing, teachers such as David are responding to more than the written text. They are also using that text to construct their version of a student's identity projected by the text, perceptions that can then shape their responses to the student's writing. In addition, in their writing, students attempt to create a persona they believe will invite a positive teacher response. At the same time, students use the teacher's feedback to derive what they believe to be the teachers' perceptions of them: "struggling," "unmotivated," or "a poor reader." Thus, teachers create images of students and students create images of teachers' perceptions, images that may or may not be valid (Taylor, 2002).

Teachers also may help students construct their identities as primary audiences by making explicit their beliefs, attitudes, and agendas related to topics or issues about which students are writing. In providing written and oral feedback to Rebecca, Clayton, and Greg, David consistently disclosed his own interests and experiences to provide these students with a sense of audience. In doing so, David created a rhetorical context in which students perceive themselves as communicating with an audience that is actually interested in learning from their writing.

Implications for Teaching

In conclusion, theory and research on responding to students' writing suggest that teachers can foster student self-assessment and revision central to improving their writing if they do the following:

Formulate criteria specific to an assignment's rhetorical task and context. In lieu of general criteria, provide students with criteria specific to a genre, rhetorical task, purpose, and audience as ground rules for use in self-assessing their writing. Involve students in formulating these criteria so that they understand and have some ownership in those criteria.

Provide specific, reader-based feedback. Describe specific, descriptive, reader-based perceptions of a student's writing, making explicit instances of engagement, comprehension difficulties, lack of direction or coherence, need for more information, and expectations based on genre conventions, for example, "In reading your opinion, I expected some supporting evidence, but didn't find any." Ground this feedback within some shared formulation of an assignment's purpose, task, genre conventions, and audience, which often need to be clarified.

Challenge misconceptions and value assumptions. At the same time, challenge students' misconceptions and value assumptions, fostering self-examination of their beliefs and attitudes. Make explicit any beliefs and assumptions about a topic or task that may reflect certain misconceptions so that students can challenge those misconceptions, for example, that a student seems to know little about a topic, when, in fact, the topic was not clearly defined in an assignment.

Vary feedback according to the phase of development. Tailor the types of response according to whether students are engaging in initial exploration of a topic; formulating an argument; organizing material; or editing, either within or across different writing phases or drafts.

Use conferences to encourage self-assessment and revision. Provide conference feedback to help students practice self-assessing and formulating possible revisions that address those limitations. Model self-assessing processes for students who have difficulty self-assessing or formulating revisions. Conclude conferences by having students specify the revisions they plan to make. Use online conferencing to create transcript records of conferences for later revisions.

Train students to provide feedback in peer conferences. Integrate reading and writing instruction by training peers to formulate think-aloud responses to texts, responses that then transfer to giving peer feedback. Model peer-conferencing strategies using videotapes and role-playing activities.

In summary, by receiving helpful feedback to their drafts, students learn to engage in critical self-assessment, leading to revision that is essential to improving their writing.

REFERENCES

Anderson, C. (2000). *How's it going? A practical guide to conferring with student writers.* Portsmouth, NH: Heinemann.

Anson, C.M. (1989). Introduction: Response to writing and the paradox of uncertainty. In C.M. Anson (Ed.), *Writing and response: Theory, practice and research* (pp. 1-11). Urbana, IL: National Council of Teachers of English.

Anson, C.M. (1997). In our own voices: Using recorded commentary to respond to writing. In P. Elbow & M.D. Sorcinelli (Eds.), *Learning to write: Strategies for assigning and responding to writing across the curriculum* (pp. 105-115). San Francisco: Jossey-Bass.

Anson, C.M., & Beach, R. (1995). *Journals in the classroom: Writing to learn.* Norwood, MA: Christopher Gordon.

Atwell, N. (1998). *In the middle: New understandings about writing, reading, and learning* (2nd ed.). Portsmouth, NH: Boynton/Cook.

Bakhtin, M.M. (1981). *The dialogic imagination* (M. Holquist, Ed., C. Emerson & M. Holquist, Trans.). Austin: University of Texas Press.

Bardine, B.A., Bardine, M.S., & Deegan, E.F. (2000). Beyond the red pen: Clarifying our role in the response process. *English Journal, 90*(1), 94-101.

Barnard, I. (2002). Whole-class workshops: The transformation of students into writers. *Issues in Writing, 12*(2), 124-143.

Beach, R. (1989). Showing students how to assess: Demonstrating techniques for response in the writing conference. In C.M. Anson (Ed.), *Writing and response: Theory, practice, and research* (pp. 127-148). Urbana, IL: National Council of Teachers of English.

Beach, R. (1993). *A teacher's introduction to reader response theories.* Urbana, IL: National Council of Teachers of English.

Berg, E.C. (1999). The effects of trained peer response on ESL students' revision types and writing quality. *Journal of Second Language Writing, 8*(3), 215-241.

Blair, L. (2003). Teaching composition online: No longer the second-best choice. *Kairos, 8*(2). Retrieved March 20, 2004, from http://english.ttu.edu/kairos/8.2/binder.html?praxis/blair/index.html

Black, L.J. (1998). *Between talk and teaching: Reconsidering the writing conference.* Logan: Utah State University Press.

Broad, B. (2003). *What we really value: Beyond rubrics in teaching and assessing writing.* Logan: Utah State University Press.

Burke, J. (2002). *Tools for thought: Graphic organizers for your classroom.* Portsmouth, NH: Heinemann.

Burkland, J., & Grimm, N. (1986). Motivating through responding. *Journal of Teaching Writing, 5*(2), 237-247.

Christian, B. (2000). The read-around alternative to peer groups. *Teaching English in the Two-Year College, 27*(3), 308-311.

Clare, L., Valdes, R., Pascal, J., & Steinberg, J.R. (2001). *Teachers' assignments as indicators of instructional quality in elementary schools* (CSE Technical Report 545). Los Angeles: National Center for Research on Evaluation, CRESST/CSE. (ERIC Document Reproduction Service No. ED457169)

Conrad, S.M., & Goldstein, L.M. (1999). ESL student revision after teacher-written comments: Text, contexts, and individuals. *Journal of Second Language Writing, 8*(3), 257-276.

Crank, V. (2002). Asynchronous electronic peer response in a hybrid basic writing classroom. *Teaching English in the Two-Year College, 30*(2), 145-155.

Crone-Blevins, D.E. (2002). The art of response. *English Journal, 91*(6), 93-98.

Dewey, J. (1934). *Art as experience.* New York: Minton, Balch, & Company.

Elbow, P. (1998). *Writing with power: Techniques for mastering the process* (2nd ed.). New York: Oxford University Press.

Emig, J. (1971). *The composing processes of twelfth graders.* Urbana, IL: National Council of Teachers of English.

Faust, M. (2000). Reconstructing familiar metaphors: John Dewey and Louise Rosenblatt on literary art as experience. *Research in the Teaching of English, 35*(1), 9-34.

Ferris, D. (2001). Teaching writing for academic purposes. In J. Flowerdew & M. Peacock (Eds.), *Research perspectives on English for academic purposes* (pp. 298-214). New York: Cambridge University Press.

Ferris, D.R. (2003). *Response to student writing: Implications for second language students.* Mahwah, NJ: Erlbaum.

Fitzgerald, J. (1992). *Towards knowledge in writing: Illustrations from revision studies.* New York: Springer-Verlag.

Flash, P. (2002). *Responding to student writing.* Retrieved January 5, 2005, from http://writing.umn.edu/tww/responding_grading/respond_student.htm

Frank, C.R. (2001). "What new things these words can do for you": A focus on one writing-project teacher and writing instruction. *Journal of Literacy Research, 33*(3), 467-506.

Freedman, S. (1987). Recent developments in writing: How teachers manage response. *English Journal, 76*(6), 35-40.

Galda, L., & Beach, R. (2001). Theory and research into practice: Response to literature as a cultural activity. *Reading Research Quarterly, 36*, 64-73.

Glasswell, K. (2001). Matthew effects in writing: The patterning of difference in classrooms K-8. *Reading Research Quarterly, 36*, 348-349.

Henkin, R. (1995). Insiders and outsiders in first-grade writing workshops: Gender and equity issues. *Language Arts, 72* (6), 429-434.

Hewett, B.L. (2000). Characteristics of interactive oral and computer-mediated peer group talk and its influence on revision. *Computers & Composition, 17*(3), 265-288.

Hillocks, G., Jr. (1986). *Research on written composition: New directions for teaching.* Urbana, IL: ERIC Clearinghouse on Reading and Communication Skills/National Conference on Research in English.

Honeycutt, L. (2001). Comparing e-mail and synchronous conferencing in online peer response. *Written Communication, 18*(1), 26-60.

Hyland, F., & Hyland, K. (2001). Sugaring the pill: Praise and criticism in written feedback. *Journal of Second Language Writing, 10*(3), 185-212.

Hunt, R., & Vipond, D. (1992). First, catch the rabbit: Methodological imperative and the dramatization of dialogic reading. In R. Beach, J. Green, M. Kamil, & T. Shanahan (Eds.), *Multidisciplinary perspectives on literacy research* (pp. 69-90). Urbana, IL: National Conference on Research in English.

Johnston, B. (1983). *Assessing English.* Urbana, IL: National Council of Teachers of English.

Jones, T., Iannacone, V., Melby-Mauer, J., & Tanner, M. W. (2003). Using e-mail assignments and online correction in ESL instruction. *TESOL Journal, 12*(2), 37-38.

Kaufman, D. (2000). *Conferences & conversations: Listening to the literate classroom.* Portsmouth, NH: Heinemann.

Kim, L. (2004). Online technologies for teaching writing: Students react to teacher response in voice and written modalities. *Research in the Teaching of English, 38*(3), 304-337.

Kooy, M., & Wells, J. (1996). *Reading response logs: Inviting students to explore novels, short stories, plays, poetry and more.* Portsmouth, NH: Heinemann.

Larson, J., & Maier, M. (2000). Co-authoring classroom texts: Shifting participant roles in writing activity. *Research in the Teaching of English, 34*(4), 468-497.

Lee, A. (2000). *Composing critical pedagogies: Teaching writing as revision.* Urbana, IL: National Council of Teachers of English.

Lensmire, T.J. (2000). *Powerful writing/responsible teaching.* New York: Teachers College Press.

Liu, J., & Sadler, R.W. (2003). The effect and affect of peer review in electronic versus traditional modes on L2 writing. *Journal of English for Academic Purposes, 2*(3), 193-227.

McIver, M.C., & Wolf, S.A. (1999). The power of the conference is the power of suggestion. *Language Arts, 77*(1), 54-61.

Mellen, C., & Sommers, J. (2003). Audiotaped response and the two-year-campus writing classroom: The two-sided desk, the "guy with the ax," and the chirping birds. *Teaching English in the Two-Year College, 31*(1), 25-39.

Mlynarczyk, R.W. (1996). Finding grandma's words: A case study in the art of revising. *Journal of Basic Writing, 15*(1), 3-22.

Monroe, B. (2002). Feedback: Where it's at is where it's at. *English Journal, 92*(1), 101-104.

Moran, M.H. (1997). Connections between reading and successful revision. *Journal of Basic Writing, 16*(2), 76-89.

Nelson, G., & Carson, J. (1998). ESL students' perceptions of effectiveness in peer response groups. *Journal of Second Language Writing, 7*(2), 113-131.

Nickel, J. (2001). When writing conferences don't work: Students' retreat from teacher agenda. *Language Arts, 79*(2), 136-147.

O'Neill, P. (1998). From the writing process to the responding sequence: Incorporating self-assessment and reflection in the classroom. *Teaching English in the Two-Year College, 26*(1), 61-70.

Patthey-Chavez, G.G., & Ferris, D.R. (1997). Writing conferences and the weaving of multi-voiced texts in college composition. *Research in the Teaching of English, 31*(1), 51-90.

Patthey-Chavez, G.G., Matsumura, L.C., & Valdes, R. (2004). Integrating the process approach to writing instruction in urban middle schools. *Journal of Adolescent & Adult Literacy, 47*, 462-477.

Rosenblatt, L.M. (1995). *Literature as exploration.* New York: Modern Language Association of America.

Schneider, J.J. (2003). Contexts, genres, and imagination: An examination of the idiosyncratic writing performances of three elementary children within multiple contexts of writing instruction. *Research in the Teaching of English, 37*(3), 329-379.

Simmons, J. (2003). Responders are taught, not born. *Journal of Adolescent & Adult Literacy, 46*, 684-693.

Sommers, N. (1982). Responding to student writing. *College Composition & Communication, 33*(2), 148-156.

Sperling, M., & Freedman, S.W. (1987). A good girl writes like a good girl: Written responses to student writing. *Written Communication, 9*(9), 342-369.

Straub, R. (1997). Students' reactions to teacher comments: An exploratory study. *Research in the Teaching of English, 31*(1), 91-119.

Sumara, D.J. (2002). *Why reading literature in school still matters.* Mahwah, NJ: Erlbaum.

Sweeney, M.R. (1999). Relating revision skills to teacher commentary. *Teaching English in the Two-Year College, 27*(2), 213-218.

Tannacito, T., & Tuzi, F. (2003). A comparison of E-Response: Two experiences; one conclusion. *Kairos, 7*(3). Retrieved February 25, 2004, from http://english.ttu.edu/kairos/7.3/binder2.html?coverweb/tannacito/index.html

Taylor, R. (2002). "Reading what students have written": A case study from the basic writing classroom. *Reader, 46*, 32-49.

Todd, R.W., Mills, N., Palard, C., & Khamcharoen, P. (2001). Giving feedback on journals. *ELT Journal, 55*(4), 354-359.

Tompkins, J.P. (1980). *Reader-response criticism: From formalism to post-structuralism.* Baltimore: Johns Hopkins University Press.

Van Gelderen, A. (1997). Elementary students' skills in revising: Integrating quantitative and qualitative analysis. *Written Communication, 14*(3), 360-397.

Vygotsky, L.S. (1978). *Mind in society: The development of higher psychological processes* (M. Cole, V. John-Steiner, S. Scribner, & E. Souberman, Eds. & Trans.). Cambridge, MA: Harvard University Press. (Original work published 1934)

Welch, N. (1998). Sideshadowing teacher response. *College English, 60*(4), 374-395.

Wilhelm, J.D. (1996). *"You GOTTA be the book": Teaching engaged and reflective reading with adolescents.* New York: Teachers College Press.

Williams, S.C. (2002). How speech-feedback and word-prediction software can help students write. *Teaching Exceptional Children, 34*(3), 72-78.

Wolfe, J. (2002). Annotation technologies: A software and research review. *Computers & Composition, 19*(4), 471-497.

Yagelski, R.P. (1995). The role of classroom context in the revision strategies of student writers. *Research in the Teaching of English, 29*(2), 216-238.

Yuan, Y. (2003). The use of chat rooms in an ESL setting. *Computers & Composition, 20*(2), 194-206.

Chapter 10

Writing and Reading Relationships in Literacy Learning

Elizabeth A. Close, Molly Hull, and Judith A. Langer

For at least the past 20 years, reading and writing relationships have been a conundrum in literacy education. We know enough about each and their relationships to each other to recognize that they are related linguistic, cognitive, and social activities that have the potential to be mutually supportive in literacy learning. But we do not yet have well-developed frameworks for optimizing these relationships in practice. We also recognize that writing and reading can work together to support not only the development of literacy abilities but also the learning of content. But here, too, we lack frameworks for how this translates into practice. We have yet to develop well-defined pedagogy that makes best use of writing and reading relationships to support both literacy and content learning. But given the history of writing and reading, all this should come as no surprise.

Two earlier papers (Langer & Allington, 1992; Langer & Flihan, 2000) trace the changing notions of reading and writing relationships, as seen in research, practice, and professional publications across the 20th century. They indicate that writing and reading theory, research, and education have very different geneses and have received overlapping attention only since the 1970s.

The teaching of writing, as well as scholarship about it, grew from Aristotelian rhetoric, which stressed invention, arrangement, style, memory, and delivery, and was intended for the elite—for learned (and usually male) college students. It had long been an academic staple of British universities when, in the 1700s, American universities assumed the British model. Over the years, expressionist and new rhetoric theories offered conceptual options, and views of rhetoric broadened. However, the teaching of writing remained rooted in some form of rhetoric until the 1970s, when in response to work in linguistics, sociolinguistics, cognition, and anthropology, the research from these diverse perspectives led to a focus on relationships among context, culture, purpose, and social interaction—and eventually to their effects on the learning and teaching of writing.

On the other hand, reading followed a very different path. While American reading education in the 1700s also followed British tradition, teaching methods were aligned with approaches used in primary instruction. By the late 1800s, scientific experiments, particularly in psychology and physiology, began to advance reading theory. While progressive views that focused on student-centered

Learning to Write, Writing to Learn: Theory and Research in Practice edited by Roselmina Indrisano and Jeanne R. Paratore. Copyright © 2005 by the International Reading Association.

instruction offered pedagogical alternatives, by the 1900s, approaches to reading instruction were deeply influenced by psychological research. It was only during the 1970s, with work in the fields of linguistics, sociolinguistics, cognition, and anthropology, that a focus on context, culture, and purpose highlighted the similar dimensions of reading and writing as linguistic, cognitive, and social language processes that could inform and support one another in learning and use.

Together, the new multidisciplinary knowledge about reading, writing, language, and sociocultural conditions led to a body of research into similarities and differences in reading and writing processes (e.g., Langer, 1986a, 1986b; Shanahan, 1984; Spivey & King, 1989; Tierney & Pearson, 1983), as well as the uses to which reading and writing are put (e.g., Cook-Gumperz & Gumperz, 1981; Heath, 1988; Squire, 1983; Street, 1993; Teale & Sulzby, 1986). And this next phase of scholarship helped form an expanded view of literacy that included not merely the acts of reading and writing, but also the social and cultural contexts that affect literacy learning and literate actions. Thus, in about a 20-year period, a great deal of research and practice focused on relationships between reading and writing to the point where, in the educational literature, their interrelationship is assumed, so much so that they have become subsumed under the broader notion of literacy. As an example, a search of all the books and articles published in the language arts field between 1984 and 1987 that contained "reading and writing," "writing and reading," or "literacy" in their title indicates a tremendous shift in emphasis. While 70% of those published between 1984 and 1987 contained "reading and writing" or "writing and reading," only 30% contained the word "literacy." Between 1990 and 1997, the balance completely inverted to 27% ("reading and writing" or "writing and reading") and 73% ("literacy").

But this seems to be where the relationship trail between reading and writing ends. A number of learner-based instructional approaches, often emanating from neo-Vygotskian notions (e.g., Palincsar & Brown, 1984; Tharp & Gallimore, 1988; Wells & Chang-Wells, 1992), relied on reading, writing, and language interactions in the teaching and learning process, as did approaches to whole language (Goodman, 1989) and Reading Recovery (Clay, 1993). Other critically important research in literacy has focused on issues of what it is and who controls it, and on issues of culture, power, and autonomy (e.g., Collins, 1995; Minnich, 1990; New London Group, 1996; Solsken, 1993; Street, 1993). But a direct line of inquiry from notions of writing and reading as mutually related and interdependent language activities to pedagogical models for using these in specific ways that foster the teaching, learning, and uses of literacy is not apparent.

We use this chapter as a reawakening, as a discussion of what we've been doing in a recent research project, and also as a call for more relationship-focused instructional research. It is cowritten by three research colleagues. Elizabeth (Betty) Close is the director of educational outreach at the Center on English Learning & Achievement (CELA); she served as an instructional facilitator in a recent research project that involved teachers who wished to improve both their own teaching and their students' learning. Judith Langer is a director of CELA and led the project. Molly Hull is an English language arts teacher who participated in the two-year project called the Partnership for Literacy. We have written our parts separately, each from her own perspective and experience. Judith has written the introduction, a brief description of the Partnership, and the conclusion. Betty's and Molly's sections make up the body of the chapter.

The Partnership for Literacy is a hybrid professional development and instructional development project that engages teachers as active investigators into the effects of their teaching on their students' learning and familiarizes them with many features that we have found to be characteristic of effective literacy instruction (e.g., Applebee, Langer, Nystrand, & Gamoran, 2003; Langer, 2002, 2004). These findings strongly support a framework for instruction where substantive and varied language experiences are used in envisionment-building classrooms, those in which teachers help students think more deeply about their reading as they question, discuss, and reflect on their understandings. The teachers and students engage with challenging subject matter about big ideas in an active and minds-on environment. Language and thought are at the heart of both the teaching and learning.

The Partnership for Literacy helps pull together what writing and reading relationships can mean for the teaching of higher literacy and also shows how they can be used effectively together, in ways that provide students with the ability not only to read, write, and understand the content they are learning, but also to relate this knowledge to larger understandings and skills they can call upon in years to come. We offer Molly and her students as one example of how writing and reading relationships can work together to support the learning of both literacy and content, with Betty linking their activities to the Partnership framework.

In Practice

Betty: Molly is one of more than 60 teachers who participated in the Partnership for Literacy, a two-year implementation study involving almost 3,000 students in 18 urban, suburban, and rural schools in two states. The study included many high-needs schools, those with underperforming students as indicated by performance on high-stakes tests, as well as schools serving a diverse range of students and those from low-income families. Using curriculum specific to their schools and programs, the teachers worked with five facilitators from the Center on English Learning & Achievement (CELA) to apply what they were learning from the center's research on literacy achievement. The teachers from participating schools met together in institutes guided by CELA instructional facilitators: weeklong institutes each summer and one-day institutes during each spring and fall. Throughout the year(s), they formed smaller professional communities within their schools, meeting regularly with their CELA facilitators to discuss articles and texts, share plans, reflect on their own teaching and their students' learning, and examine taped lessons as well as student work.

Initially, facilitators focused on literary discussion and ways to help students comprehend and interpret the works with greater depth: How can we support students so that they raise authentic and substantive questions (Nystrand, Gamoran, Kachur, & Prendergast, 1997) and can share them with the class? What is envisionment building? And how do the stances readers take during reading work to build deeper understanding during a discussion (Langer, 1995)? What does it mean to focus on big issues and connect class work and conversations to these issues (Applebee, 1996)? And of course, how can writing, as well as reading and discussion, be used in classrooms in ways that support and extend students' understandings both of the texts they are reading and the larger life issues they bring to mind?

Teachers experienced activities with their groups and then adapted them for their students. Throughout, writing was used as a tool to clarify thinking, to share experiences, to plan the next steps for the group, and to move thinking along, as well as to create texts. For example, the teachers marked texts, developed questions, wrote in journals, responded to others' entries, responded to questions posed by the facilitators or by one another, reflected on experiences, and described lessons. Soon, teachers were using writing for similar purposes with their students.

As teachers began to develop a professional community within their schools, their instructional concerns about the match between their teaching and their students' learning became the focus of the meetings. Often there were concerns about connections: How do we connect the kind of thinking our students are doing about literature with what we are asking them to do with their writing? Are there ways in which writing, discussion, and reading can become more effective language and thinking tools for students to use?

These connections are an important concern for Molly, a seventh-grade teacher in a large, suburban middle school. For several years before the Partnership began, the language arts department in her district had invited experts from the field to provide workshops on writing and reading. Molly found these very helpful and wanted to blend what she had learned from them with what she was gaining from the Partnership.

Molly: As students enter my classroom in the fall, I know that they are walking in with strong basic skills. It happens every year. They are, for the most part, literal thinkers who approach reading, writing, listening, and speaking as separate work, separate activities, separate ways in which they perform in language arts. I like to think of my September students as novice jugglers. They each have four balls and know how to throw each one in the air, one at a time. Most can even handle two balls simultaneously. Very few can do three, and I want to challenge them to keep all four in the air at once. They don't yet know that the balls are all part of a bigger whole and that each separate movement affects the others. This is my goal: By the end of the year, they will be able to not only juggle the different skills in conjunction with one another, but they will also learn to make them work together in ways that enhance their understanding and performance. My job is not only to show them that it is possible, but also to reveal to them the secret that they already know how to do it.

One way in which I make the secret visible to my students is by using a big idea. In developing my year-long curriculum, I use the big idea of change. As the students navigate their way through each unit, we also have a larger, year-long discussion about how the reading and writing they are doing relates to this broader idea of how people are shaped or changed by the world around them and vice versa. In making these connections, students are able to see how one unit builds to the next and how much they are growing in their reading and writing.

On our first day in September, I ask my students to teach me about what they know of writing. They get out a sheet of paper, and I ask them to write whatever they choose. They look at me strangely, wondering what the right answer is. Do you want me to write about myself? Should I write a full page? An essay? I simply shake my head as if I am stumped. "Whatever you want is all," I reply. It may take some time, but gradually every pen and pencil begin to move. Some finish quickly, only producing a paragraph. Some take the whole time and are still not done. When time is up and class ends, I collect their papers and tell them they are free to go. I get anxious looks as I paper clip their first attempts at finding their writers' voices.

When they return for class the next day, I hand back their writing and give yet another brief activity: revise and edit your draft. Do you mean fix the spelling? Does it need to be longer? Should I rewrite it on a new piece of paper? And again, I respond with a shrug of my shoulders and ask them to tell me. Some walk purposefully to the dictionary and place it on their desk, some work swiftly, and others thoughtfully take their time. As class ends, I again collect their papers and thank them for their efforts. From these papers, I gather a snapshot of the writers I have in my classroom. I can tell who grasps the concepts of genre, who can ace a spelling test, and who has trouble mustering a few sentences and has no idea what revision, particularly a focus on the ideas, truly means. It gives us a place to start.

During our first unit of study, my students look at the idea of change in their writing. We walk through the steps of the writing process so that they can see the work they are expected to do, realize how an idea can change and grow during the writing process, and examine their roles in my class as students and writers. I begin this work by sharing a piece of my writing, from my initial thoughts; to writing in my notebook; to drafting, revising, editing, and publishing. We talk about how one idea grew and changed forms many times before I came to my final product. The students gaze nervously yet eagerly up at me, half curious to see what I have, half amazed that I have the courage to stand up front and put it on display for them. They listen and tell me what they think of my writing. They nod in understanding as I talk and read about my family, my childhood, and how I tried to put the topic of my relationship with my dad into a memoir, revising my writing until I had said what I wanted to say. Showing my work helps to cultivate the workshop atmosphere in our classroom and makes it clear that we are all writers struggling to be better.

Betty: All of Molly's activities support the students' envisionment building (Langer, 1995). They focus on their own and their classmates' ideas and collaborate to develop them more clearly and fully. They also work toward changing and developing ideas when they read and discuss pieces in class. In doing this, they develop a literate classroom community. Molly's goal is to have the students be open to and respectful of the ideas of their classmates. She wants a classroom in which her students value conversations around important issues in language arts (Applebee, 1996), and where diverse experiences and thinking enhance learning for all.

Molly: To begin, my students work in their writers' notebooks. They write daily, cultivating ideas for the writing they will do during the year in language arts. They work on big issues. They read and think about and learn that choosing a topic for their writing is not the same as choosing a genre. We look at the multitude of possibilities that an entry in their notebook can have and how to nurture those ideas to help them once they have decided upon a genre. We also use our notebooks to help understand what makes a good piece of writing—to reflect on texts we've read, potential topics, or possible original literary works. As we read, we note what good writers do and try them out in our notebooks. I share the ways in which I write in my notebook to help them to see its potential. To help them to take ownership of their notebooks, their first assignment is to personalize the

Figure 10.1   Suggested Ways for Students to Approach a Notebook Entry

Finding Ideas for My Writer's Notebook:

1. I write about what is around me...
   -news   -family   -friends, etc.
2. I write because of something I have read.
3. I write questions, lists, etc.
4. I write about clippings, tickets stubs, photos, a sketch, song lyrics, and old letter, or other item that I have placed in my Writer's Notebook (WBN).
5. I write about my feelings (good or bad).
6. I write entries that bump off from, extend, contradict, or link with earlier entries.
7. I experiment with different writing stuctures in my WNB, such as dialogue, narrative, detail.
8. I plan for writing in my WNB by creating characters, asking questions, writing about what I am smart about, etc.

Figure 10.2   Rubric Used to Grade Student Notebooks

Writer's Notebook checklist:

☐ Do I write EVERY DAY?

☐ Am I varying my topics? Do I try different kinds of entries?

☐ Am I getting inside my head stuff? No "Today, I..." lists.

☐ Am I caring for my notebook? (No ripping out pages, doodling, crossing out entries.)

☐ Am I dating all of my entries?

☐ Is there evidence of what I am learning in class?

☐ Is my notebook in school EVERY DAY?

cover to reflect who they are and to make the notebook distinguishable as their writer's notebook. One way they do this is to find a quote about writing that speaks to them, copy the quote, and glue it to the cover. Once students have personalized their notebooks, we begin to talk about what is to go inside. I hand out two slips of paper, which we glue to the inside front and back covers for quick reference. On one is a list of different ways for them to approach an entry (Figure 10.1). The list ranges from writing about what they are passionate about to writing about a song that they enjoy or reading they have done. The second slip is the rubric that I use to grade their notebooks (Figure 10.2). This lets them know what my expectations are in terms of quantity and quality of their entries.

Betty: Judith Langer (2001) found that teachers in higher achieving schools often share and discuss rubrics and other means for evaluating performance with their students and sometimes even involve students in their development. In addition to helping students reflect on and revise their work, rubrics can also help them become familiar with the components that contribute to success on high-stakes tests. Langer says that this helps them see qualitative differences in thought and language use.

Molly: In the first few weeks of school, I keep close tabs on students' work in their notebooks. I share entries from my own notebook and ask them to try similar entries; I confer one-on-one with students who seem to be struggling; we discuss different ways to nurture a topic when getting ready to draft. I read, comment on, and grade everyone's notebooks. I do this frequently during the first quarter as students learn how to use their notebooks. As the year goes on, comments and grading become less and less frequent. Students come to understand the importance of their notebooks and how they contribute to the quality of the writing and reading they do. They also learn that writing can be used for a range of other, more informal purposes—collecting ideas for writing topics, jotting down questions and thoughts when reading, noting critical remarks, or writing plans for future work.

Betty: This process is one example of how Molly scaffolds student learning. Her students learn to use reading, writing, and discussion in more fluid ways, as tools to move their own understandings along. As students are engaging in new tasks, she provides additional support as needed, but she removes that support as they internalize the strategies and become independent.

Molly: As my students prepare for their first formal piece of writing, they look through their permanent blue writing folders, a collection of selected written pieces from each year they have been in the district. To incorporate our big idea of change, they find a topic from an earlier piece they would like to revisit. Once this is determined, they use that topic but write about it in a different genre. As their work begins, we explore how our writers' notebooks can help them to figure out what they will be writing. Reflection on what they have read, experienced, or imagined, about both content and form, is something I ask my students to do throughout. As we take our time working through the steps of the process, they continually reflect on the decisions they are making as writers. What are the strategies or techniques that work best for them? I ask them to explain the strategies that did and did not work. They write about what they have learned and what they still struggle with. I have them put themselves in the minds of their readers—to use all they know as readers and writers. They also write about what they would like to do differently in their next writing piece. I believe that only by reflecting on our work can we truly improve.

Betty: In Partnership meetings, teachers are asked to be reflective practitioners. They keep journals and share their thoughts with their professional community. They also ask their students to be reflective learners. Similarly, when Molly asks her students to reflect on their learning, she helps them understand the demands of a task, develop an awareness of the strategies needed to successfully complete it, and move toward independence.

Molly: Even as the students get their writing "balls" into the air, I am also working on changing views of reading. In sixth grade, my students kept a daily reading calendar that included pages read each day, a response to that reading, and plans for the next reading. I want my students to do more—to think about the difference between hearing someone and actually listening to the person, and to be open to the changing ideas this might bring to mind individually as well as collectively.

In order to do more critical reading and thinking, we not only look at different ways to comment on a text but also, more specifically, at how we question a text. We discuss how reading often can be done superficially, which usually doesn't make for an interesting or thoughtful read. On the overhead projector, I model my questioning as we read through a short article together. We discuss how my examples don't necessarily have a right or wrong answer. Instead, my questions get me deeper into why events are happening. They also help me anticipate future events, revise my understanding, and make connections to other readings or experiences. I explain to them that the only "bad" questions are those we already know the answers to (Tovani, 2000). At first, as my students begin to look at their questions during and after reading, they usually tend to focus on the "right there" questions (Raphael & Pearson, 1985), those that have an answer in the text. As we practice asking questions about the texts we read in class, they start to ask broader questions, authentic questions (Nystrand et al., 1997) that provoke discussion rather than lead to only one right answer. As the students gain more confidence in their questioning, I gradually step out of discussions and merely facilitate their literary conversations as they ask their own questions and listen to and build on others' ideas.

Betty: As Molly's students read and think and write and think, they come to see questioning as something all readers do. They ask questions, posit hunches, anticipate, revise, reject, and build on ideas. Their envisionments change and grow (Langer, 1995). Molly uses reading, writing, and discussion to push students beyond immediate understanding. She develops activities that will move them to deeper understandings and generativity of ideas (Langer, 2001, 2004).

Molly: We talk about how what we do in writing is similar to what we do when we read. As Cris Tovani points out (2000), we have a reciting voice in our heads that reads the words but doesn't pay attention to what is being read, but we also have a conversation voice that interacts with texts as we think about what we are reading.

I ask my students to jot down their thoughts as they read, using either notes on the text or sticky notes. This helps them prepare for class discussion by having comments and questions already at hand. Their marks and notes can also help them to read and understand the content or genre better.

Betty: Helping students find ways to identify their questions, concerns, and observations as they read is an important issue for Partnership teachers. They use various ways of helping students to capture ideas during reading—bookmarks with guiding questions, sticky notes to record thinking. At times, teachers duplicate a short piece so that students can record their thinking directly on the text and then reflect on their comments—how their thinking changed during the reading and what caused the changes. Some teachers have students do two readings using different colored inks. By doing this, students are able to reflect on the changes in their understanding between the two readings.

Molly: As they read, my students are thinking and noticing how and what the author has written. For example, when we were reading commentary, many students noted that they could really connect to what one particular author was saying. These responses helped them realize that connecting to your audience is a key feature of writing commentary. I heard a lot of "Oh, I get it!" as the students were trying to write their own commentaries and to connect to their own audiences. This awareness is a change for most of them, but it is something that they all need to learn so that they can think more deeply about what they read and write.

Betty: Molly's students begin to see connections between what they read and what they write. As they read and question each text, they develop a richer understanding of it and its connections to their big idea of change. They also discuss the techniques writers use to communicate ideas and ways they can use these techniques in their own writing.

Molly: Once students are attending to their thinking while reading as well as writing, we put both the reading and writing balls in the air as we discuss how we use our conversation voice when discussing what we have read or when conferring on a piece of writing. They practice this with the drafts they are working on as they confer with a partner and explain what they are thinking as they share and read pieces. From there, a conference is no longer just a talk about whether a piece of writing is good, but a talk that seeks to answer these questions: Does it make sense? Does it appeal to the reader? Is there anything missing? They learn that if the reader's conversation voice says that it is confused, then there is work they as writers must do to fix that: rethinking and rewriting to make it better. In their conferences, they write as they read one another's drafts, making clear what information they need from the writer. The writer reflects on those comments and plans what to do next. All at once, they are reading, writing, listening, and speaking—using each skill toward a common, fuller goal.

As we progress through the year, I ask my students to think more deeply about genre. We talk about similarities and differences among genres and then get deeper into specific genres. For example, when discussing the writer's craft in a variety of realistic short stories, they connect their reading and writing and learn that a short story usually has five distinct elements: character, plot, setting, movement through time, and change. We talk about the ways a person is shaped or changed by the world. We make a bulleted list of all the various factors that affect us as people. We read realistic short stories about young adults dealing with personal change. As we read and discuss, students vocalize that conversation voice in their minds during class discussions. They comment on how ideas in each story connect to our big idea of change. By now, they also use a variety of kinds of writing to help them react to and think about what they read, and to develop their own ideas about change and how it can be crafted—in writing and in life.

Betty: In the Partnership, the teachers participate in many literary readings, writings, and discussions that serve as models for the lessons they plan for their students. During discussions, teachers consider the importance of making connections to earlier learning and to the bigger ideas in their curriculum and life (Applebee, 1996). Molly decided that focusing on the concept of change would help students see connections in their reading, writing, and personal learning. During the initial discussions of the stories they read, Molly's students share their questions and changing understandings of the characters. Then Molly helps them take a more critical stance (Langer, 1995) and focus on the writer's craft.

Talk about reading and writing permeates Molly's classroom. She provides many opportunities for students to learn through interaction with one another. This shared cognition has been identified as a feature of classrooms in higher achieving schools (Langer, 2001).

Molly: We call on all we have read, written, and discussed when students write their own short stories. We start by creating a character together. On the overhead projector, I collect their ideas about who this person should be. Sometimes it is an aspect of someone they've read about or have discussed. But that is only the beginning. Each class comes up with a distinct and unique personality for its character. Once we have our class character, the students work in their notebooks to create the characters for their personal stories. We build on this work as we develop the story elements, first together with our class character, and then individually. This way, I am able to model the work that I want them to do independently. I also share some of my short story ideas from my notebook. As they are working, we are continually going back to the importance of how their character will change by the end of the story. We are able to draw on the stories we read together as models for the work we are doing.

Next, my students build on their knowledge of short story by thinking about change in different ways: how a person is shaped by the larger world and how a person can contribute to change in society. As we brainstorm about major historical events that have happened during their lifetime (e.g., September 11, 2001; terrorism; the war in Iraq), I write them on the board as they think about ways circumstances in their lives have an impact on the people they are becoming. Applying the strategies we have learned in earlier units, students will now use novels as a starting point for research and as models for their writing. Each student reads a historical fiction novel set during one of the phases of African American history: slavery, abolition, the Civil War, Reconstruction, segregation, the Harlem Renaissance, and the Civil Rights movement. As they read books such as *Watsons Go to Birmingham—1963* by Christopher Paul Curtis (1995) and *Francie* by Karen English (1999), they write down what they notice about a person's life and the different events that affect it. They talk and wonder about how some people experience terrible hardships and yet are able to change what is happening, while others cannot.

Betty: In this major unit, Molly first asks the students to read and discuss the novels they have selected. They share their growing understandings in small groups and write in their notebooks. Then they step back and take a critical look at how the writers have developed their texts. What makes historical fiction different from other fiction? How are the characters changed by the events and conditions of the world? How do the characters respond? What makes a character able to take a role in shaping events? What kind of work does the writer do to develop this genre? How can I use what I see this writer doing to help me with my writing?

Molly: As this work concludes, they spend two weeks of class time in the library, where they research the time periods of their chosen novels and dig deeper into the events and the ways people reacted to them, ideas they were discussing as they read their novels. In essence, they are doing the work that a writer must do to be able to write historical fiction.

As they are researching and writing, they are also reading and discussing examples of historical-fiction short stories. They talk in small groups, discussing how authors create realistic characters living in a specific time period and imagining challenges that people of that time faced and how they responded to them. They work in their notebooks to develop characters for the stories they will write. They create webs about the "inside" and "outside" of their characters to explore how certain people—black, white; adults, children—dealt with the conditions of the times in which they lived. They write entries brainstorming how those conditions might change a person. They talk to each other and share the work they are doing to see if the seeds they are planting in their notebooks will grow into strong stories. Returning to the classroom, they begin to write. The students easily shift into workshop mode as they continue planning in their notebooks and talking eagerly to each other about their ideas. The most common discussion that can be heard is about how their characters are going to change in the story. Some students can easily create a plot line; others find it harder, but as we talk about our big idea and the ways in which we have looked at this issue all year long, they are able to figure out what they want to write—and how.

As drafts are written, conferring becomes more and more important. As writers, they ask others to offer feedback on needed revisions (e.g., "Can you tell that this is during the Civil Rights movement by my description of how people reacted to segregation?"). As readers, they let the writer know if they get pictures in their minds of where and when their characters are living. They talk and write, giving feedback and cultivating the seeds of the workshop planted in the fall. They are most certainly juggling as they read, write, speak, and listen. It is similar to what happens when they look to and listen to each other as they discuss a published piece of literature—trying out ideas, agreeing and disagreeing with each other, unpacking the ideas and their own reactions to them.

At the close of the year, I step back to see the how well they now can manage these skills that they began growing in September. We begin by reading *The Giver* by Lois Lowry (1993). We note and discuss how our world and we might change in the future. I want the students to move slowly through the story and focus on the consequences of change—how changes made to society that are intended to improve life can sometimes have negative results. I want them to consider connections they can make to other pieces we have read and to their own lives, and so I choose to take the book out of their hands and do it as an in-class read-aloud. This gives us time to read each chapter carefully and discuss the novel more deeply. As I read, the students are recording ideas. Some use their notebooks while others use a thinking guide I provide (Figure 10.3). They effortlessly write down comments, connections, or questions, and discussions come directly from their writing rather than from me.

Reflection is something I ask my students to do throughout the year. At the end of class each day, the students reflect on not only what they thought about the reading, but also on what they heard in discussions or wrote in their notebooks.

Figure 10.3   Thinking Guide for *The Giver*

I wonder...	I hope...
I don't understand...	I think...because...

Use back of the sheet for a quick-write. Quickly record what you are thinking now.

This sometimes comes in the form of a written conversation with a partner, which is not directed by me but totally by the student partners.

Betty: Written conversation is one way to use writing to capture thinking about reading. Students work silently in pairs, and all conversation is done on a shared paper. The students have the opportunity to develop and clarify their ideas with a partner, and the teachers have a record of the students' current thinking. Figure 10.4 presents an example of a written conversation between students; the writing in the example supports the students' developing understandings and also provides starting points for class discussion, such as:

What exists outside this community?

How would the people in this community react if they had this knowledge?

What does trust mean to this community?

How do you think Jonas will change as he gains knowledge?

How is your understanding of this community changing?

Molly: Sometimes I ask students to tear a piece of paper in half, reflect on the work that day in class, and hand it to me as they leave. I might ask them to write

Figure 10.4   Written Conversation Between Students A and H About Chapters 9 and 10 of *The Giver*

A: It hadn't occured to me that they wouldn't have snow or sleds. I wonder how they change the seasons?

H. Yeah, that too crossed my mind. It makes me wonder whether or not they live in some sort of dome or something. I wonder how Jonas feels about this job and if he's anticipating pain.

A: I would be afraid of the knowledge, It would be like finding out that someone had known that there were aliens out there but hadn't told us. I also don't understand how they wouldn't see out of the community because we live in Guilderland but at certain points we can see right over to other towns.

H: If someone had found out about aliens and hadn't told us, but some information leaked out it'd be very difficult to trust that community, and that's probably what happened to Jonas' community. Maybe the communities are very spread apart, so they never make contact, like in Gathering Blue, there was another outside community, but they never interacted.

A: That makes sense. I wonder if there are other communities w/strict rules that are different or if they have free will?

Note: No changes have been made to the original student text.

about the discussion, describe what they learned that day, or tell me if they enjoyed an activity. I like knowing what they are taking from class each day. Then, when they come back in for the next class, I can pass the responses back and pick up where we left off. These short writings allow me to address questions that we may not have had time for during the previous class and to take a pulse of the class to see who is with me and who is not. These reflections also lead to my own reflections: How can I better teach and reach my students?

Betty: Reflection is an ongoing process that supports both teachers and students in their growing and changing understandings. Sometimes students write reflective responses at the end of the class; sometimes the responses are written at home or at the beginning of class as a means of identifying issues still needing attention. Some teachers have students use a notebook as a place to collect these reflections; others prefer to have students write on separate sheets of paper. Teachers in the Partnership keep journals and experience similar opportunities for reflections in their biweekly meetings.

Molly: While the students are listening to the novel, they are also reading and making connections to short texts, such as newspaper articles and poetry. For example, we discuss Lois Lowry's Newbery Acceptance Speech (1994). These texts enrich the class discussions as students make meaning of the novel; they talk about our big idea of change and the possibilities for causing change in the world.

Another connection my students make is to their own lives. As we continue in the novel, I give them several prompts to think and write about in their notebooks.

They examine the ways in which they have changed through the years. The prompts run parallel to our study of *The Giver* and allow students to make connections to the main character, Jonas. For example, they are asked to discuss someone in their lives who has been influential and has had some impact on who they are; they are not allowed to write about a family member. The purpose of these prompts is twofold: They help students to enrich thinking for the current reading unit and to look toward the final major writing of the year, a memoir. Students write about themselves in ways that plant seeds for a possible memoir while cultivating their understanding of the changes that Jonas is experiencing in the story. While writing facilitates discussion of the novel, it also gives students a jumping off point as we turn to writing a memoir, where they explore change in themselves.

As our discussions of *The Giver* wind down, we consider Lowry's example of how a memory about change (in self or society) can truly have an impact on one's life. The students start thinking and writing in their notebooks about important events, places, and people in their lives who have helped shape who and what they have become, and they begin work on a memoir. They reflect in their notebooks on those things that have made an impact on who they are. They write about divorce, love, death, babies, disappointment, responsibility; they make personal connections to our big idea and see how they have changed in ways they have read and written during the year. They notice how the time they live in affects the way in which they live. We read and examine other memoirs to notice the craft that writers use to bring their memories to life for readers. I reach for my memoir that I shared with them in the fall. We discuss what further revisions I could make based on what we are learning of memoir. They juggle. They read, write, speak, and listen to each other as they work to produce their final piece of writing.

I give my students one final assignment. This time I want them to use their understanding of change to rework their writing. I pass back the pieces from that first day of class. They murmur and chuckle as they look over what they had written. Some have no recollection at all of the writing they had done. Some laugh out loud at how silly their ideas look jammed into one solitary paragraph. I once again ask them, as I had in September, to revise their work. We discuss what they now know that to mean: I need to figure out what genre I am writing; this isn't really anything. I want to use this and turn it into a short story. Should I go back to plan in my notebook? I think I might just use one of the ideas in this piece and just focus on that in my next draft. No longer am I met with stares of confusion or asked questions about length. Instead, my students' writerly minds began looking at the possibilities. They talk and listen excitedly about what they might do to revise or re-see this piece. They read and reread their drafts, notebooks, and each other's work as they come to decide what to do next. They write revisions, plan in their notebooks, and jot comments to each other as they flourish in their community of readers and writers. They demonstrate what revision now means to them, and before I read a single word, they are able to show me and talk to me about all that they have learned. They know that they will need to read, write, speak, and listen in order to complete the assignment, and the reading and writing they have done all year will help them through. They juggle all four seamlessly and without dropping a single ball. (See Figure 10.5 for an example of a student's drafts and reflections.)

Figure 10.5   Example of a Student's Drafts and Reflection*

Initial Draft, September 9, 2003

Last year I went skiing at Jimminy Peak with my brother, Dad, and my friend Keith. Jimminy Peak is not to big for me anymore because I concqured it that day first I went down the Glades with my brother. Glades are trails that go through the woods. All that they do is clear out all the saplings and keep all the big trees and rocks

Then I went down the hardest trail The Jerico it is a double black diamond. That trail is a 60' 70' drop with Ice.[Add more details about the ride] My dad twisted his ankel that day. When I got home that day My Mom got real mad at my dad because he hurt his ankle. After that day my feet were hurting.

Revised Draft, June 2004

I seems like yesterday that I concured Jimniy Peak ski Resort. I went down all of the hardest trails on the mountain. It actually wasn't that hard to do. Compared to things I'd done afterwards, now it just seem like a breeze and I could do it all day long.

The hardest trail on the mountain was called Jerico, It was a double Black Diamond, The next hardest is a Triple Black Diamond which is the hardest in the world. I have never seen any of those in my life. The Jerico was very steep at first, from a few feet away from the trail entrance it looks like a cliff. I got one of those feelings when you are all mixed with feelings. I was excited nervous, scared, and anxious all at the same time.

It took my dad about half a day to convince me that it wasn't so bad. My brother was also with us that day. He has been skiing about 4 years more than I have so he obviously thought that it was a smidge. Now relived that I listend, I decided to do it.

When I just started to make my way down a bunch of snowboarders came flying down the mountain to my right and left I started to freak out and really decided that if I didn't want to take a couple of nasty falls down this trecherous hill, I better get going or else one of those snowboarders is going to hit me down the mountain.

The first 20 feet or so were a little bit icy but I knew I couldn't turn back. The farther I went the less steep it became. When I was about halfway down I saw a speedboarder go zooming down. I could hear the swish of the ice on my skies as he went by. Finally, it was the final stretch. A very steep dropoff merging onto the main trail.

I stood up straight then then hunched over making myself as small as possible to slice through the wind. A half second later, it was over I did it I concured the mountain.

Student Reflections (to prompts), June 2004

1a. The new draft that I brought today is about the day that I conqured Jimniy peak. Although I really didn't actually conqure it. I had just completed all of the trails including a double black diamond, Jerico. This piece of writing is about my experences on my way down the mountain along with my experences leading up to my ride. This peice has a genre of memoir because it is one of the vague memories in my life.

1b. I spent about 2 hours on my piece. I had done most of it on the computer a few days ahead but had not printed it though. I had planned to finish the final touches on the computer the night before this test but my power went out therefore I had to spend about 2 more hours to redo the whole thing by hand because I didn't print it. I mainly wish I had worked on it earlier that day and finished it before the storm hit.

2. My first revision stragty was Add more. I thought about what I had left out then wrote notes in the 1st draft on what I could do to enhance the writing. I had mainly focused on my experience down the mountain and my inner thoughts. I chose this stragty because my writing was missing a lot of detail.

(continued)

Figure 10.5   Example of a Student's Drafts and Reflection* (continued)

The second revision stragty that I used was take a sentence and turn it into a page. I took the sentence "That trail is about a 70'-90' drop with ice" and turned it into almost my whole story about my other experiences while on the trail. I used this stragty because I really needed this story longer and I wanted to make a focus point to my story.

My third revision stratgy that I used was "Did I tell the internal story." I really thought that I needed some inside voice of this story that even the people that were there beside me could not hear. So I added a lot of feeling and thought that was going through my mind at the time.

3. One main thing that I would do is add more figurative language in my writing to try and bring out more emotions and looks for the people who have not experenced the same experences that I have.

Although this student has yet to write his final draft, we can see the writing growth made throughout the year. In addition, the students' reflections indicate an awareness of the role change plays in sharper writing and thinking. In this class all students use what they have learned across the year to make changes that improve their writing.

* These are examples of the changes in students' writing and thinking before the editing and publication stages.

At the end of the year I ask for a final reflection. Students talk about how they have changed as readers and writers. Each sees the changes differently, but all can identify ways in which they have grown. They speak about how what they have experienced in class has had an impact on how they view themselves as readers, writers, and thinkers. In addition, they consider our bigger idea—the ways the events in the world can change people and the ways people can change the world. They revisit earlier units and discuss changes they see in people and in the world around them. They refer to the texts we read together and those they read independently. For example, some note that the courage that Jonas needed to leave his world was similar to the kind of courage people needed during the Civil Rights movement to change society. Many mention the ways that being aware of how society changes people and people change society will help them in their future studies and in life.

Betty: Through their shared experiences, the students in Molly's class grow as a community of readers, writers, and thinkers. They reflect on how their experiences are changing them. They use writing and reading to identify their questions and wonderings and to clarify what they know and understand. They also use reading and writing to develop and deepen understanding of the literary works they are studying, and the big idea of change. Talking is essential. They learn to listen to one another; accept and reject ideas respectfully; and rethink, refine, and deepen their understandings by hearing one another. They make connections across texts and to their own lives.

They learn to become more critical thinkers, and more highly literate individuals.

Conclusion

The examples Molly has selected to include in this chapter can offer us a backdrop from which to think about the ways in which writing and reading can skillfully be used to help students make connections not only among the various topics they encounter in class (e.g., the big issue of change), but also among the skills and knowledge they can call upon when they read and write. In Molly's classroom, students are minds-on reasoners as well as learners all the time. Their new writing and reading skills and knowledge are made overt, connected within activities that help them try them out, see their effect, and go beyond. Throughout the school year, her students use writing, reading, and talk to question, learn, and act in highly literate ways. But Molly's class is just one example. In Partnership classes, equally effective teaching can occur within a context of very different activities, but the underlying pedagogical framework remains the same:

1. Envisionment-building classrooms. Students' growing understandings are the center of class work. They use purposeful reading, writing, and language to ask questions; make predictions; reflect on meanings; take perspectives; consider alternative views; and examine, explain, and elaborate their understandings. Their mental envisionments about reading, writing, and content keep developing.

2. Curricular connections. The topics students study are connected to large issues to which they can relate their new knowledge. This provides continuity and coherence within and among lessons over time, and helps students apply new learnings to big ideas that are central to them and the field of study.

3. Substantive conversation. Teachers and students ask thought-provoking questions that lead to high-level conversation about the topics at hand. Through conversation they learn to agree or disagree (and tell why), build on each other's ideas, and engage in sustained and thoughtful discussion that moves their understandings along. Students see models of thought in action as their teachers, as well as other students, use language to inform as well as to refine understandings.

All this occurs in an environment where reading, writing, and talk are used to bring, try out, examine, and refine new ideas and connect them to old ones. Class becomes a time when students attempt, explore, analyze, reflect, apply, communicate, and critique about and with language. In doing so they gain knowledge of language and content and grow as writers and readers. Across the school year, students overtly and implicitly relate writing and reading; they use their knowledge in one to inform performance in the other—a major step in their growth toward higher literacy.

REFERENCES

Applebee, A.N. (1996). *Curriculum as conversation.* Chicago: University of Chicago Press.

Applebee, A.N., Langer, J.A., Nystrand, M., & Gamoran, A. (2003). Discussion-based approaches to developing understanding: Classroom instruction and student performance in middle and high school English. *American Educational Research Journal, 40,* 685-730.

Clay, M.M. (1993). *Reading recovery: A guidebook for teachers in training.* Portsmouth, NH: Heinemann.

Collins, J. (1995). Literacy and literacies. *Annual Review of Anthropology, 24,* 75-93.

Cook-Gumperz, J.J., & Gumperz, J. (1981). From oral to written culture. In M. Whitman (Ed.), *Variations in writing* (pp. 89-108). Hillsdale, NJ: Erlbaum.

Goodman, K.S. (1989). Whole language research: Foundations and development. *The Elementary School Journal, 90*(2), 207-221.

Heath, S.B. (1988). Protean shapes in literacy events: Ever-shifting oral and literate traditions. In E.R. Kintgen, B.M. Kroll, & M. Rose (Eds.), *Perspectives on literacy* (pp. 348-370). Carbondale: Southern Illinois University Press.

Langer, J.A. (1986a). *Children reading and writing: Structures and strategies*. Norwood, NJ: Ablex.

Langer, J.A. (1986b). Reading, writing and understanding: An analysis of the construction of meaning. *Written Communication, 3*(2), 219-267.

Langer, J.A. (1995). *Envisioning literature: Literary understanding and literature instruction*. New York: Teachers College Press; Newark, DE: International Reading Association.

Langer, J.A. (2001). Beating the odds: Teaching middle and high school students to read and write well. *American Educational Research Journal, 38*(4), 837-880.

Langer, J.A. (2002). *Effective literacy instruction: Building successful reading and writing programs*. Urbana, IL: National Council of Teachers of English.

Langer, J.A. (2004). *Getting to excellent: How to create better schools*. New York: Teachers College Press.

Langer, J.A., & Allington, R. (1992). Curriculum research in writing and reading. In P.W. Jackson (Ed.), *Handbook of research on curriculum* (pp. 687-725). New York: Macmillan.

Langer, J.A., & Flihan, S. (2000). Writing and reading relationships: Constructive tasks. In R. Indrisano & J.R. Squire (Eds.), *Perspectives on writing: Research, theory and practice* (pp. 112-139). Newark, DE: International Reading Association.

Lowry, L. (1994). Newbery acceptance speech. Retrieved July 26, 2004, from http://www. loislowry.com/speeches.html

Minnich, E.K. (1990). *Transforming knowledge*. Philadelphia: Temple University Press.

New London Group. (1996). A pedagogy of multiliteracies: Designing social futures. *Harvard Education Review, 66*(1), 60-92.

Nystrand, M., with Gamoran, A., Kachur, R., & Prendergast, C. (1997). *Opening dialogue: Understanding the dynamics of language and learning in the English classroom* (Language and Literature Series). New York: Teachers College Press.

Palincsar, A.S., & Brown, A.L. (1984). Reciprocal teaching of comprehension-fostering and comprehension-monitoring activities. *Cognition & Instruction, 1*, 117-175.

Raphael, T.E., & Pearson, P.D. (1985). Increasing students' awareness of information for answering questions. *American Educational Research Journal, 22*(2), 217-235.

Shanahan, T. (1984). The nature of the reading-writing relation: An exploratory multivariate analysis. *Journal of Educational Psychology, 76*(3), 466-477.

Solsken, J.W. (1993). *Literacy, gender and work in families and in school*. Norwood, NJ: Ablex.

Spivey, N.N., & King, J.R. (1989). Readers as writers composing from sources. *Reading Research Quarterly, 24*, 7-26.

Squire, J.R. (1983). Composing and comprehending: Two sides of the same basic process. *Language Arts, 60*(5), 581-589.

Street, B. (1993). *Cross-cultural approaches to literacy*. New York: Cambridge University Press.

Teale, W.H., & Sulzby, E. (1986). Introduction: Emergent literacy as a perspective for examining how young children become writers and readers. In W.H. Teale & E. Sulzby (Eds.), *Emergent literacy: Writing and reading* (pp. vii-xxv). Norwood, NJ: Ablex.

Tharp, R.G., & Gallimore, R. (1988). *Rousing minds to life: Teaching, learning, and schooling in social context*. New York: Cambridge University Press.

Tierney, R.J., & Pearson, P.D. (1983). Toward a composing model of reading. *Language Arts, 60*(5), 568-580.

Tovani, C. (2000). *I read it, but I don't get it: Comprehension strategies for adolescent readers*. Portland, ME: Stenhouse.

Wells, G., & Chang-Wells, G.L. (1992). *Constructing knowledge together: Classrooms as centers of inquiry and literacy*. Portsmouth NH: Heinemann.

LITERATURE CITED

Curtis, C.P. (1995). *Watsons go to Birmingham—1963*. New York: Bantam Doubleday Books for Young Readers.

English, K. (1999). *Francie*. New York: Farrar, Straus, and Giroux.

Lowry, L. (1993). *The giver*. Boston: Houghton Mifflin.

Chapter *11*

Why Writing Is Technology: Reflections in New Media

Bertram C. Bruce and Sharon L. Comstock

Over 20 years ago, James Squire was one of the first to understand how open-ended computer tools and environments, such as Quill (Bruce & Rubin, 1993), could amplify the possibilities for writing. Every aspect of the writing process—collecting and organizing ideas, collaborating, drafting, revising, and sharing—could be facilitated through the new technologies then emerging. Of course, we have witnessed the shadow aspects of these technologies as well: misuse—or abuse—of networked information, lack of information ethics, and the digital divide, to name but a handful. Despite all this, today many of the innovative tools of the late 20th century have become commonplace, so much so that a teacher might say, "I don't use computers in my teaching; my students just write."

Just write—the movement from novelty to tool to transparency is remarkable when we consider what it means to write today. Models of writing have internalized the technology to such an extent that new genres are now becoming as commonplace as the computer: Hypertextuality is no longer a buzzword of academics or postmodern literati, but an accepted form of both fiction and nonfiction; online diaries have flourished in a networked environment that offers both anonymity and audience for creative construction of identity; and blogging has reached professional culture, with corporations and libraries alike posting to the world. What all of these new genres—and the tools used to create them—share at their core is *transformation*; the technologies we use are essentially transformative of the writer, the community, and even of the tool itself. Whether in the classroom, library, workplace, or neighborhood center, new digital technologies are making possible new ways to communicate, create, and collaborate. This chapter discusses how technology is not only expanding the environments for writing, but also changing how the craft is practiced. We consider the transactional as well as the transformative relationships intrinsic to the writing process.

Googling, blogging, instant messaging, text chatting—new media are becoming increasingly important in the practice of writing. From word processing that allows for collaborative drafting of a single document to peer-to-peer file sharing that supports real-time collaboration, so many aspects of writing are witnessing change. Few would question that metamorphosis. Yet the impact of these new technologies on writing is often poorly understood and rarely analyzed critically. Our goal here is to understand the impact of new media on writing; to begin to tease out the implications technologies pose for reframing our relationship to the tools we use, and how they shape the creative dynamic we call "writing." Key to our exploration is that the impact is two-way, requiring us to look at how the technologies themselves are being affected by the writing process. We see reflection and experience as twin, central functions of writing, and take this as our lens for analysis. Ultimately, this investigation leads us to conceive technologies neither as genies nor gadgets, panaceas nor passing fancies, but as an integral part of the human experience that demands thoughtful and critical understanding.

Writing as Reflection

Writing serves many purposes, and we do not wish in any way to limit an examination of those many purposes. However, one essential role writing plays is to provide a means of reflecting on experience. This reflection on different aspects of experience has three major facets:

1. On self: Writing offers one way in which individuals make sense of their own experiences and their roles within their communities. This facet is evident today in blogs and online diaries.
2. On other: Writing is also a way to describe, investigate, and articulate experience, then to communicate that emerging understanding with others.
3. On community: Writing becomes the means to reflect on society and one's role within it, in particular building a critical analysis on a macro level.

One could say that writing becomes the "tool" by which experience is made manifest; through it, we are able to reflect on the very essentials of being human. Curiosity, creativity, community building—these are but a few of the human impulses that writing as reflection enriches and new media further enhance.

Materiality of Writing

In some ways, it may seem that the oft-heard dichotomies that describe technologies are as new as new media. In fact, technologies have always been a part of the writing process, and the history of writing might well be structured around the series of transformations that have evolved: from cave drawings to early writing systems, printing press to current digital publishing. Writing, as a social practice, has been inseparable from the tools that have produced it. Christina Haas (1996) critiques the autonomous view of technology, in which technology is conceived as a new and outside agent that causes changes to social practices. This view leads to an instrumentalist, even deterministic, way of thinking about technology. Instead, Haas argues that literacy, technology, and other human functions take place in the whole context of an activity. Her view thus recalls John Dewey's (1938) conception of situation as a coordinated system in which no element—individual, others, objects, texts, and so on—can be seen as determinate. Applied to the question at hand, this view leads us to reject both the conception of technology as an independent agent that in and of itself creates change and the idea that writing activity can be understood separately from its technologies (cf.

Bruce, 1997). The evolution of the technological media by which we express ourselves is the very story of literacy.

Today, many people argue that new media are leading to fundamental changes in writing practice, a "writing revolution" of a kind we have not witnessed before in our lifetimes. Although there may be some (quite valid) reasons for enthusiasm, our stance here is neither to argue for the existence of a qualitative change in writing nor to deny that writing is changing, but rather to understand in concrete terms what is happening in writing practices with new media today. In this section, we look at the three areas of reflection identified above and explore how new media—as a form of creativity—are practiced.

On Self

The Blogosphere. Blogs were originally maintained by computer programmers as a way to communicate updates to software or information systems. (For an early example of this type of blog, see an archived page at the University of Illinois, Urbana-Champaign [UIUC] website: http://archive.ncsa.uiuc.edu/SDG/Software/ Mosaic/Docs/old-whats-new/whats-new-0693.html.) A spirit of a shared informational space that could be created for and by a community established the basis for continual experimentation. Tim Berners-Lee provides a historical overview of these issues in Internet development (see www.w3.org/People/ Berners-Lee). Librarians, information specialists, and library staff now use blogs as a critical piece of their service roles, as well as a way to build professional community and identity. (See the ubiquitous professional—and not-so-professional —uses of the blog at http://pscontent.com/od2/opendirectory.php?browse=/ Reference/Libraries/Library_and_Information_Science/Weblogs.) The word *blog* appears routinely now in reference to the vast "third-space," where the written word has the consumptive speed of wildfire as rumor, art, and innuendo merge to become legitimized. Recently a metagenre has emerged—blogging about blogging— in which writers claim being "first" to keep a Web-based log.

New media provide dynamic environments for the construction of self-identity tantamount to an electronic mirror. There are online journals popularized by such sites as Blogger (www.blogger.com), LiveJournal (www.livejournal.com), and Open Diary (www.opendiary.com), where regular diarists-bloggers write for a sometimes-adoring audience. Once-private musings are now prime-time reading. (However, some suggest that even the "private" diaries of the past had an intended reader [see Mallon, 1995].) Take, for instance, this piece from a young woman's blog (modified somewhat to preserve anonymity):

> Then I got really drunk with my friends down the street, and ended up becoming extremely upset and sobbing and talking about a whole bunch of [expletive] to my good buddy/..., including all my problems with lying and my mom in high school and the fact that feeling guilty about failing authority figures had made me become semi-obsessed for two weeks with the idea of cutting myself.

Another young woman admits to making fake identification cards in order to buy liquor, while a young man writes about a having an affair with an older man. All of this is marked "public," even though the blogger may say explicitly, "I hope my parents never find out about this." Clearly, particularly for the young adult diarist-bloggers, writing is a form of exploration as they navigate and struggle with emerging maturity.

The blog format is also a place where the young writer can test his or her voice (carving out safe space in which to write creatively) as well as create an ad hoc "writer's workshop." Following is a poem from Open Diary on what role the blog-diary takes in this process:

> This is my home
> A safe keeping for my jumbled
> Thoughts
> Perhaps they are senseless
> Or even unfinished
> But this is my outlet
> A quiet place to scream
>
> (Story_Queen)

The writer ends her poem with a quick "please leave a note or email me" to solicit feedback on her experience as a teen as well as her poetry. Often, teen diarists use their online journals to express in poetry what they cannot express in any other form. The diary provides a cocoon in which to create. Clearly, the diary's role in creating self-identity and being, itself, a work of art dovetail to make the diary fertile ground for public creative work to take root—a place where that "silent scream" can be heard.

The diary allows a writer—a young adult in particular—a safe space in which to test his or her voice in a world that often discounts the young adult's thoughts and creativity. A diary has always allowed the disenfranchised a place to speak: Prisoners, wives, slaves, and children all have turned to this medium in the past (Kagle, 1979). A young adult often is one of these disenfranchised, and with new media, the diary genre has become a dominant creative presence on the Web. The audience, then, is always present in the online diarist's mind. Whether it serves as a critic or a support, a mirror of the present or a reflection on a past, the audience for the blog is not that much different from the reader of a novel or short story. Writer and reader share the same relationship, albeit a more intimate one, and the diarist can claim the mantel of "creative writer" as surely as that of any poet or novelist.

Here is another poem written by a different online diarist:

> Pretty Blue Haze
>
> Picture your hand on my face
> Your eyes searching mine
> Now take what you feel
> No it's better than real
> Down, underneath, say it's fake
> A lake, a pretty blue haze
> A place you can stay
> A place you've made.
>
> (Ender)

Note those last lines, "A place you can stay/A place you've made." Perhaps this more than anything sums up the online diary-blog for the young-adult diarist.

The diary-blog is a haven, a defined space of one's own creation, its parameters self-determined; a place where "it's better than real/down, underneath"; a place where the teen self and that of the teen creative writer can be fashioned out of view from his or her everyday life—but very much in view for that online one— where it's "better than real." This view has implications for what defines experience: The online experience, or rather the writing as represented online, becomes absolute engagement at the same time it is an artifact of the authentic.

On Other

Research and writing are always done in context; purpose defines design. When we consider new media's impact on research, we naturally turn toward the classroom as a laboratory to investigate how technologies are actually used by the students we teach. By way of illustration, we examine one collaborative work group's depiction of their research process. Each semester in their LIS (Literacy in the Information Age) 391 course, students carry out a group project on a self-selected topic relevant to literacy. At the end of this project, as a way for them to reflect, they are asked, "So, if you were to draw a picture of your research process this term, what would it look like?" One semester, every one of the students' drawings included computers, usually represented as a schematic computer monitor near the top or middle of the page, implying how early it entered the process. Meeting with others to discuss what was found "on the computer" was also an early part of nearly every research path. Another common thread was an impending sense of a critical shortage of time to find, analyze, discuss, and write. Interestingly, many represented too much time spent trying to find materials via search engines, and then—in desperation, almost as a last hope—turning to the physical library on campus, where the student stick-figure faces smile as they carry books back to their work group. New media, in many cases, have contributed to the "information overload" students encounter, where Googling—once thought to be the fastest way to gather sources—overwhelms. The utility of the technology diminishes to such a point that the user simply abandons it out of sheer frustration.

The ubiquity of technology in the research and writing process, as well as its different functions in that cycle, are illustrated in Figure 11.1. The student researcher begins with a question, a guiding line of inquiry. She shows the further refinement of the initial question by moving toward community, and then enlarging that community to ultimately share a "eureka" moment where the idea is structured enough to motivate. She turns to the "square box," presumably the online catalog, which guides her through the library stacks and back (and forward) to more significant questions. She goes "back to the box" that allows her to access the library, and on to a discussion with her community for more insights. She returns to the computer again, this time for information and tools available on the Web, from which she prints, has a new idea again, and meets with her group. There is this idea of returning, of spiraling inward—and out again—as a labyrinth, following Ariadne's web in these stages of the creative process. New media here are used invisibly and seamlessly, integrated into the work. A slight shift occurs, however, in the creation—not to imply that what preceded was not "creative"— where, as a collaborative team, they use digital technologies and peer-to-peer environments to create and present their work to the larger community of learners.

Figure 11.1　Student Drawing of the Research Process

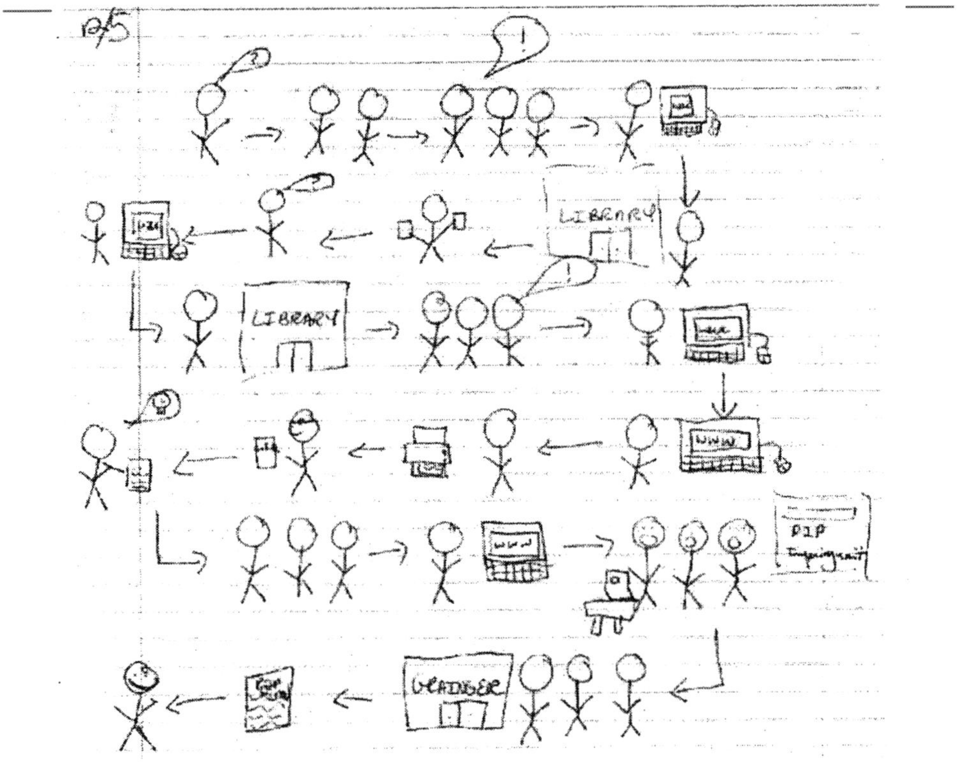

Ultimately, the final "product" of their process is represented as a written, traditional document.

　　For these learners and for all of the students in the class, technology is represented as deeply integrated into the entire process. Yet there is still a sense of "it" being something "over there," some thing in a box on a desk. What the students may not have been able to represent was this idea of technology—in and of itself—being an experience, not simply the *means* to an experience. But it is beyond dispute that technologies have penetrated and altered their experience of research.

On Community

If the relationship between writer and research has been reframed, then the relationship between writer and community has been redefined as well. Collaboration has grown considerably in networked environments. We examine here a genre that exists because of the essential flexibility of that networked space: hypertext.

　　At John Dewey's University of Chicago Laboratory High School, students in their senior year can create a spring-long independent study termed "May Project." This project-based learning allows students to examine a problem in depth, conduct a study or experiment, or create an artistic portfolio or piece. One student knew she wanted to write a series of autobiographical stories, but also wanted to do something "on the Web." After some discussion with her advisor, she was pointed to the Electronic Literature Organization (ELO; www.eliterature.org), where she discovered—not without some surprise—a genre she had never heard of: hypertext narrative. The form would allow the student to take advantage of the multilinearity of stories she wanted to tell, making transparent Roland Barthes's (1974) lexias (small units of reading through which a reader comes to understand and reconstruct the meaning of a text) and reconfiguring the author-reader-text relationship (see Landow, 1992). She agreed that this form of writing was exactly what she wanted to try.

The student maintained a blog on the Inquiry Page (http://inquiry.uiuc.edu) in order for her to keep track of her Web resources and citations, certainly, but also for her to see her project as a nonlinear process. Hypertext fiction and nonfiction draw so much on post-postmodern theory that maintaining a chronological blog would help her be more conscious of the very real craft involved. (See her Inquiry Unit at www.inquiry.uiuc.edu/bin/update_unit.cgi?command=select&xmlfile= u11824.xml.) This in itself allowed not only a way for advisor and student both to keep track of the student's process, but it also gave the student's peers a view on an ordinarily invisible part of creative writing.

A community of peers developed as she created her online presence. Other students regularly asked her if she'd "done any more" on her May Project, and she found that her friends were reading her pieces as soon as she put them up. Some of these friends made suggestions about what she should cover or write about, and what not to write about. The student struggled over these "censorship" moments, and she wrestled with what should or should not be included in her hypertext narrative. Here it became obvious that the sheer scale of her audience made her second-guess her creative process. In contrast, if this were a piece written only for her advisor, she might not have wrestled with the ethical—and very real—issue of creative license and privacy. The form itself raised issues distinct from a traditional portfolio.

The hypertext genre is unwieldy and daunting to an expert, much less a novice, and the electronic literature writer-artist needs community, whether as a high school student or adult author. Part of building this community meant reaching out to those who have blazed trails, including, in particular, the authors of a hypertext novel called *The Unknown* (2002; see www.unknownhypertext.com): Scott Rettberg, cofounder and first executive director of the ELO, and a new media faculty member at Richard Stockton College of New Jersey; William Gillespie of UIUC, a playwright, poet, and fiction writer employing collaboration in his work (see Gillespie's "literature laboratory" at www.wordwork.org and his "publishing house" at www.spinelessbooks.com); and Dirk Stratton, a writer and poet (see www.unknownhypertext.com/biodirk.htm).

The student interviewed them via e-mail, eventually cutting and pasting the text of this exchange into her own hypertext narrative (with permissions granted, of course), linked via the words *lesson* and *novel*. She was implying, with these single lexias, that she was not only learning how to write a "novel," but that this was a "novel lesson"; in other words, her experience with this genre and these authors was unlike any other English lesson she had had up to this point. They spoke often about what words she would link to what essays, and she eschewed formal architecture for a much richer intertextuality. She began to grow a sense of personal "author-ity" as she defined for herself what themes she would stress by the creation of a link, discovering in the process what meanings *discourse* and *author* held for her (see Foucault, 1977, for discussion of these terms). These were conscious decisions made often in an environment of collaboration with her peers, other writing teachers, and advisor. Ultimately, she was still struggling with what meaning and implications she had crafted when the time came to demonstrate her May Project for the school, but she felt successful at having experimented. Her hypertext (available at http://fade.to/llawred) represents her experience of genre experimentation and of new media and reflections on both her life and the tools that allowed her to shape her narrative.

We stress here the idea of "relationship" within the contexts of the writing process at many levels: writer to text, writer to writer, writer to reader, writer to tool, reader to writer, and tool to writer. These last two are aspects of technology-enhanced processes that are emergent: the participatory nature of the intended reader-audience on the author as well as the influence of the writer on his or her tool. In the spirit of participatory design practices, the tool itself does not remain static, but emerges as the writer and reader interact. The dynamic tool echoes the dynamism extant in interaction; it illustrates that the technology, the writer, and the written are, in fact, a single, inextricable experience.

Discussion

The examples in this chapter raise more questions than answers. Indeed, different commentators may arrive at widely differing interpretations of phenomena such as those we have discussed. For some, the new forms of writing we see in the blogs, instant messaging, e-zines, and webpages of children and young adults presage a radical shift in the fundamental nature of representation and communication. This shift is seen as comparable to, if not exceeding, that of mass distribution of books, the introduction of the printing press, or even the invention of the alphabet. The shift includes not only new forms, such as hypertext and multimedia, but also new modes of distribution and response.

Gunther Kress (2005) explores this ongoing realignment in culturally valued modes of writing, specifically the widely held view that text is being displaced by image. Assuming this realignment, he asks a variety of questions, such as whether "depiction is a better means of dealing with much in the world than writing or speech could be." Does speech or writing distort the world by forcing the automatic expression of temporality and causality? Does "the specificity of depiction" provide more truth than "the vagueness of word"? Could we all become authors of apt and accurate representations if we were to establish authority and knowledge for ourselves?

A number of other writers have examined similar questions. Cynthia Selfe and Gail Hawisher (2004) explore in detail the meaning of these changes for individual lives. Chapters in a collection edited by Bertram Bruce (2003) examine the implications for learning as well as ethical and policy dimensions. Those in a collection edited by Donna Alvermann (2002) adopt a similar stance as they consider the implications of e-zines and other elements of adolescent literacy. Jay David Bolter and Richard Grusin (1999) study the process by which new media technologies refashion prior media forms, one aspect of the "genealogy of new media." In these and a wide variety of other studies, a central assumption is that important changes are occurring and need to be examined carefully and critically.

Despite the change in form, the same issues of making sense of experience and communicating that to others, developing identity, and solving problems have not substantially changed. A brief survey of the recent International Reading Association conference papers indicates that many still view new technologies as having little—or even a negative—impact. Perhaps most importantly, they see these technologies as separate from "real" reading and writing. Even the language we use in this chapter reflects this sense that technology is somehow "over there," when, in fact, technology is an extension of—and is itself—our experience and engagement with our world.

We argued in the beginning that writing is a technology; hence the history of writing is a history of its tools. The new communication technologies are not a break with the history of writing, but a further evolution of it. The new tools offer us new ways for reflecting on experience; even technologies like computer programming or digital video recording (DVR), such as TiVo (a device that allows users to find and digitally record via satellite or other Internet connection various media content such as television programs, movies, and music to replay later), can thus be viewed as a kind of writing. We conceive writing as a form of technology, but the converse is true as well: Technology is a form of writing—of "story." Through this lens, then, we see technology as an integral part of human experience, not as an outside agency that is somehow changing us against our will. Rather, it is our process of using—and re-creating—these technologies that is essential human experience.

REFERENCES

Alvermann, D.E. (Ed.). (2002). *Adolescents and literacies in a digital world.* New York: Peter Lang.

Barthes, R. (1974). *S/Z* (R. Miller, Trans). New York: Hill and Wang.

Bolter, J.D., & Grusin, R. (1999). *Remediation: Understanding new media.* Cambridge: MIT Press.

Bruce, B.C. (1997). Literacy technologies: What stance should we take? *Journal of Literacy Research, 29*(2), 289–309.

Bruce, B.C. (Ed.). (2003). *Literacy in the information age: Inquiries into meaning making with new technologies.* Newark, DE: International Reading Association.

Bruce, B.C., & Rubin, A. (1993). *Electronic Quills: A situated evaluation of using computers for writing in classrooms.* Hillsdale, NJ: Lawrence Erlbaum.

Dewey, J. (1938). *Logic: The theory of inquiry.* New York: Holt.

Foucault, M. (1977). What is an author? (D.F. Bouchard & S. Simon, Trans.). In D.F. Bouchard (Ed.), *Language, counter-memory, practice* (pp. 124–127). Ithaca, NY: Cornell University Press. Retrieved May 2, 2002, from http://foucault.info/documents/foucault.authorFunction.en.html

Haas, C. (1996). *Writing technology: Studies on the materiality of literacy.* Mahwah, NJ: Erlbaum.

Kagle, S.E. (1979). *American diary literature, 1620–1799.* Boston: Twayne.

Kress, G. (2005). Gains and losses: New forms of texts, knowledge, and learning. *Computers & Composition, 22*(1), 5–22.

Landow, G.P. (1992). *Hypertext: The convergence of contemporary critical theory and technology.* Baltimore, MD: Johns Hopkins University Press.

Mallon, T. (1995). *A book of one's own: People and their diaries.* St. Paul, MN: Hungry Mind.

Selfe, C.L., & Hawisher, G. E. (2004). *Literate lives in the information age: Narratives of literacy from the United States.* Mahwah, NJ: Erlbaum.

LITERATURE CITED

Rettberg, S., Gillespie, W., & Stratton, D. (2002). *The unknown.* Retrieved May 1, 2002, from http://www.unknownhypertext.com

Chapter 12

Breaking Ground: Constructing Authentic Reading–Writing Assessments for Middle and Secondary School Students

Robert C. Calfee and Roxanne Greitz Miller

When examining student achievement on writing assessments, particularly large-scale writing assessments such as the National Assessment of Educational Progress (NAEP) or state-level writing assessments, it is apparent from the results that such assessments are problematic for many students. The 2002 NAEP (National Center for Educational Statistics [NCES], 2003) showed 72% of fourth-grade students performed at or below the Basic level of achievement, and that by eighth grade, the students still did no better. Moreover, only 28% of fourth graders and 31% of eighth graders performed at or above the Proficient level. These writing assessments measure two distinct, albeit highly related, abilities: (1) reading comprehension and (2) transforming comprehension into composition.

The goal of this chapter is to propose a theoretically grounded and empirically tested method to design, administer, and evaluate an authentic writing assessment for students in the late elementary grades and beyond. We present this method from the perspectives of researcher, teacher, and student. Rather than a linear view of the transmission of curriculum, instruction, and assessment design—researchers to teachers to students, with little interaction—we take a collaborative–reciprocal or reflective approach. Researchers, teachers, and students interact with one another within a concentric circle, where a dynamic development process replaces the separate stages for designing, administering, and grading. In this process, teachers become "reflective practitioners," inquisitive of their own practice and responsive to the particularities of the classroom (Schön, 1983, 1987). For students, learning mirrors teaching, demonstrated by the use during assessment and instruction of metacognitive strategies, or thinking about thinking.

In the chapter, we first focus on the linkage between comprehension and composition, between reading and writing. For the grade levels considered here,

Learning to Write, Writing to Learn: Theory and Research in Practice edited by Roselmina Indrisano and Jeanne R. Paratore. Copyright © 2005 by the International Reading Association.

authentic classroom projects call for the translation of students' ideas and cognitions, garnered from various sources, into written text that transforms those ideas and cognitions into new constructions. Theoretical bases for these tasks rest on schema theory and the reading–writing connection (Anderson, Spiro, & Anderson, 1977; Nelson & Calfee, 1998). Next, we examine the importance of informing teachers and students about text analysis and rhetorical structure (often overlooked components of reading instruction) as strategies to support reading comprehension and effective writing. Against this context, we then present practical, hands-on suggestions for constructing an authentic assessment—start to finish—including characteristics of appropriate reading samples (target texts) that can serve as the basis for writing assessments, creation of reading–writing prompts, and support for the move from reading to writing.

Schema Theory and Reading Comprehension

What does research have to say about reading comprehension? A RAND Corporation reading study group (Snow, 2002) approached this question to set the stage for a research and development program aimed toward increasing K–12 reading comprehension. The report begins on the pessimistic note that "the current knowledge base on reading comprehension...is sizable but sketchy, unfocused, and inadequate as a basis for reform in reading comprehension instruction" (p. xii). The group then proposes a tripartite conceptualization of reading comprehension: the reader, the text, and the activity or purpose for reading. In its review of comprehension assessments, the reading study group finds fault with current methods when viewed through this framework; rather than operationalizing reading comprehension as "the process of simultaneously extracting and constructing meaning through interaction and involvement with written language," current instruments "conflate comprehension with vocabulary, domain-specific knowledge, word reading ability, and other reader capacities" (p. 53).

We are more optimistic about the conceptual and empirical foundations in the field, although we share the criticisms of current assessment strategies. Our reason for optimism springs from the work of the Illinois Center for the Study of Reading (CSR). Although remarkably few of the center's findings can be found in current practice, the CSR has produced valuable studies in the comprehension area for more than 25 years. The hallmark of the CSR work falls under the label of *schema theory* (e.g., Adams & Collins, 1977; Anderson, Spiro, & Anderson, 1977; Armbruster, 1976), with origins in cognitive models, later expanded to incorporate social-constructivist elements.

At the center of schema theory is the notion that understanding a complex message depends on instantiation by the comprehender of a template, or schema, that serves as a tentative framework for organizing the incoming information. Consider the following passage, used in research projects as a prototypical illustration of the importance to the reader of connecting with an appropriate schema:

> The procedure is actually quite simple. First you arrange the pieces into different groups. Of course, one pile may be sufficient depending on how much there is to do. If you have to go somewhere else due to lack of facilities, then that is the next step. Otherwise you are ready to go. (Bransford & Johnson, 1973, p. 400)

Several other paragraphs follow this introduction, leaving most "readers" thoroughly confused about the message. What is the problem? The vocabulary is familiar to most adults. The sentences are not especially long or complex. The problem is that the reader cannot connect to a familiar schema—what is the passage about? In this instance, a connection is easily established by suggesting that the reader think about doing laundry. Suddenly the text clicks—words and sentences fit together, the reader can anticipate upcoming material, and assessments show that the message has been understood.

A substantial body of research (Anderson, Spiro, & Anderson, 1977) supports the basic idea that comprehension of new material depends on connections to existing knowledge and previous experiences. But similar to 19th-century phenomenology, which captured audiences' attention with vivid examples, schema theory left important questions unanswered: What elements and dimensions are essential in defining a schema? What processes link a new text to an existing schema? How are schemata created and transformed? The examples typically relied on concrete experiences (doing laundry, going to a restaurant) that entailed shared commonplaces, or on "scripts" (fairy tales, fables) also commonplace but more generalizable; "heuristics" appear as a strategic version of the concept. The schema construct nonetheless provides a powerful foundation for reflecting on both comprehension and composition. To understand (or construct) a text, the individual relies on an existing memory template, which provides "slots" into which information can be placed, and that establishes tentative relations among existing and incoming elements. The linking process is dynamic, as shown by garden-path studies where the reader is led to instantiate an inappropriate schema, and must then move the information from one framework to another. In a favorite study of cognitive researchers, the reader is led to believe that the text is about a burglary, and then realizes at the end that it's a wrestling match; short story writers such as Guy de Maupassant use the same technique to startle readers. A similar conceptualization applies to the writing process, where an author chooses a particular framework to guide the assembly of a set of elements, which then serves to begin the composing activity. But we have all had the experience of stopping midway through a work with the often-distressing realization that we need to reframe the argument.

For present purposes, we will rely on two related concepts to extend and particularize schema theoretic notions: *text structure* and *latent semantic analysis*. Text structure concepts emerged during the CSR heyday as a substantial line of research and development (for an overview, cf. Chambliss & Calfee, 1998). Also driven by cognitive and social-constructivist notions, the idea was that written texts are more than collections of words and sentences. "Written" was an important determiner because the structure of casual conversations was less obviously the result of purpose, construction, revision, and permanency. A text, whether oral or written, resulted from the writer's or speaker's application of design principles.

While an oversimplification, the division of texts into narrative and expository categories provides a useful first cut for academic purposes. Story grammars (Stein, 1978) captured the universal human capacity to grasp slices of life, ranging from jokes to fairy tales to *Heart of Darkness* (Conrad, 1899/1999). The underlying elements are familiar territory—character, plot, setting, and theme. Human beings are remarkably adept at making sense of story "stuff" if they can fit a few elements into the basic story schema, whether it is a child's story or James Joyce's *Ulysses* (1922/1990).

Expository or informational texts, generally associated with formal communication, build on a collection of schemata that emerge not through natural development, but as societal artifices. The instantiation of extended structures, such as research reports, newspaper articles, and op-ed pieces, comes not from casual conversation but academic activities. The textbook, a daunting challenge for most readers, exemplifies the concept. For novices, the topic is unfamiliar, the cognitive schema has yet to be established, and the writing style is unfriendly. One of the primary outcomes of formal education is to support the creation of abstract schemata, along with detectors that alert the individual that the incoming message is not a simple story but requires genuine comprehension—the origins of which condense to "wrestling with ideas." When a speaker announces, "Let me lay out the three points that frame this presentation," you know she is not going to tell a story and that you should establish three slots in working memory to capture the three points. Before long, "three points" will be a schematic structure in long-term memory.

Text structures have their foundations in rhetorical principles but are also increasingly related to the application of graphic organizers (Chambliss & Calfee, 1998). The latter can serve several functions. One is the use within a text to lay out text structure. For example, a matrix displays three muscle types crossed with critical features, providing a summary of the textual content. A second provides the reader a way to create a visual summary of a complex text; if the writer did not provide a matrix for the muscle text, then the reader can construct one. In writing, organizers can set the stage for the design of a composition and serve as a framework for organizing information. If the task is to prepare a paper on muscles, then a matrix serves to display the results of various explorations in preparation for writing.

Text structures are inherently abstract, but comprehension eventually comes down to linking words and ideas—to establishing associations. During the past decade, a new set of conceptualizations and procedures has emerged around the notion of semantic space (Landauer, 1999). The origins of this work arise from efforts to define a "concept"—what does a person understand in response to *dog*, *house*, or *snowflake*? Viewed as a vocabulary matter, the question often centers on responses to a stimulus, following associative traditions. But the question also touches on schema theory; what comes to mind when you think about *restaurant*? A template emerges for most of us, which can be fleshed out more completely by suggesting labels like McDonald's or New York's Four Seasons. Finally, concepts can be connected to text structure. A primary aim of courses in physics and government is to (re)shape the individual's semantic space in the content domain. For instance, consider how adolescents define and interrelate the following words prior to a course in mechanics: *speed*, *force*, *accelerate*. They have some familiarity with this vocabulary, but as they make their way through the physics text (and other course-related experiences), they construct new schemata and transform existing ones.

Research on latent semantic analysis (Landauer, 1999) captures conceptual maps through a computer-based procedure (Intelligent Essay Assessor, or IEA) that constructs a student's associative structure following experience with a target text through analysis of a composition written in response to the text. Practically speaking, the procedure begins by providing IEA with a target text, along with a large collection of student essays written in response to the text. For instance, the target input might be a chapter on human memory from an introductory psychology textbook; additional input comes from responses to exam questions on the chapter, including the grade for each exam. The "word" is the foundation for IEA analysis, where "word" is operationalized as a physical entity (written or spoken) along with all the conventional associative correlates. Practically speaking, IEA uses a standard thesaurus as a guide, so it "knows" that *dog, hound, mutt,* and *pooch* refer to the same concept. IEA "digests" this body of material, including the chapter and the graded responses, and generates an associative "kernel," a multidimensional nugget that incorporates the critical conceptual relations in a compact package. The associative core features the textbook information along with the compositions that receive high grades, but the model also includes information about departures from the ideal.

Once a core has been constructed, IEA can be used to grade new sets of essays, including responses not only to previous questions but also new ones. The intro psych instructor can ship off a collection of student essays on human memory to the IEA website, and will quickly receive ratings and comments about each essay, based on the match of each essay to the kernel generated from the previous inputs. Automated and responsive grading is the primary practical application from the IEA system. From our perspective, a more interesting question centers around the nature of the kernels generated for a particular topic. What does IEA, using latent semantic analysis as the foundation, produce as the package that represents near-ideal understanding of a particular text? What is the relation of this associative network to corresponding schemata and text structures? Exploration of these issues using IEA as a foundation both conceptually and practically holds promise for the design and assessment of students' capacity to collect, analyze, and organize a complex body of information, and then transform the material into a novel construct—the kinds of tasks that become more essential as students move through the middle school years and beyond. Valid assessment of students' competence as academic writers begins with the acquisition of a clearly defined knowledge base rather than sole reliance on personal experience, which can vary substantially and inequitably. The most appropriate foundation for an academic writing assessment thus begins by presenting the candidate with a target text designed around a clear rhetorical structure and corresponding semantic associations, with provision for connections to existing experiences (schemata). Comprehension brings together the rhetorical, conceptual, and semantic perspectives in a dynamic mental entity that enables and organizes the writing task. The writer can then approach the task from various cognitive perspectives, but always with a clearly defined text as the starting point.

Assuming the availability of a target text, how does the process move ahead, based on the use of the conceptual elements presented thus far and with the focus on assessment of the written product? A text-based writing assessment can take three basic forms: summarization, extension, and transformation. Summarization highlights the key semantic elements in the text and reflects the text structure of the target text. Extension goes beyond summarization, including not only information from the target but also other relevant knowledge and experience. More than for summary, audience becomes critical in extension because the writer must select knowledge that is relevant to the designated purpose or reader of the text. Finally, transformation calls for creating a new construction from the original information and extensions. An example might call for a student to consider the consequences if the Civil War had ended in a stalemate, or to weigh Jefferson's proposal that public schooling be required only through eighth grade.

Designing an authentic writing assessment requires consideration of the writer's knowledge base, the purpose of the exercise, and a clear explication of the task, if the aim is to ensure optimal performance by all students. Comprehension is the starting point of the process in this model, hence our detailed attention to the various treatments of this construct. Somewhat surprisingly, current discussions of the construct seem to lack grounding in the research of the previous few decades. The RAND study (Snow, 2002), for instance, focuses on reader, text, and activity, but does not consider lessons from schema theory, gives only passing attention to text structure, and makes no reference to semantic analysis. Similarly, the linkage between reading and writing, between comprehending and composing, between oral and written language—is not discussed. In the following section, we will attempt to demonstrate the value of the "conceptual kernel" as the basis for defining comprehension and for linking comprehension and composition.

Let us summarize the preceding background and set the stage for the remainder of the chapter with a concrete example: "Where do rocks come from?" Most young people know something about rocks, and they may have some ideas about their origins. Your assessment task is to delve into a student's understanding of this topic during an instructional activity. You begin with your expert "kernel knowledge" of the topic; we assume you approach assessment grounded in pedagogical content knowledge. Your task is to determine the student's initial understanding (fraught with intriguing preconceptions), and then track the transformations in this kernel as the student undergoes a course of study—a month-long unit on the rock cycle. The student produces artifacts along the way—discourse, written reports, and a final report. The assessment process can be couched in fairly traditional terms: a needs assessment (what does the student already know?), formative evaluations (tracking the growth of knowledge), and summative performance (the final project). The model presented below combines substantive content with rhetorical structure, all bound together in the kernel. The ideal assessment provides an image of the student's understanding templated against the kernel during the project, to support assessment and instruction.

The Reading–Writing Connection

Ideas about reading-writing connections are not new, with origins in colonial times (Nelson & Calfee, 1998). In the past several decades, the two literacy components have been largely *disconnected* in U.S. classrooms. Yet process-based correlational studies suggest that reading and writing share underlying cognitive processes, that is, reporting (reproducing and paraphrasing), conjecturing, contextualizing, structuring, monitoring, and revising (Nelson & Calfee, 1998; Sperling & Freedman, 2001; Tierney & Shanahan, 1996). Some analyses emphasize the differences. For instance, the typical view is that readers absorb and organize information, while writers construct and express knowledge. The question, as Timothy Shanahan (1997) put it so pointedly, is whether the cognitive processes underlying reading and writing are sufficiently similar to allow for cross-learning opportunities yet sufficiently different to enhance learning. In particular, does processing information through reading *and* writing increase chances of raising comprehension by providing distinctive cognitive perspectives on text and knowledge?

Our hypothesis is that the answer to Shanahan's questions is "yes." Research by Tierney, Soter, O'Flahavan, and McGinley (1989) showed (a) students who wrote prior to reading tended to read more critically than did students who were either involved in a background-knowledge activation task or were given a simple introduction to the story, and (b) writing together with reading prompted more thoughtful consideration of ideas than did writing alone, reading alone, or either writing or reading in combination with questions. Similarly, in *How Writing Shapes Thinking* (1987), Langer and Applebee found that writing in conjunction with reading prompts students to be more thoughtfully engaged in learning. They found that, for high schoolers, writing activities contributed to better learning than when reading was done without some form of writing, especially if the material was less familiar to the student. Additionally, the results supported Langer's 1986 study that different writing tasks prompted different kinds of cognitive engagement. For example, essay writing prompted the learner to focus more deeply on specific sections and led students to engage in a greater variety of reasoning operations than either note-taking or study guide questions. Overall, these studies confirm that learning through writing *and* reading deepens student comprehension and engagement. (See chapter 6, this volume, for further development of these ideas.)

Aside from cognitive processing, effective reading and writing are connected by a rhetorical, transactional, "cyclical" relationship. Writers, as they produce text, consider their readers. Readers, in turn, respond to what they perceive writers are trying to communicate, interpreting the text based on their own knowledge and experiences (Brown, Campione, & Day, 1981; Rosenblatt, 1978). To be sure, these interactions reflect an ideal that is not always realized in the classroom. Tierney, LaZansky, Raphael, and Cohen (1987) suggest that failure to understand the author's intention can cause problems in text comprehension. By studying the response of readers to inconsistent ideas, they found that better readers relied upon a consideration of an author's intent to comprehend meanings, a strategy that helped them with less familiar texts and texts without dialogue. Also, Salvatori (1986) argues that enhancing a sense of authorship can contribute to more critical thinking. College-level basic writers who had undergone a carefully developed sequence of writing experiences acquired a more "dialogical," or transactional, attitude toward reading than students who just "read" text. Salvatori's finding suggests that writing can enhance a sense of authorship and with it, comprehension skills, making readers more thoughtful as they critically approach meaning of texts through authors' intentions. These analyses are consistent with a view of deep, substantial, and purposeful comprehension as a (re)constructive process closely akin to composition.

This selection of studies from the field of reading–writing connections suggests that integrating reading and writing can have a beneficial impact on reading comprehension, can enhance writing performance, and can serve as a powerful tool for assessment design. Leading students to understand and practice processes that underlie both reading and writing offers possibilities for improving students' reading comprehension and writing skills. Instruction in the use of these cognitive processes and strategies provides a scaffold that equips students with the means and attitudes to become active learners and researchers rather than passive consumers of knowledge.

From Theory to Practice: Elements of Authentic Reading–Writing Assessment

We now turn to the practical elements of authentic reading–writing assessments. First is the classification of writing assessments into two basic formats: text-based and stand-alone assessments. Text-based assessments employ a reading sample or *target text* followed by the writing task or *writing prompt*. Stand-alone assessments consist of a writing prompt only, relying on students' prior knowledge as the basis for the composition. For reasons argued earlier, we think that large-scale, high-stakes writing assessments should be text-based, giving students the opportunity to extend and reconstruct information provided to all participants, and reducing experiential differences. Text-based assessments emphasize reading–writing connections, encouraging thoughtful analysis through writing, deepening a feeling for rhetorical structures through an enhanced sense of authorship and audience, and so forth.

Text-based writing assessments do pose particular challenges for assessment design: (a) selection of the target text, (b) development of the writing prompt, and (c) establishment of the reading–writing context. We will discuss the first two design elements and then move to the issue of constructing rubrics that assess not only writing ability, but also the actual transformation of ideas from reading into writing.

Target Text

Choice of the target text poses a host of challenges, some obvious, others more subtle. Reading level must be appropriate for the range of students. Vocabulary, both technical and "plain," must be embedded in contexts that provide clues, enabling students to comprehend unfamiliar words or usages. Substitutions and paraphrasing may be necessary to provide sufficient explanations of concepts introduced. Layout features of the target text (font, type size, paragraphs, columns, word breaks) all must be examined for potential problems. Texts may help level the playing field, but they are by no means "culture free." To the contrary (Kaplan, 1966), for example, recent immigrant students unfamiliar with American history may be at a disadvantage when asked to read a target text and write to a prompt about the importance of Sacagawea to Lewis and Clark's expedition. To be sure, students born in the United States who may have heard of Sacagawea's journey with Lewis and Clark may also have difficulty locating a "history" schema for processing the information.

Aside from content, schema theory suggests that text structures (narrative, compare–contrast, cause–effect, etc.) are important considerations for text selection. As examples, Driscoll (1994) and Halliday and Hasan (1989) note that readers' text structure schemata allow them to organize text information. To ensure that the target text supports student access to the information, the target text structure must "click" for students, providing memory slots into which the new information can be placed, establishing relations among the incoming elements. The assessment should include elements that facilitate students' linkage to the appropriate schema, through obvious devices such as headings or topic sentences, along with analogies, similes, and metaphors.

The choice of narrative versus expository genre for the target text can substantially influence writing performance. In high-stakes assessments through grade 3, the narrative genre is most common for reading and writing instruction and assessment. In our judgment, exposition offers advantages for assessing reading comprehension and writing ability, especially in the mid-elementary grades and beyond. Exposition rests not so much on everyday experiences but on academic, school-learned schemata that are more likely to reflect content area standards. Narratives are often the basis for cultural portrayals, which are important outcomes from schooling, but are more problematic as the basis for assessment activities. "Real-life" reading-writing demands are primarily in the expository genre, preparing students for future professional and social demands.

Writing Prompt

The structure and content of the writing prompt is critical in designing an authentic writing assessment. Our ongoing reviews of writing prompts in a variety of large-scale assessments at the national and state levels have revealed substantial design variations (Calfee, Miller, & Associates, 2002, 2004). In the Reading and Writing About Science Project (RWS) (Miller & Calfee, 2004b), we developed a set of guidelines for the construction of writing prompts based on the existing literature (Mathena, 2000) and in dialogue with teacher collaborators (Miller & Calfee, 2004a, 2004b). In brief, these guidelines call for the design of prompt structure around five elements—focus statement, identification of audience, type or form of writing, purpose for writing, and supporting details—to provide the student an optimum base from which a text can then be composed:

- Begin writing prompts with a focus statement, such as "You are learning about different kinds of rocks and how they are formed through the rock cycle process." The focus statement has a twofold purpose: (a) it activates students' prior knowledge, and (b) it models implicitly to students that thinking before writing is critical to writing a coherent and effective essay. Focus statements may be separated from the actual writing directive by placing them in separate paragraphs, folding over the sheet of paper, or using two separate sheets.

- Provide students with work space to create webs, weaves, or graphic organizers of their own design to help organize their thoughts prior to writing. This space may be provided between the focus and directive statements or on a facing page. A statement such as "You may use this space to plan your writing," should be included in the prompt (or after it) so that students (a) are encouraged to develop a written organizer, and (b) know they are allowed to write in the blank space (obvious to us—but not to students accustomed to being told "don't write in the book"). Younger students may be provided with an advanced organizer.

- Tell the students what specific form (also referred to as type) the writing is to take: a letter, paragraph, essay, article, or so forth. (Students should never be instructed to "write a paper.")

- Offer specific and simple instructions about the purpose of the students' writing. Use phrases such as the following:

"Write a story that tells..."

"Write an essay to explain..."

"Write a letter to convince..."

"Write a letter to persuade..."

- Tell the students who the audience is for the composition. Giving the students an idea of whom they are writing to or for gives them essential information about tone, vocabulary, and structure. It also makes the writing more real for students and encourages them to consider audience in their writing and, by extension, authorship in their reading.

- Emphasize the importance of supporting details and elaboration. In particular, inform the writer about the relative importance of text-based and background knowledge in the composition. The following messages can evoke quite different responses:

"Use your personal experience in your essay."

"Keep the passage in mind as you write, along with your personal experience."

The Role of Rubrics

To most effectively support student understanding and performance, the prompt should mesh closely with the rubrics used to evaluate the composition. Ideally, students should know the rubrics (i.e., what matters?), and should have learned how to digest a prompt in light of the expectations. For classroom exercises, these linkages are within the teacher's control and can be built into the design of all assignments. Large-scale assessments tend to be more secretive, of course, which is understandable in some ways, though not others.

While many rubrics are available in the literature and are in practice in schools and assessment programs at the state and national level, our experience is that rubrics for content area writing present a unique challenge for assessment. First, all writing components, including grammar and spelling, must be addressed. Second, and of equal if not greater importance, the conceptual ideas relating to the content area must be rated and measured. It is for this reason that we believe that a "one-size-fits-all" rubric that addresses both the writing and the concepts is impractical and ineffectual. We have all read papers that are fluent, grammatically correct, and well written, but completely miss the point on the critical concepts. On the other hand, while some assessors assign a score of zero to all writing that is deemed "off-prompt," we do not agree with this practice; a well-crafted essay, even if off-target, merits some recognition.

We have employed a five-rubric scale for writing assessment (cf. Miller & Calfee, 2004b), based on work originally done in Project READ (Calfee & Patrick, 1995) for measuring the traditional areas addressed by many writing assessments: length, coherence, grammar and mechanics, spelling, and vocabulary. It is important to note that spelling and vocabulary are separate elements. The importance of vocabulary in reading comprehension has been mentioned previously. Using new vocabulary in writing is an essential goal of text-based writing assignments. In our experience, spelling and vocabulary use in writing share an inverse relationship when examined by writing scores (as vocabulary scores go up, spelling often goes down because more complex words are more difficult to spell). If students are not rewarded for taking risks with vocabulary usage (as is the case with many existing rubrics that consider spelling only), then they will simply not take the chance and thereby constrain their writing.

When student writing is based in content area knowledge, we advocate that a sixth rubric—content—be added to the evaluation process. We have found in the RWS Project (Miller & Calfee, 2004b) that reliance on a coherence rubric as the sole indicator of successful expression of content knowledge through writing is insufficient and sometimes actually misleading. Therefore, a generic content rubric was developed to serve as the framework for evaluating content knowledge through writing, with the intent that specific content goals for each score level be developed for each assessment according to the writing prompt directive(s), content knowledge to be transmitted, and writing task assigned.

Finally, we reemphasize the importance of informing students about the rubrics and how they specify the skills and knowledge that are important. If students do not know what is desired or have no idea what a "great" paper looks like, then they are not likely to produce one. This idea is a variation of the "writing to models" approach from many years ago. It is important that teachers share with students (and that testing administrators and developers share with teachers) the goal statements for each level prior to the administration of the assessment, give students opportunities to read papers at various levels of achievement, and provide opportunities to discuss the reasoning underlying the papers' scores. We have discussed the importance of student metacognitive reflection on their writing; by sharing the assessment framework long before requiring an on-demand writing task, students are enabled to construct papers that meet high standards.

Reading–Writing Context: Linking Assessment and Instruction

Authentic writing assessments function best not in isolation but when closely aligned with classroom instruction. To demonstrate their best performance on standardized writing assessments, students benefit from opportunities to develop well-established schemata for carrying out the reading-writing task in a variety of settings and subject matters, coupled with developmentally appropriate support and feedback along the way. Explicit instruction in reading and writing strategies at the classroom level (i.e., prewriting and metacognitive strategies, along with classroom and small-group interaction to activate background knowledge and schema) provides students with the cognitive schemata to display what they know during assessments.

The aim of this section is to explore the benefits of fusing instruction and assessment by describing the Read-Write Cycle (Miller & Calfee, 2004a), an integrated instruction and assessment model shown in Figure 12.1. The curriculum of the Read-Write Cycle utilizes varied reading comprehension strategies and text-based student writing as a vehicle to increase students' reading comprehension and composition skills and, simultaneously, to assess students' comprehension of texts as reflected in the their writing. Although much is known about strategies for improving comprehension in controlled settings (Palincsar & Brown, 1984), less is known about translating existing research and instructional

Figure 12.1   The Read–Write Cycle

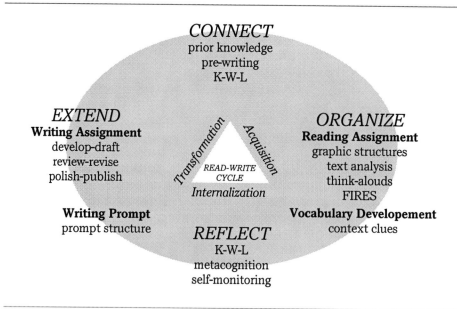

Adapted from Miller, R.G., & Calfee R.C. (2004a). Building a better reading–writing assessment: Bridging cognitive theory, instruction, and assessment. *English Leadership Quarterly, 26*(3), 6–13.

techniques into classroom activities that impact large-scale reading and writing assessments (see also Wilson, 2004).

The Read-Write Cycle combines the techniques of the CORE Model (Chambliss & Calfee, 1998), the California Learning Assessment System (CLAS) (Underwood, 1999), and varied reading comprehension and writing strategies in the domain of expository text, where we refer to both the prose and figural representations typical of exposition. Metacognitive reflection is emphasized throughout the model, and reading comprehension is assessed continually by both oral and written methods. Individual activities within the Read-Write Cycle provide practical models for classroom teachers for planning and implementing research-based reading and writing instruction.

We developed the Read-Write Cycle in response to the following challenge: How do we translate what we know from research on reading comprehension into a generalizable instructional method that teachers are willing to implement, able to internalize, and can apply across subject areas and grade levels? To be feasible and successful, such educational strategies must be efficient (they cannot require enormous amounts of time and money), effective (they must apply to a broad range of texts, grade levels, and subject areas), and adaptable (teachers can employ the strategies within the same classroom for a range of students, from gifted to special education).

To illustrate the Read-Write Cycle in practice, we will draw on an example from the RWS Project. During an introductory lesson from the Connect phase on the rock cycle, for example, the teacher first identifies for students what they will be studying (in this case, different kinds of rocks and how they are formed).

Teachers activate students' prior topic knowledge, or specific topic background knowledge (Alexander, Schallert, & Hare, 1991), and existing schema by having them actively reflect, share with others, and use prewriting (Tierney et al., 1989) and K-W-L (What I Know–What I Want to Know–What I Have Learned; Carr & Ogle, 1987) as focusing techniques. Students write down and share their knowledge and experiences in both whole-class and small groups regarding different kinds of rocks and their origins, and they make predictions about the content of the upcoming reading sample.

Meaning is not inherent in text but constructed as readers transact with the text and draw upon their knowledge and experiences to make sense of it (Brown, Campione, & Day, 1981; Rosenblatt, 1978). Having students share their prior knowledge in class not only increases students' reading comprehension but also assists the teacher in identifying the academic experience of the class as a whole, including particular preconceptions held by the students. For example, during the rock cycle unit's introductory lesson, a fourth-grade student shared with the class that "rock cocaine" was derived from rocks. The teacher gently corrected the student's confident claim.

During the Organize phase, students (a) read the reading sample on the stages of the rock cycle (igneous, sedimentary, metamorphic), use think-aloud strategies when reading individually, and conduct analysis of text structure, purpose, and audience; (b) organize their pre- and post-reading ideas using graphical structures (e.g., web, matrix, linear string, or FIRES [Facts, Incidents, Reasons, Examples, Statistics]); and (c) apply contextual clues in the text to translate new and unfamiliar vocabulary—all of these activities done individually, in small groups, and through whole-class discussions. Graphic organizers have been shown to aid in reading comprehension and writing ability (e.g., Calfee & Drum, 1986). In the RWS Project, we found that matching the type of graphic organizer (e.g., falling dominoes, web) to the type of text (for example, sequential, descriptive) maximized the effect of the organizer on writing coherence. The match seems to help students arrange the new information received from the reading into an existing text-structure schema (for example, compare–contrast, narrative), thus aiding comprehension. Note that graphic organizers are not given to the students; rather, the students, with teacher guidance, actively create them. Students are asked to justify their organization of the content matter into the graphic structures during the process. This active creation of the organizer further strengthens the student's metacognitive and reasoning ability and enables students to choose which type of organizer "works" best for a given situation (Chambliss & Calfee, 1998). In a target text on the stages of the rock cycle, for instance, students often organized their information into a format that we describe as a sequential web; each stage in the cycle was represented by a cluster on the web, and the stages were then linked to each other with arrows representing transformations from one stage to another.

After reading the text sample during the Reflect process, students examine their graphic organizer's structure and content and make revisions as necessary. Students may discard, reorder, or restructure ideas they had during prewriting. Prewriting ideas may prove incorrect, inaccurate, or simply irrelevant to the reading. Students share their reflections on the reading both in small groups and with the teacher. K-W-L (Carr & Ogle, 1987) serves again during reflection to further solidify students' reflections on the content knowledge.

Between Reflect and Extend, the teacher introduces students to the writing prompt. Students also reflect on the writing assignment. The RWS writing prompts follow the guidelines described earlier, and students are taught how to "dissect" the prompt into its constituent elements to help locate key ideas from the reading, and to translate the information into a coherent compositional structure. Here is the prompt from the introductory lesson of the rock cycle unit:

> You are learning about different kinds of rocks and how they are formed through the rock cycle process. Although rocks can have many differences, they all are related to each other through the rock cycle.
>
> Suppose you want to explain to your parents about the rock cycle. Write to explain (a) what the rock cycle is, (b) what the different kinds of rocks formed by it are, and (c) how the rocks can be changed from one kind into another. Use paragraphs to group your ideas and make sure your writing has a clear beginning, middle, and end. Use as many details and examples from what you have read to explain your ideas clearly and completely.

Students identified the audience (parents), type of writing (paragraphs), purpose (writing to explain), and the source of the supporting details (reading sample).

The final task is the individual composition, which occupies the Extend phase. This task provides an opportunity for individual students to synthesize their knowledge and transform it into new shapes and for new applications. This "extension" is performed individually, with little or no assistance from peers or the teacher, as during a regular assessment. Students go through the traditional phases of the writing process (develop, draft, review, revise, polish, publish) while composing. Once the paper is completed, RWS students typically have an opportunity to share their writing with other audiences—peers in small or large groups, the "public" (which means posting the papers outside the classroom), or their parents—raising the level of relevance of the assignments and providing valuable feedback to students on the effectiveness of their efforts.

Closing Thoughts

The No Child Left Behind (NCLB) era confronts everyone in the educational enterprise with high-stakes punitive outcomes, modest rewards, and limited resources. Depending on the regional context, the consequences and demands descend from administrator to teacher to student. The one constant in the U.S. federal program, mirrored in many state programs, is the emphasis on externally mandated testing. Ralph Tyler (1950), who fathered the concept of national assessment, might be surprised at these developments. Current policies and practices, driven by bureaucratic more than educational considerations, emphasize cost (cheaper is better), standardization (flexibility and accommodation are to be minimized), and central control (disconnection from the classroom curriculum). The consequences are substantial for students (diploma denial, retention, summer school), for teachers (mandated in-service activities and imposed classroom activities), and for administrators (especially for principals, whose positions rise or fall with yearly spikes in average test scores). These practices and policies, popular though they may be, fly in the face of international research showing the limitations of externally mandated testing and the benefits of authentic instruction and performance-based assessment.

The message in this chapter revolves around national trends that (a) emphasize reading comprehension and (b) neglect writing assessment. These trends are understandable. Multiple-choice comprehension tests are easy to construct and cheap to administer. Writing assessments are expensive, "subjective," and difficult to control—all features certain to provoke bureaucratic distress. The typical response is to limit the number of grades tested and to standardize the task through "on-demand" procedures, constrained rubrics, and minimal weighting of this domain in decisions.

The Read–Write Cycle approach presented in this chapter provides a valid strategy for linking reading, writing, and language development while also offering opportunities for assessment in the equally neglected content areas of science and social studies. One might question the workability of the model, especially as it proposes demanding instruction for all students. In fact, some reviewers have criticized the model as being too demanding for students of lower achievement levels, despite documented success with such students (Miller & Martinez, 2004). In the RWS Project, we have applied Robert Maynard Hutchin's premise that "the best education for the best is the best education for all" (as cited in Adler, 1982, p. 6).

Our programmatic focus is on the classroom teacher's crucial role in the implementation of cognitively demanding, transformative instruction and assessment as prescribed by the Read–Write Cycle. The National Reading Panel (National Institute of Child Health and Human Development, 2000) reports that the preparation of teachers is intimately linked to students' achievement in reading comprehension but then bewails the lack of research-based evidence on this issue. Hence, the central question: What do teachers need to know in order to produce lasting improvement in students' reading comprehension and writing ability? We propose that elementary and nonlanguage arts teacher specialists do not need intimate knowledge of the research on reading and writing instruction to raise reading comprehension and writing skills. Rather, they need to know a few things well, such as understanding how different reading and writing skills can be combined and used in context to improve reading comprehension, how to communicate what they know to their students, and how to reflect on and improve their teaching. Central to these activities is the "assessment schema" that guides the teacher through the daily and weekly complexities of the classroom.

Of course, the consequence of this requirement for good teaching is the need for ongoing professional development to enable teachers to tailor their knowledge and skills to particular demands. It has been our finding, during implementation of the RWS project, that relatively little time (three to five days of inservice training, implemented in various formats, ranging from hour-long sessions to concentrated full-day programs) can be highly effective in teaching teachers the components of the Read–Write Cycle, and in assisting them to develop lessons of their own around "scripts" that incorporate these elements. To address the task of constructing authentic writing assessment, from start to finish, appropriate and supportive professional development of teachers must be addressed and provided. The challenge, of course, lies with emphasizing professional development versus "program training," where teachers learn to implement a prescribed program. The key here is control—professionals exercise independent judgment and resist efforts to override their autonomy as individuals and collectives. If the goal is a cadre of workers who follow instructions to produce graduates who possess basic skills, then training is the appropriate model. A different vision highlights the concept of "high standards for all students," which requires professionals capable of informed decisions and accountable for meeting the societal ideals of quality and equity. The practical challenge, in this age of assessment, is to develop models that can move school communities from where "we" are to where "we" would like to be.

Support for preparation of this paper was provided by the National Science Foundation Interagency Education Research Initiative Grant No. 9979834.

REFERENCES

Adams, M.J., & Collins, A. (1977, April). *A schema-theoretic view of reading* (Tech. Rep. No. 32). Urbana: Illinois University, Center for the Study of Reading. (ERIC Document Reproduction Service No. ED142971)

Adler, M.J. (1982). *The Paideia proposal: An educational manifesto.* New York: Macmillan.

Alexander, P.A., Schallert, D.L., & Hare, V.C. (1991). Coming to terms: How researchers in learning and literacy talk about knowledge. *Review of Educational Research, 61*(3), 315-343.

Anderson, R.C., Spiro, R.J., & Anderson, M.C. (1977, March). *Schemata as scaffolding for the representation of information in connected discourse* (Tech. Rep. No. 24). Urbana: Illinois University, Center for the Study of Reading. (ERIC Document Reproduction Service No. ED136236)

Armbruster, B.B. (1976, July). *Learning principles from prose: A cognitive approach based on schema theory.* (ERIC Document Reproduction Service No. ED134934)

Bransford, J.D., & Johnson, M.K. (1973). Consideration of some problems of comprehension. In W.G. Chase (Ed.), *Visual information processing: Proceedings.* New York: Academic Press.

Brown, A.L., Campione, J., & Day, J. (1981). Learning to learn: On training students to learn from text. *Educational Researcher, 10*(2), 14-21.

Calfee, R.C., & Drum, P.A. (1986). Research on teaching reading. In M.C. Wittrock (Ed.), *Handbook of research on teaching* (Vol. 3, pp. 804-849). New York: Macmillan.

Calfee, R.C., Miller, R.G., & Associates (2002). *Analytical report of the 1998, 2000, 2001, 2002 Delaware Student Testing Program Writing Assessments.* Riverside: University of California, Riverside, Graduate School of Education.

Calfee, R.C., Miller, R.G., & Associates (2004). *Analytical report of the Spring 2003 Delaware Student Testing Program Writing Assessment.* Riverside: University of California, Riverside, Graduate School of Education.

Calfee, R.C., & Patrick, C.L. (1995). *Teach our children well: Bringing K-12 education into the 21st century.* Stanford, CA: Stanford Alumni Association.

Carr, E., & Ogle, D. (1987). K-W-L plus: A strategy for comprehension and summarization. *Journal of Reading, 30*, 626-631.

Chambliss, M.J., & Calfee, R.C. (1998). *Textbooks for learning: Nurturing children's minds.* Malden, MA: Blackwell.

Driscoll, M.P. (1994). *Psychology of learning for instruction.* Boston: Allyn & Bacon.

Halliday, M.A.K., & Hasan, R. (1989). *Language, context, and text: Aspects of language in a social-semiotic perspective.* Oxford, UK: Oxford University Press.

Kaplan, R. (1966). Cultural thought patterns in inter-cultural education. *Language Learning, 16*, 120.

Landauer, T.K. (1999). Latent semantic analysis: A theory of the psychology of language and mind. *Discourse Processes, 27*(3), 303-310.

Langer, J.A. (1986). Reading, writing and understanding: An analysis of the construction of meaning. *Written Communication, 3*(2), 219-267.

Langer, J.A., & Applebee, A.N. (1987). *How writing shapes thinking: A study of teaching and learning* (Research Report No. 22). Urbana: National Council of Teachers of English. (ERIC Document Reproduction Service No. ED286205)

Mathena, T.J. (2000, Fall). Prompting kids to write. *American Educator, 24*(3), 16-21.

Miller, R.G., & Calfee R.C. (2004a). Building a better reading-writing assessment: Bridging cognitive theory, instruction, and assessment. *English Leadership Quarterly, 26*(3), 6-13.

Miller, R.G., & Calfee R.C. (2004b). Making thinking visible: A method to encourage science writing in upper elementary grades. *Science and Children, 42*(3), 20-25.

Miller, R.G., & Martinez, W.T. (2004, April). *The Reading and Writing About Science Project: Demonstrating successful literacy techniques for scientific text.* Paper presented at the annual meeting of the American Educational Research Association, San Diego, CA.

National Center for Education Statistics. (2003). *The nation's report card: NAEP data.* Retrieved December 1, 2003, from http://nces.ed.gov/nationsreportcard/naepdata

National Institute of Child Health and Human Development. (2000). *Report of the National Reading Panel. Teaching children to read: An evidence-based assessment of the scientific research literature on reading and its implications for reading instruction* (NIH Publication No. 00-4769). Washington, DC: U.S. Government Printing Office.

Nelson, N., & Calfee, R.C. (1998). The reading-writing connection viewed historically. In N. Nelson & R.C. Calfee (Eds.), *The reading-writing connection: 97th yearbook of the National Society for the Study of Education* (Vol. 97, Part II, pp. 1-52). Chicago: University of Chicago Press.

Palincsar, A.S., & Brown, A.L. (1984). Reciprocal teaching of comprehension-fostering and comprehension-monitoring activities. *Cognition & Instruction, 1*(2), 117-175.

Rosenblatt, L.M. (1978). *The reader, the text, the poem: Transactional theory of the literacy work.* Carbondale: Southern Illinois University Press.

Salvatori, M. (1986). The dialogical nature of reading and writing. In D. Bartholomae & A.R. Petrosky (Eds.), *Facts, artifacts, and counterfacts: Theory and method for a reading and writing course* (pp. 137-166). Portsmouth, NH: Boynton/Cook.

Schön, D.A. (1983). *The reflective practitioner: How professionals think in action.* New York: Basic Books.

Schön, D.A. (1987). *Educating the reflective practitioner: Toward a new design for teaching and learning in the professions.* San Francisco: Jossey-Bass.

Shanahan, T. (1997). Reading-writing relationships, thematic units, inquiry learning: In pursuit of effective integrated literacy instruction. *The Reading Teacher, 51,* 12-19.

Snow, C. (2002). *Reading for understanding: Toward an R&D program for reading comprehension.* Washington, DC: RAND.

Sperling, M., & Freedman, S.W. (2001). Research on writing. In V. Richardson (Ed.), *Handbook of research on teaching* (4th ed., pp. 370-389). Washington, DC: American Educational Research Association.

Stein, N.L. (1978). *How children understand stories: A developmental analysis* (Technical Report No. 69). Urbana: Illinois University, Center for the Study of Reading. (ERIC Document Reproduction Service No. 153205)

Tierney, R.J., & Shanahan, T. (1996). Research on the reading-writing relationship: Interactions, transactions, and outcomes. In R. Barr, M.L. Kamil, P.B. Mosenthal, & P.D. Pearson (Eds.), *Handbook of reading research* (Vol. 2, pp. 246-280). Mahwah, NJ: Erlbaum.

Tierney, R.J., LaZansky, J., Raphael, T., & Cohen, P. (1987). Author's intentions and reader's interpretations. In R.J. Tierney, P.L. Anders, & J.N. Mitchell (Eds.), *Understanding readers' understanding: Theory and practice* (pp. 205-228). Hillsdale, NJ: Erlbaum.

Tierney, R.J., Soter, A., O'Flahavan, J.F., & McGinley, W. (1989). The effects of reading and writing upon thinking critically. *Reading Research Quarterly, 24,* 134-173.

Tyler, R.W. (1950). *Basic principles of curriculum and instruction, syllabus for Education 360.* Chicago: University of Chicago Press.

Underwood, T. (1999). *The portfolio project: A study of assessment, instruction, and middle school reform.* Urbana, IL: National Council of Teachers of English.

Wilson, M. (Ed.) (2004). *Towards coherence between classroom assessment and accountability: 103rd yearbook of the National Society for the Study of Education* (Part II). Chicago: National Society for the Study of Education.

LITERATURE CITED

Conrad, J. (1999). *Heart of darkness.* New York: Penguin. (Original work published 1899)

Joyce, J. (1990). *Ulysses.* New York: Vintage. (Original work published 1922)

Epilogue: Effective Professional Development for Improving Literacy Instruction

P. David Pearson, Barbara M. Taylor, and Anamarie Tam

In honor of James Squire's legacy, we have chosen to share some of the insights we have gained about effective professional development in our work in high-poverty schools around the country as a part of the Center for the Improvement of Early Reading Achievement (CIERA) School Change Project. While reading reform was the goal, professional development was the fuel for the reform, as we soon learned once the project was underway.

In 1999, a group of us from CIERA embarked on a four-year project to study the process of change and school improvement on key indicators of reading performance and pedagogy. We wanted to know how schools who voluntarily agree to engage in the hard work of improving programs, pedagogy, and performance go about their work, and which aspects of the improvement process truly account for improvements in the all-important variable—student achievement. It was in this context that we learned our lessons about professional development.

Our work has not been conducted in a vacuum; we did not start from scratch and discover everything on site. To the contrary, we have grounded our work in the recently growing field of professional development research, relying on those theorists and researchers who have reached strong consensus about what makes professional development effective (Killion, 2002; Lieberman & Miller, 2002; Richardson & Placier, 1991). From a range of efforts, we know that teachers who receive quality, ongoing professional development stressing higher order thinking and concrete learning activities are more likely to use effective classroom practices associated with gains in student achievement (Wenglinsky, 2002). We have found that sustained and intensive professional development—work that is tied to active learning and daily school life—is more likely to have an impact than shorter, more encapsulated professional development experiences (Garet, Porter, Desimone, Birman, & Yoon, 2001). We also know that professional development has both an internal face and an external one. School-based professional development—in which entire teaching staffs work on a problem, issue, or activity for extended periods—is effective (Richardson, 2003; Taylor, Pearson, Peterson, & Rodriguez, 2005). But external sources of support, whether subject matter collaboratives, reform networks, or school–university partnerships are also important (Lieberman & Miller, 2002).

Professional development is better, more effective, when it has a collaborative flavor (Killion, 2002; Lieberman & Miller, 2002). In professional learning communities, teachers who share a common purpose for their students and engage in collaborative activities to achieve this purpose see improved student learning (Newmann & Wehlage, 1995). As Richard Elmore (2002) eloquently postulates,

> If professional development is to play a role in sustained instructional improvement, it should probably be based on the premise that teachers learn to teach by teaching, and by engaging in new forms of practice in the presence of people who have some expertise in that practice, by observing others engaging in new forms of practice, and possibly by observing themselves on videotape and analyzing their practice with others. Professional development should probably be based on the premise that changing instruction requires coherence and focus in professional development—working, for example on a manageable set of new practices in a sustained way over time until they become part of a relatively stable set of repertoires with which a teacher is comfortable. (p. 118)

These contexts, ideas, scholars, and findings have guided our work over the last several years.

Description of the School Change Framework to Improve Reading Achievement

One research-validated model of effective professional development is the CIERA School Change Framework. Although designed to improve reading instruction and reading achievement, it could easily be adapted for use in writing or other school subjects. The following account is adapted from Barbara Taylor's (2004) description of the School Change Framework.

The School Change Framework (Taylor, 2004; Taylor, Frye, Peterson, & Pearson, 2003; Taylor et al., 2005) was designed to support schools as they (a) improved their reading program based on local needs, (b) worked collaboratively in both professional development and developing classroom models for crafting reading instruction, and (c) used research from a variety of domains to guide their efforts—effective practices related to reading instruction, school reform, effective schools, effective teachers, and parent partnerships. The framework is based upon the following assumptions:

- No single solution to reform exists. Schools are at different places with different needs.
- Schools will benefit from becoming collaborative, learning communities.
- Teachers will benefit from reflection and change efforts related to their teaching practices.
- All educators at a school site must put the children first.

In the final two years of research on this model, we were able to demonstrate its effectiveness in 13 high-poverty elementary schools across the United States (Taylor et al., 2005). Through complex statistical analyses (hierarchical linear modeling, or HLM) of school-level and classroom-level variables, we found that success in implementing the reform explained a substantial proportion of the between-school variance in reading growth (as measured by comprehension and fluency scores). The teachers in the high reform effort schools used more effective reading instruction practices than teachers in the low reform effort schools and made more research-based changes in their reading instruction. The model has also been used by 23 schools participating in the Minnesota Reading Excellence Act Program with good success (Taylor & Peterson, 2003) and is currently being used with 30 Reading First schools in Minnesota. The School Change Framework process is described in greater detail in the National Education Association (NEA) publication *Steps to School-wide Reading Improvement* (Taylor, Frye, et al., 2003).

Program Components

At the start of the project, teachers learn about effective reading instruction and effective teachers of reading, characteristics of effective schools, and characteristics of effective school improvement. Teachers also learn about the major components of the School Change Framework for reading improvement. The beginning point is commitment and buy-in for the use of the framework, with at least 75% of the teachers within a building voting to use the model. This commitment obligates everyone to participate in the framework and the professional development activities. In addition to working within grades, teachers agree to get involved in cross-grade and cross-role collaboration (e.g., regular ed, special ed, ESL teachers working together). Without substantial buy-in, it is doubtful that a school is ready to embark on the project.

The major goal of the model is to improve reading instruction. In addition to improving classroom instruction, a school must have interventions in place for children in grades K–3, as needed. Also, the school agrees to work on developing and implementing a plan for involving parents as partners.

Leadership Team. Each school appoints a literacy coordinator (at least a half-time person in this role) and a school leadership team made up of the principal, literacy coordinator, and teacher leaders, usually one per grade. Ideally, each school has the resources to support a 20–40% time external facilitator to ensure the influx of new ideas. Together this group will plan the reform effort, lead small focused study groups and schoolwide staff development meetings, monitor the implementation of new instructional techniques in classrooms, provide support to teachers, solve problems, and keep the reform effort moving along successfully.

Study Groups. All teachers participate in hour-long study-group meetings three times a month. Study groups undertake analyses of research-validated practices on a range of topics, such as comprehension strategy instruction, vocabulary, fluency, rich discussions, phonemic awareness, guided reading, and the like. In a typical school, there might be three to five separate study groups, each pursuing a single topic over several months or an entire year. Schools and teaching staffs are given wide berth in selecting topics. However, it is important that (a) the focus of each study group be grounded in documented needs (as evidenced by student performance on tests used to monitor progress or teachers' perceived needs—from questionnaires that all teachers complete at the beginning and end of every school year), (b) study group members apply what they are learning to their daily teaching, and (c) study groups share the fruits of their labor with their colleagues in schoolwide meetings.

In their thrice-monthly study-group meetings, teachers focus on improving instruction through three major activities: (1) enriching their knowledge base by reading and discussing research-based practices, (2) sharing videos of their classroom instruction with peers, and (3) closely examining student work (either everyday assignments or test performance). The goal is to improve the moment-by-moment enactment of effective pedagogical practices. We have found that an optimal study group size is 4–6 members. Study groups also set action plans to guide their work in between sessions; this creates a sense of communal accountability. Study groups get support from the external facilitator, if one exists, and from the internal leadership team. Although leadership for study group meetings should rotate, we recommend that each study group include a representative who is a member of the leadership team.

The leadership team meets at least once a month to gauge progress and address problems in the various study groups. They take steps to assist study groups that may have gotten off track. Study groups are vulnerable to many obstacles and pitfalls, but four recur often enough to merit the attention of project directors. Leaders should be on the lookout for these four obstacles:

1. A group may pick a topic with a research base too weak to support systematic study.

2. A group may flit from topic to topic without going in depth on anything (our experience suggests that they need at least four months per topic).

3. Study group members may get stuck on discussion and never get to the close analysis of instruction necessary for real progress (e.g., video sharing, looking at student work).

4. Study groups that remain within grade deny colleagues in other grades access to new knowledge.

Whole-Group Meetings. In the CIERA School Change model, teachers also meet once a month as a whole group to share study-group activities and to discuss issues related to the schoolwide delivery of reading instruction. In whole-group meetings, staff members share what is happening in study groups and negotiate needed changes in the schoolwide reading program. We have found that things work more smoothly when the leadership team plans the whole-group meetings for the entire year.

As a school and individually, teachers examine several kinds of data in order to shape professional development activities. We have found that the leadership team needs to help the teaching staff in the systematic and honest evaluation of three kinds of important data:

1. *Student performance data.* School data, district-mandated data, and state-mandated data on students' reading, and preferably writing, performance need to be considered. In addition, teachers need to voice their concerns about what they perceive to be particularly problematic areas for their students.

2. *Classroom observation data.* We have had remarkable success with an instrument we developed just for our project, the School Change Classroom

Observation System (see Taylor, Pearson, Peterson, & Rodriguez, 2003). It includes protocols for examining the entire range of classroom instructional activities and recommendations using data to help teachers set priorities for study groups. The final step in this process is engaging teachers in a set of self-reflection questions that help them identify strengths and weaknesses in their classroom reading instruction. It is in this reflective process that teachers find a focus for study group topics.

3. *Self-study questionnaire.* This instrument codifies teachers' perceptions of various school-level factors known to be important in successful schools. All teachers in each building complete the two-part self-study questionnaire. The first part deals with teachers' perceptions of factors within their school that have been found to affect students' achievement. The second part deals with teachers' opinions of their schools' needs in terms of priorities for school change efforts. The items deal with the topics of school change, school climate, and leadership; professional development; schoolwide decisions about reading instruction; classroom reading instruction; reading interventions for struggling readers, and school–home–community connections.

Summing Up the Process. All of these activities should be intimately related to the school improvement plan that the teaching staff and the school leadership, most likely in concert with parents and community members, have created. We believe that these activities should be informed by the school improvement plan, but we also believe that they should inform—and serve as the basis for modifications in the school improvement plan, particularly on issues such as schoolwide curricular and instructional emphases. Useful tips from numerous facilitators and school leadership team members on implementing the School Change Framework are listed in the appendix at the end of this piece.

One School's Experience in the CIERA School Change Project

Of all the schools in our four years of implementing the CIERA School Change Framework, one stands out above the rest in terms of progress on student achievement and professional development—Howard Elementary School (our account of Howard School draws heavily from Tam, 2002). At Howard Elementary School, situated in a large urban area, 81% of the students qualify for subsidized lunch and 78% of the students are English-language learners. At Howard, everything in the framework clicked. They used the data on teaching practices, along with the study group process, to imagine and then implement changes in classroom teaching practices. And most important, Howard demonstrated substantial and significant increases in students' reading growth from the first year of the project to the second.

During Howard Elementary's first year in the project, the overall focus area was improving students' reading comprehension. Teachers agreed that most students could decode grade-level text, but many struggled to understand it. Eight study groups were formed:

1. Kidlit (initial focus on emergent literacy, subsequent emphasis on parent involvement)

2. Dazed and Confused (focus on guided reading with primary students),

3. Guided Reading Gurus, also known as "GUREES" (focus on guided reading with upper-grade students)

4. Reading Comprehension

5. Higher Level Thinking (initial focus on higher level questioning, subsequent emphasis on strategies to promote higher level thinking)

6. Reading Assessment

7. Struggling Circle of Reading Friends, also known as "SCORF" (focus on reading interventions within the classroom)

8. Modeling–Coaching–Scaffolding (initial focus on teaching vocabulary, subsequent emphasis on ways to provide scaffolding)

Initially, the study groups focused on becoming more familiar with the purpose of the CIERA project as well as the nature of study groups. They established group norms and routines, and learned how to work with one another. Group dynamics at Howard Elementary, a four-track year-round school, varied from month to month as some team members diverted off-track, while others returned from being off-track. This inconsistency of group membership each month made it difficult for groups to be responsible for providing their own professional reading materials. Over time, the internal leadership team, or the support staff—the principal, assistant principal, facilitator, and teacher specialists—played a more active role to contribute to the success of the meetings. The support staff learned how to preempt these derailments by, for example, locating and providing more of the professional readings themselves.

After three or four relatively unproductive meetings, groups started struggling to define "what do we want to achieve?" Over the course of the year, some of the groups that initially had selected broader topics sharpened their focus as reflected in the earlier list of study group topics. Some groups struggled with interpersonal dynamics; others seemed to revel in the cross-grade interaction. Several teachers emerged as leaders within their groups. Although the group facilitator and recorder for each meeting rotated, "unofficial leaders" helped to keep the meetings going. Each support staff member joined a different study group. Their presence helped to keep the teams more focused and on task.

The most effective groups had a clear picture of what their group was trying to accomplish within the first few meetings. They worked "with the end in mind." These groups had a specific classroom application they were working toward. By the end of the year, when the groups shared their accomplishments, this variability in the groups' level of emphasis on direct classroom applications was most evident. The "Dazed and Confused" group developed a more consistent picture of implementing guided reading and incorporating language arts standards and instructional strategies to teach reading, such as the timeless Directed Reading–Thinking Activity (DRTA). The GUREES shared the benefits of talking to other teachers about guided reading in upper grades. Because this has been an important strategy emphasized at Howard, they felt more assured about what it should look like in upper grades, and how it differed from primary guided reading. The Reading Comprehension group narrowed their focus each week so that by the final meeting, the members were sharing how they applied the questioning strategies within their classroom or with a particular book. The SCORFS tried reading intervention strategies in their classroom and created a booklet of selected strategies to share with the rest of the teaching staff.

Implementation of study groups was much more efficient, effective, and seamless during the second year in the project. Teachers were already familiar with the purpose and format of meetings; they knew how to stay with and complete an activity, and how to report back to the facilitator and, ultimately, the entire faculty. A survey administered at the end of the first year provided feedback to adjust the year-two study group activities.

One important difference in year two was narrowing the focus of study groups. Although year-one study-group topics related to reading comprehension in general, the topics tended to be broad, such as reading comprehension, interventions, or guided reading. In year two, topics were related to a more specific aspect of reading comprehension, for example, an instructional strategy that combines some specific comprehension strategies, such as Students Achieving Independent Learning (SAIL) or DRTA, written response to reading, or vocabulary development within the context of reading. The facilitator helped make action planning easier and more focused by suggesting some specific classroom applications and activities and some recommended resources to help groups move to practical applications sooner. Professional development funds were used to purchase some professional books as resources for the groups.

Also, instead of focusing on a topic for the entire year, study groups focused on two topics for half a year each. The beginning of the year was devoted to learning about graphic organizers to represent ideas from what students were reading during language arts and the content areas and organize these ideas into well-developed paragraphs and essays. Groups learned various strategies from two programs being implemented widely in the district. This focus reinforced some research unearthed by one study group that highlighted the benefits of using graphic organizers as an effective technique to support reading comprehension.

During the second half of the year, teachers selected their choice of topic, resulting in this set of study groups:

1. Phunky Fonix (phonics)
2. Dream Readers Together Again (Directed Reading–Thinking Activity, or DRTA)
3. SAIL (Student Achieving Independent Learning)
4. Word Wise (strategies to develop vocabulary)
5. 76ers (summarizing and responding to text as more meaningful independent work)

The phonics group read selections from *Phonics They Use* (Cunningham, 1995), reviewed the district's phonics scope and sequence, and planned a Family Reading Night to share phonics games parents could use at home with their child. The DRTA group read about and practiced using prediction and verification strategy during guided reading and content area instruction. The SAIL group read several research articles about this transactional reading strategy, and selections from *Strategies That Work* (Harvey & Goudvis, 2000). They discussed the need for explicit modeling of strategies and tried several strategies in their classrooms, such as visualizing, making predictions, questioning, and summarizing. Word Wise read selections from *Teaching Vocabulary in All Classrooms* (Blachowicz & Fisher,

2002). Each member tried various maps to increase retention and understanding of vocabulary. The 76ers also selected visual tools to help students construct written responses that demonstrate their understanding (including main idea, inferences, and summary) of the texts they read during guided reading.

Based on responses from teacher surveys at the end of the year and from interviews of teachers participating in classroom observations, several successes were noted. Most teachers agreed on the following benefits of being part of the CIERA project and participating in study groups:

- Opportunity to talk with and collaborate with other teachers; teachers and administrators learning together
- Sharing ideas and lessons related to a specific topic; sharing what works and doesn't work
- Reading and sharing professional books and reading research on a topic of choice

Teacher interviews also reflected the belief that school goals, especially related to reading, were becoming clear and more focused over time. Teachers also mentioned the importance of school leadership and ongoing support to help the school achieve its goals. At the end of the first year in the CIERA project, one teacher reflected on the project's professional development activities, "It gave us an opportunity to meet and talk. Our school is getting a clearer definition of what we are trying to do, and we're feeling more expertise. Before we were trying to find our way."

The interviews were clear regarding the importance of interval professional support. Teachers appreciated instructional support, not only from the administrators, but also from the three teacher specialists. Most interviews acknowledged the role of the internal facilitator to help provide leadership for project activities. As one teacher stated, "She helps with planning, sharing, organizing, training, and finding research materials to read." Yet this teacher acknowledged that leadership is a group effort: "Everyone provides leadership— the facilitator, teacher specialists, administrators, teachers, and even students. Leadership is not in one person's hands. Everyone does [his or her] share. It all connects...It has a direction. We are all going in same direction. All are pushing it forward."

Howard is a year-round school, rendering communication more difficult than in traditional schools because, at any given time, some group of teachers will be absent. When teachers return from vacation, a "track-back meeting" is held by the principal to try to update teachers about school activities during the month of their vacation. In addition, weekly bulletins are mailed to teachers to keep them informed.

Communication within and between study groups was also a challenge, partly because of the year-round feature and partly because communication, even in a close-knit group, is tricky. Each study group was formed from a mix of teachers from different tracks (tracks define teachers who are on the same teaching and vacation schedule) and grades. Despite the challenge, many teachers commented that this was one of the few opportunities they had to collaborate with teachers who were not in their same grade level or same track. Some primary and upper-grade teachers rarely see or interact with each other because they have different recess and lunch times.

Although the flow of communication and the degree of collaboration varied by group, each group maintained a team binder with weekly reporting forms and sections to save articles they read. Teachers rotated the roles of facilitator of the meeting and recorder of the notes. During the year, several *CIERA News* newsletters were written by the facilitator and given to the teaching staff to review recent professional development activities related to reading comprehension and highlighting the work of study groups. At the end of the year, each group prepared a presentation to share their successes and suggestions for follow-up. Some teachers suggested planning more sharing between groups so that they would know what other groups were doing throughout the year.

Even though Howard Elementary has concentrated its school improvement efforts in the area of reading achievement during the past 5-6 years, its recent involvement in the CIERA project has strengthened this effort. The overall reading instructional program has not changed significantly: Howard continues to promote a balanced reading program with the adopted textbook materials as the core for shared reading, books at students' instructional levels for guided reading, and a variety of trade and little books for independent reading. Yet an emphasis on improving guided reading instruction continues. Thus, while the core components of the program have not changed much, more emphasis is being placed on the quality of the implementation. Thus, the use of study groups has been a valuable professional development strategy. Even after funding for the CIERA School Change Project ended, the school has continued to use the study group motif. In the past, while various topics were covered, there was neither a consistent focus nor much follow-through from one week to the next. In contrast, building upon the work of the last two years, the most recent selection of study group topics concentrated on several specific reading strategies that have direct classroom applications, including reciprocal teaching, questioning the author, question-answer relationships, and comprehension monitoring strategies. Purchasing a book for each teacher related to these topics has helped to provide a common reference tool and to encourage more links between groups. Several whole-faculty professional development sessions for all study groups have been included in the meeting schedule to provide some common training for all teachers. Topics for these meetings have included: strengthening guided reading lesson design, effective teaching techniques to improve students' reading engagement, and balancing strategic teaching and standards-based teaching. Promoting effective and more consistent teaching throughout the school continues to be an important goal, especially in such a large year-round school with many new teachers.

Although teachers did not drastically transform their repertoire of instructional strategies, the staff development activities and readings helped them learn a few effective strategies. More important, staff development helped them become more knowledgeable and reflective about their own practice, as well as more aware of schoolwide improvement efforts. One teacher captured this sentiment when she said,

> A challenge for school is thinking critically about what it gives students or gives without having them analyze. We are working toward it with this research project. Analyzing what we do has been the focus of most of our study groups. It

is very important in life, too. You need to analyze yourself and the world to bring change.

Participation in the CIERA School Change Project helped to validate and build on Howard Elementary's efforts to improve reading achievement as it has added a stronger research base to these efforts. The School Change Framework has helped to serve as an analytic tool and a scaffold for focusing school efforts at several levels. At the classroom level, the framework helped identify several instructional strategies that can improve students' reading achievement, such as the use of coaching, active student involvement, and higher level questioning. At the school level, the framework helped to structure focused, collaborative, and ongoing whole faculty/staff development. At the macro level, the school was included in a small network of schools across the country, and it received support and feedback about grade-level and schoolwide practices, as well as access to research resources.

Fortunately, because the School Change Project emphasizes each school's homegrown reform efforts, these efforts can continue (and more importantly have continued) after the project has ended. At least as of this writing, Howard Elementary continues to address areas of need and build on its successes to help its students become stronger readers.

Conclusions

So what have we learned about effective professional development across our years of work with these schools that began the process only aspiring to achieve excellence and equity for their students? We can and will discuss our insights from both a global and local perspective—spelling out broad principles that we think apply to this sort of work, but also offering practical tips (see the appendix) for staff developers who would venture to travel though this difficult, but rewarding, landscape.

Our first major conclusion about professional development is that it must, above all, be based on the best evidence we can muster. And evidence is important in two distinct senses: (1) We are obligated to use the best research about the nature and effectiveness of staff development (e.g., Lieberman & Miller, 2002; Richardson, 2003; Wilson & Berne, 1999) that we as a collective of scholars have developed, and (2) when we study new practices in our local professional development workshops and implement them in our classrooms, we must use evidence of changes in our knowledge and in student learning as the basis for determining the practices we will keep or discard. We must be both critical consumers of research and action researchers in our own settings.

Second, we should decide upon our professional development emphases in a bottom-up, grassroots fashion—even if we end up implementing approaches that could have been mandated or handed to us from an external source (e.g., the state or a district mandate or set of guidelines). We know that professional development works better, is more likely to result in teacher uptake, and builds greater local capacity for the future when teachers have a clear voice in its direction. Just telling people what to do does not work well—even if the tellers are right. This should not surprise us—from what we know about the need for buy-in and building commitment as a prerequisite to effectiveness, we should expect no less.

Third, we have learned that staying the course—sticking with a single topic until we, as a group, develop a sense of mastery and expert control over it—is much preferable to the typical "topic of the month" pattern in which groups flit from topic to topic. It takes a long time to develop control over certain approaches, such as reciprocal teaching, writer's workshop, or even methods of providing feedback.

Fourth, we have learned what the scholars in professional development have long told us—that it is important to build a strong sense of community within the group engaged in the professional development. The need for community is important in both school-based professional development groups (Richardson, 2003) or volunteer groups (Lieberman & Miller, 2002).

Fifth, we have learned that both internal and external leadership are important. An internal leadership team, a strong principal committed to improved classroom pedagogy, even a strong teacher leader can make all the difference in getting a school moving on the course of improved instruction. Just as important, an external facilitator can come in and notice things that don't occur to the insiders or say certain things that are difficult for an insider or even a principal to say. Ideally, use both internal and external sources of insight, ideas, and support.

Sixth, professional development and school change need a celebratory component—an opportunity to acknowledge accomplishments by individual teachers and by students who have made the sorts of gains that we aspire to on their behalf. Finding a time, a place, and a way of nurturing these celebrations is as important as ensuring that teachers develop new and useful research-based knowledge of pedagogy and that they bring a disposition of inquiry into their examination of their current teaching practices and their students' learning. Teachers must be prepared to find that new ideas have the potential to trump established practices, and professional development leaders must find ways of celebrating the work of teachers who personify those critical dispositions of learning and inquiry. It is only through the regular application of these two teacherly dispositions—learning and inquiry—that we can be assured that our children will always have access to the best knowledge that we, as a profession, can provide.

We think that if James Squire were around to read these conclusions about what we have learned in our journey into the world of professional development, he would have liked what he saw. Our insights certainly would have been consistent with the model underlying his own seminal work in creating professional development communities. If we can promote these principles in our schools and our classrooms, we would do justice to the legacy of the man who is honored by the scholarship in this book.

REFERENCES

Blachowicz, C.L., & Fisher, P. (2002). *Teaching vocabulary in all classrooms*. Upper Saddle River, NJ: Prentice Hall.

Cunningham, P. (1995). *Phonics they use: Words for reading and writing* (2nd ed). New York: HarperCollins.

Elmore, R.F. (2002). Local school districts and instructional improvement. In W.D. Hawley & D.L. Rollie (Eds.), *The keys to effective schools: Educational reform as continuous improvement* (pp. 111-122). Thousand Oaks, CA: Corwin.

Garet, M.S., Porter, A.C., Desimone, L., Birman, B.F., & Yoon, K.S. (2001). What makes professional development effective? Results from a national sample of teachers. *American Educational Research Journal, 38*(4), 915-945.

Harvey, S., & Goudvis, A. (2000). *Strategies that work: Teaching comprehension to enhance understanding.* York, ME: Stenhouse.

Killion, J. (2002). *What works in the elementary school: Results-based staff development.* Oxford, OH: National Staff Development Council and National Education Association.

Lieberman, A., & Miller, L. (2002). Transforming professional development: Understanding and organizing learning communities. In W.D. Hawley & D.L. Rollie (Eds.), *The keys to effective schools: Educational reform as continuous improvement* (pp. 74-85). Thousand Oaks, CA: Corwin.

Newmann, F.M., & Wehlage, G.G. (1995). *Successful school restructuring: A report to the public and educators.* Madison: Center on Organization and Restructuring of Schools, Wisconsin Center for Education Research, University of Wisconsin.

Richardson, V. (2003). The dilemmas of professional development. *Phi Delta Kappan, 84*(5), 401-406.

Richardson, V., & Placier, P. (2001). Teacher change. In V. Richardson (Ed.), *Handbook of research on teaching* (4th ed., pp. 905-950). Washington DC: American Educational Research Association.

Tam, A. (2002). *The CIERA school change project: A case study of Howard Elementary School.* Minneapolis: University of Minnesota.

Taylor, B.M. (2004). *The school change framework for improving reading achievement: Implementation manual.* Minneapolis: University of Minnesota.

Taylor, B.M., Frye, B.J., Peterson, D.S., & Pearson, P.D. (2003). *Steps for school-wide reading improvement.* Washington, DC: National Education Association.

Taylor, B.M., Pearson, P.D., Peterson, D.S., & Rodriguez, M.C. (2003). Reading growth in high-poverty classrooms: The influence of teacher practices that encourage cognitive engagement in literacy learning. *The Elementary School Journal, 104*(1), 3-28.

Taylor, B.M., Pearson, P.D., Peterson, D.S., & Rodriguez, M.C. (2005). The CIERA school change framework: An evidence-based approach to professional development and school reading improvement. *Reading Research Quarterly, 40*, 2-32.

Taylor, B.M., & Peterson, D.S. (2003). *Year 1 Report of the Minnesota REA School Change Project.* Minneapolis: University of Minnesota.

Wenglinsky, H. (2002). How schools matter: the link between teacher classroom practices and student academic performance. *Educational Policy Analysis Archives, 10*(12). Retrieved February 13, 2002, from http://epaa.asu.edu/epaa/v10n12

Wilson, S.M., & Berne, J. (1999). Teacher learning and the acquisition of professional knowledge: An examination of research on contemporary professional development. In A. Iran-Nejad & P.D. Pearson (Eds.), *Review of educational research* (Vol. 24, pp. 173-209). Washington DC: American Educational Research Association.

Appendix

Tips From Facilitators and School Leadership Team Members for Implementing the School Change Framework

Issue/Question	Tip
Promoting staff commitment	At a staff meeting early in the school year, ask staff to brainstorm about all the concerns that they have, record this information, and categorize the concerns. Use these to help address concerns and set priorities for the year.
	Make sure the staff has adequate time to make informed decisions. Allow staff time to talk informally about their commitment to the project.

(continued)

Issue/Question	Tip
	Clarify roles in the process. Who does what? Why? This will go a long way toward building trust.
	As a leader, make yourself available to individuals and small groups who are uncertain about their roles.
	Continue to ground your activities in demonstrated need—based on student performance, staff perceptions, and, if available, parent and community concerns.
	Always follow through when you make a promise or commitment to someone. (If you forget a time or two, you will not earn their trust and confidence.)
Promoting evidence-based decision making	Begin with a topic and an initiative for which progress is easily measurable. This can give a study group a baseline and a benchmark. Using the data in a graphic form to show change over time is a powerful means to help teachers reflect on the progress their groups made.
	Encourage teachers to look at data across grades and talk about moving forward as a school. Data need to be put in user-friendly forms before staff will use them.
	Ensure that this activity is an ongoing and regular component of action research. Create a consistent framework for examining data. Here is one set of questions a group of teachers came up with:
	1. Here are the data. What do they say to us about student performance?
	2. What do they say to us about instructional need?
	3. Based on the data, what practices would most significantly impact growth?
	4. What professional development is needed in order for us to be proficient with these practices?
Providing feedback about data from classroom observations	Take time to share the purpose and the focus of the system with the entire staff, so that they know why the observations are being conducted.
	Remind teachers that the observations are like snapshots. They are descriptive, not evaluative.
	Reinforce the positive practices that are evident in the observations. Listen to what the teachers want feedback on.
Working with study groups	Get each teacher to commit to trying one or two new things before the next meeting and to report back to the group on the results.

(continued)

Issue/Question	Tip
	Distribute an agenda two to three days before the meeting to remind teachers of their responsibilities.
	To facilitate video sharing, ask teachers if they had any strategies they were proud of as candidates for videotaping.
	Once the schedule is set for study groups, honor it. Don't let the study group agenda be interrupted or disabled by other school needs and priorities.
Increasing your effectiveness as a school leader/facilitator	Come into classrooms as a helper, not an evaluator. Initially, work with individuals or small groups to facilitate the teacher's agenda. Demonstrate your value added. Then get on with your professional development agenda.
	Help the groups reach consensus about their collective (and individual) action plans.
	Ask questions that refocus the reform on student performance and more effective pedagogy. Learn from those who are more experienced. Try to structure opportunities to talk with more experienced facilitators.
	Use every opportunity to discuss your role with the principal and leadership team. Get regular feedback on how the leadership team and teachers feel you are doing and how they feel about the study group time.
	When you visit classrooms, work with children on whatever they are doing at the time. Send the message to teachers you and they are in this together to improve instruction.

Adapted from Taylor, B.M. (2004). *The school change framework for improving reading achievement: Implementation manual.* Minneapolis: University of Minnesota.

Author Index

Subject Index

Note. Page numbers followed by *f* and *t* indicate figures and tables, respectively.